ONE

LIFE & GLORY

MIRACULOUSLY NORMAL
LIVING AND SERVICE

HENRY HON

TABLE OF CONTENTS

PART 2 – GLORY FOR SERVICE

DEDICATION

I am dedicating this book (*One in Life & Glory*) and the other two books (*One Ekklesia; One Truth*) to the ministry of One Body Life, which has a mission to support and build up the Lord's ekklesia everywhere. This trilogy includes the preaching of Jesus Christ as the good news, encouragement for believers to focus on and enjoy the Lord Jesus, and the practical gathering of diverse believers in the Lord's ekklesia, His one Body. One Body Life has no intention to federate or organize home assemblies. Our vision is simply to connect believers together in our common fellowship with Jesus Christ. All proceeds from the sales of this book and the other two in this trilogy will be used for the sole purpose of this mission. For tax purposes, One Body Life is a 501(c)(3) non-profit organization approved by the IRS. For more information about One Body life go to: www.onebody.life.

Personally, I will continue to commit myself to my loving family: my beloved Sylvia, my four children and their spouses, and my grandchildren (seven as of 2019). I sincerely pray and hope they will continue to love and serve the Lord for the rest of their lives, even when I am away in body. I want them to remember how they were raised to enjoy and serve the Lord in our home through the years and continue this pattern in their homes, and in the homes of their friends. I also pray that all my grandchildren will grow up loving the Lord Jesus for the building up of His ekklesia. Thank the Lord for His mercy and grace.

FOREWORD

As one part of a trilogy, *ONE LIFE & GLORY* will continue to take you into what Henry Hon sees as miraculously normal living and service. It is a clear call for every believer, through God's empowering grace and our inspired obedience, to become the answer to the prayer that Jesus prayed to our Father.

> "... that they may be made perfect in one, and that the world may know that You have sent Me, and have loved them as You have loved Me."
>
> John 17:23

Hon has a clear insight into the centrality of the *ekklesia* (church) that Jesus said He would build. While it may seem more divided than ever, he demonstrates how we can become one without dismantling "church" as it exists in many parts of our world today. Simultaneously, he is committed to seeing the same experience of life and vibrancy of early Christians expressed today as they carried the life of Jesus into the very centers of their living in homes – from house to house.

When it comes to meeting from house to house, Hon is not a novice. His journey has had him assembling in this way since 1986. His experience has taught him that this form of worship is not in itself the answer. Rather, it is obedience to Jesus' Command to "love one another," just as He has loved us.

He clearly demonstrates that God has given us all we need to become one – the Eternal life, Truth and Jesus' Glory. However, Hon is not content to leave us with profound theological truth alone; this book is filled with practical examples of how we can both embrace the truth and live the life God calls us to live – miraculously normal.

This life work is given to us by one who has lived its reality. I urge you to take the time to digest the truth contained in *ONE LIFE & GLORY!*

Gaylord Enns
Author of *LOVE REVOLUTION: Rediscovering the Lost Command of Jesus*

PREFACE

In 2016, I published my first book *ONE: The Vision and Practice of God's Eternal Purpose from House to House*. That book expounded on the Lord's prayer in John 17 where Jesus gave three gifts to His people for them to manifest oneness. I expanded and improved on the first book by breaking it down into a trilogy: *One Ekklesia, One Truth,* and *One Life & Glory*. *One Ekklesia* was published in 2018, *One Truth* in 2019, and this book, *One Life & Glory* in 2020. My plan is to revise the first book, *ONE*, and make it into a condensed "Cliff Note" version of the trilogy.

My Testimony

I was born in Hong Kong, the youngest of five boys. My parents were divorced, so my mom raised me. Our family immigrated to the USA when I was eight years old. Since we were poor, I started working when I was nine years old to contribute to our family — I haven't stop working since! I grew up in Berkeley, California, and was graduated from UC Berkeley with an IEOR engineering degree. I have been a serial entrepreneur since then.

Through the introduction by one of my brothers, I was fortunate enough to earn a good income from computer programming and an insurance business. So, I decided to invest and started a folding bicycle company with my oldest brother. It started a trend and became the largest folding bicycle company in the world. Since then I also started a few technology companies. Though I am now officially retired, I am still involved in some businesses.

I have been married to Sylvia since 1976 — a wonderful and beautiful woman both inside and out who has the same vision as I. Sylvia and I have raised our two sons and two daughters here in the Bay Area of Northern California. All four of our children were likewise graduated from UC Berkeley and are now married raising their own families. By 2019, we now have 5 grandsons and 2 granddaughters. Our family is a "melting pot" reflecting American society: My wife is European American; my kids have married Americans with ancestry from Africa, Europe and Southeast Asia. As you can imagine, we are looking forward to more beautifully blended grandchildren.

I consider myself just a regular guy in this world, working in businesses my whole life with their temptations and unending challenges while

ONE Life & Glory

enjoying the task of raising a family with its typical struggles. Yet, the life of Christ and God's purpose is intertwined with mine. I thank God that I can directly contribute to the building up of His ekklesia, the Body of Christ.

My Life in Christ

I began my spiritual journey as a follower of Jesus Christ when I was sixteen in 1969 during the Jesus People Movement. At the time, I was not seeking God or desiring to be a Christian. Though raised by a Christian mom, I had abandoned Christianity and was enjoying my teenage years as an accomplished athlete in high school. However, one weekend, after succumbing to my mom's nagging, I finally agreed to attend a Christian conference. It was not in the church service, but outside with a group of young people singing impromptu that attracted me. Ten to fifteen minutes or so after joining in their singing, I was filled with the joy of Jesus and the Holy Spirit. That weekend I decided to serve the Lord Jesus and give Him my life. I became so vocal in preaching the gospel at my high school I was given a derogatory nick name: "Jesus Freak."

Since those early years, I have pursued the principles and experiences of various Christian persuasions: Evangelical—a strong desire to preach the gospel, with a focus on missions while bringing people to a new birth in Christ; Fundamentalism—a focus on the inerrancy of the Bible; therefore, a strong emphasis on Bible study and adherence to its teachings; Charismatic experiences—a focus on being Spirit-filled under the power of the Spirit and the release of the spirit; and "Mysticism"—a focus on seeking to know and experience constant union with God by knowing the value of the cross through self-denial, and following the Spirit's leading through inner intuition. In pursuing each of these, I have received help. However, eventually and invariably, I grew frustrated. I found deficiencies with each. Today, I would not be classified by any of these associations; however, I still possess elements of each, therefore, I am comfortable accepting and fellowshipping with all kinds of believers, no matter their proclivity or denomination.

It has been my good fortune to be a diligent student of the Bible. My scriptural understanding is influenced by the theology of the Plymouth Brethren (Darby, Mueller, Mackintosh, Vine), Watchman Nee, and Witness Lee. I have never been to Bible school, but through learning a great spectrum of Bible teachings, and having them as a foundation and influence, I have received fresh insight and understanding into the Word (not heard from others). This has affected my journey with the Lord. Also, it has affected how I reach out in fellowship with all kinds of believers. Whatever I have understood and written in my books has been curated and condensed from what has practically guided every aspect of my life. I have no intention of passing on inane biblical doctrines and theories. My desire is to impart the revelation of God's eternal purpose which is practical and positively effective in everyday living.

Over the last 50 years, I have actively participated in various forms of ministry with sundry Christian communities. In my younger years, it was open air public preaching, street evangelism, and communal living. For over a decade I had a youth ministry, and for the most part I found myself responsible for weekly Sunday sermons. I started speaking in conferences by my late 20s. I have served for years as a church-planting elder and as a teaching/shepherding elder in both small and large churches. I've also practiced for decades via meeting in homes as a kind of simple/organic home group or house church facilitator. Thus, over the decades, I have functioned in a variety of environments and have witnessed and learned much through insider observation and experience in the arena of ministry and "church."

Out of all my experience—until I was 60 years old—the most outstanding period was when my wife and I were raising our four children. We moved back to Berkeley when our eldest started attending high school. Since all four of our children were graduated from UC Berkeley, we were privileged to have them in our home for an extended period. During this time my desire was to focus spiritual activities in our home wherein the need to raise our children for the Lord perfectly fitted together. Our house was always opened to their friends with a weekly meal and fellowship. Through their network of friends and being close to the university, over 100 young people came to the Lord and many were established in the faith growing in the Lord as they were shepherded in a community around Christian homes. Additionally, a wide variety of people and believers were attracted to our community and home assembly.

I began to understand and experience the life of fellowship in the one body of Christ and how it should take place from house to house. Even though I was still going to church, my heart and focus of service and fellowship was in the homes, house by house. It is in this environment oneness was manifested. It was here people from diverse backgrounds were received and accepted. Additionally, any differences that would normally divide Christians have become a non-factor in our one fellowship with Jesus

Christ. The more I see this oneness among believers spread to more and more homes, house to house, the more I see our real enjoyment as His One Body. This environment has always been attractive to both believers and unbelievers. Just about everyone coming into this environment, sooner or later, has come to faith in Christ and has grown in the faith.

Since our four children not only enjoyed the Lord in this environment, they were also contributing partners in this fellowship community; their positive outcome has been lasting. Our four children with their spouses continued their faith in the Lord, and most of them also host gatherings for fellowship in their own homes. They foster a loving care for people and a desire to build up the Body of Christ.

Inspiration for Writing the Trilogy of ONE

I was associated with a church which considered they were part of God's restoration movement: Exposing the errors of institutional Christianity, while recovering the original understanding and practices of the New Testament. One of the main focuses: all believers should be in unity—one in the Body of Christ. I was helped by this ministry to receive a real vision of God's eternal purpose; likewise, I desired to contribute toward bringing God's people together in oneness. This church movement declared it received all Christians into fellowship; however, if any genuinely desired such fellowship in the one Body, they would have to leave their denominational churches to join ours. Needless to say, that didn't work out well; rather, it produced more divisions in the Body. It turns out, virtually every restoration movement in history has had a similar message: Our movement has the latest revelation from Scripture; therefore, our church is superior to any others — leave yours and join ours.

When this church movement I was involved in started, it was a time of innocence. I was active at the early stage of this church movement in the USA. The joy, love, and excitement in witnessing people coming to salvation, and the organic growth and dynamic spread of this church, covered up the divisive foundation the church was tragically built upon. However, as it grew and increased, a hierarchy emerged where the freedom to follow the Lord's leading was replaced by human orchestration, wherein the gulf between this church and Christians in other groups was widening. I became increasingly disturbed; eventually, when I confronted the leadership with my objection to the hierarchical control, I was finally ostracized. Now, I recognize they were merely building up their own ministry, like many other churches.

It was at this juncture I started reconsidering the entire counsel of God in the New Testament about the Lord's ekklesia ("church"), His eternal purpose. My questions: 1) How did this church which started seeking and preaching the oneness of the Body of Christ become so exclusive, so sectarian — like the groups which they had vociferously condemned? 2) What else can be learned from Scripture in order to truly build up the oneness of God's people to fulfill God's eternal purpose, without causing additional divisions in the Body?

New enlightenment began to unveil in Scripture which I had not heard or read from other teachers. Major portions included: John 17 concerning the Lord's prayer where He gave His people three gifts in order for them to become one; the practice of ekklesia as found in 1 Corinthians 11:17 to the end of 1 Corinthians 14; and Romans chapters 9-16 concerning the gospel of peace and the vital practice of "greeting" diverse believers found in Romans 16. Many new understandings, as described throughout my three books: *One Ekklesia*, *One Truth*, and *One Life & Glory,* were enlightened by the Holy Spirit.

The Lord has graciously satisfied my quest and prayer. He continues to answer my questions by wonderfully liberating believers into the joy of the Lord by these biblically based practices regarding real-life ekklesia in action. The solution in bringing diverse believers into one fellowship into His one Body is clearly unveiled in Scriptures. I am absolutely convinced the Lord will have a testimony of His ekklesia, His one Body, Bride, and Kingdom before His second advent. This will occur without having to denigrate any Christian churches or by starting another church movement. I have no intention in forming another defined group of believers or federating groups and churches into a movement. The Lord has already done everything necessary to build up His Body. Now, we just need revelation of what He has accomplished and walk in it. My hope is my books will generate discussions, challenges, confirmations, awareness, and increasing interest in the topic of God's eternal purpose centered on Christ and living out of His ekklesia.

The Lord's intention is a joyful and purposeful life for His own. No one is meant to be a passive spectator. On the contrary, each person is needed to function as a member of His body during their everyday lives. In various capacities, all believers need to become teachers, shepherds, ministers, and good-news-bearers in their normal environments for His Body.

Reading through the Trilogy, one will discover a wide variety of Scripturally-based doctrine and practice: Many points of theology relating

ONE Life & Glory

to the Trinity, steps to salvation, discipleship, spiritual growth, ecclesiology, holiness, spiritual warfare, gospel preaching, inner life, bearing the cross, eschatology and much more. Unfortunately, many of these doctrines and practices are usually taught or considered as separate disjointed topics, which can lead to confusion, disagreements, and divisions. Diverse churches have been raised up due to differing emphases by Bible teachers throughout the centuries. Positively, they have brought light to many portions of the Bible. However, negatively, teachers have used their insights into these topics as a kind of niche marketing to differentiate themselves from others in order to build their own followers and churches — causing many divisions and factions.

By having an overarching view of God's eternal purpose for the building up of His ekklesia, all these various diverse doctrines and spiritual topics in the Bible can be harmonized; they can be synchronized for the building up of His ekklesia. God's eternal purpose is like the rim of a bicycle wheel, the spokes are the many spiritual topics generated from a connection to the Triune God, the hub. Without the rim, all the spokes can be very confusing and pointing in all sorts of directions; although, they all have something to do with God. All the spokes need to be connected to the rim. It is only when all the various topics are connected to, and for the purpose of God's eternal purpose, will there be a complete wheel upon which God can move.

Therefore, students of the Bible will be able to appreciate the development and application of each of these various topics along a single theme of the building up of God's eternal desire which is the Lord's ekklesia. This may be considered a comprehensive systematic theology of God's ekklesia. Typically, systematic theologies have been developed with the salvation of humanity in view. This Trilogy includes soteriology, but also intentionally advances toward the building up of the Lord's ekklesia, His eternal purpose.

I pray people of all ages, backgrounds and spiritual inclinations will be inspired by the unveiling of the truth of the complete Gospel and begin to enjoy the Lord as eternal life in their daily living. Simultaneously, this enjoyment will cause a revival in serving others while entering the delight of the one fellowship we now have with all other believers for the building up of the one Body of Christ.

".. . that they may be one even as we [Father and the Son] are one."
                                                    –Our Lord's Prayer

ACKNOWLEDGEMENT

In 2017, I met Douglas Krieger again after 43 years of losing contact. When I was a teenager and began my years at the University of California at Berkeley, he was one of the elders in the church I attended even though he was only 12 years my senior. He was "excused" from that church soon thereafter. So, we went our separate ways until meeting again in Sacramento, California.

He has been a prophetic voice relating to Eschatology – the study of the end times. He has written 10 books and has been a frequent conference speaker on numerology, Old Testament prophecies specifically relating to Israel and the Jewish nation. He was an early proponent of Commonwealth Theology and serves as chair of the Commonwealth of Israel Foundation. He was also the President of the National Prayer Breakfast in Washington DC from 1983 to 1985 held during the annual National Religious Broadcasters Convention

When Doug heard my presentation at a home gathering concerning the Lord's ekklesia, it resonated with him – He was drawn to connect with me to have more fellowship on the initial presentation. Since then he has been a huge supporter of this message and has assisted me in extending the message of oneness.

Not only did he help edit my trilogy to improve my English, but he also provided help with additional prophetic passages from the Hebrew Scripture, as well as from the New Testament, to support and amplify this message. He has committed himself for the rest of his life to advance this message for the oneness of God's people, the building up of His ekklesia according to what the Lord has laid out in this trilogy; and, as Doug says: "Whatever happens to you Henry, I'm pressing on with this vision!"

I appreciate His dedication and consistency to team up for the Lord's move. I pray his remaining days on earth will be long and more useful for God's purpose than ever before. May his voice speak forth the message of oneness ever more clearly and may it be anointed by the Spirit. It is God's mercy that we can co-labor with God for the building up of His ekklesia.

ONE
LIFE & GLORY

MIRACULOUSLY NORMAL LIVING AND SERVICE

HENRY HON

1

INTRODUCTION

*O*ne in Life & Glory is the last book in this three-book series. Here are the titles of the first and second in this trilogy:

- One Ekklesia: The Vision and Practice of God's Eternal Purpose.
- One Truth: Liberating – Nourishing – Unifying

These three books are a further development from my first book: *ONE: The Vision and Practice of God's Eternal Purpose from House to House*. This first book shall be replaced by this trilogy; likewise, a curriculum with study guide and practicum will be developed to enhance the understanding, vision and practice found in the trilogy.

The inspiration of the trilogy is from the Lord's prayer at the last supper the night prior to His crucifixion. He earnestly prayed three times petitioning for His people to be one in unity. Their oneness would be as one as the Father and the Son are one in the Trinity. This manifested oneness would take place in the current world where Satan is still the ruler, and this oneness would cause the people of this world to believe *into* the reality of Jesus Christ.

Three gifts were distinctly given by the Lord in His prayer. After giving each gift, He petitioned: "*that they may be one.*" The mysterious and divine oneness of His people can only be a result of these three gifts. Without receiving, understanding, and enjoying these three gifts, it is impossible to have the same unity as the Father and the Son within the Trinity. The three gifts are:

- Eternal Life (the Father's name)
- The Truth (God's Word)
- The Glory Jesus received as a man

God's people have been divided over the centuries. There is an increasing number of denominations and churches around the globe. Many of the divisions are so deep with such animosity that those belonging to one faction will not fellowship with believers in an opposing camp. Some of these are centuries old divides such as between believers attending the Catholic church and those in Protestant churches or between the Roman Catholics and the Orthodox. Even among the Protestants there are huge gulfs between churches influenced by the Calvinist/Reform theology and those on the Arminianism side of theology. Additionally, among these two major divisions in Protestantism are many other factions based on the differing shades of understanding relating to salvation, holiness, Pentecostalism, church government, worship styles, the practice of the inner life, prosperity, discipleship, sanctification, eschatology and more. Additionally, there are celebrity ministers who command the following of tens of thousands of Christians. No wonder God's people are so divided.

By in large, all Christians have the same faith of Jesus Christ. Just about all Christian churches, Catholic, Orthodox, and Protestant proclaim there is only one saving faith:

- Jesus Christ is God who put on flesh and became a man
- He died on the cross as a sinless God-man for redemption for the forgiveness of sin
- He resurrected on the third day and ascended to become the Lord of lords
- He indwells all who have received Him in faith as the Spirit

Nevertheless, Christians with this one faith in Jesus Christ are splintered throughout the globe. It seems there is no solution. The Catholic Church initiated the ecumenical movement trying for a political unity by bringing churches under one organizational umbrella. That itself is also a very divisive idea with much opposition from Christian groups.

It seems there is no solution to this disunity among Christians. However, Jesus Himself prayed for His people to be one. He literally went to the cross and died in order to bring into one diverse people who were otherwise hostile to each other. If the Lord's prayer is not going to be answered then His death does not accomplish His purpose for the unity of His people; furthermore, the very foundation of the Christian faith disintegrates into "spiritual nihilism." How can Christians have faith to pray when Jesus' own prayer is not answered? How can Christians believe in their redemption and forgiveness through the cross of Christ if the other reason for His death, which is unity, is not fulfilled? This cannot be! Yes, the Lord inaugurated the New Covenant, the New Commandment and provided the Promise of the Spirit in His going to the cross during the last supper; however, He went much further in His high-priestly prayer for the oneness of His people in that same upper room — in other words, the ultimate goal was not only for the salvation wrought through the blood of His cross, but unity among His people!

This trilogy is based on full confidence in the Lord's prayer in John 17 for the manifested oneness of His people. This prayer will be answered; the work of His cross has wrought peace to all divided people making them one New Man. However, Christians need to enter into the same vision Jesus has in the building up of His ekklesia, His Body. Additionally, they must have the knowledge of these three gifts seen in John 17 and enter into their appreciation and enjoyment. Without immersing into the gifts given in His prayer, there is no way for unity to occur. Why? Because this is not an organizational unity ministered by worldly means but by His provision, grace and love.

Many may hope for a miracle: somehow God will do something supernatural and with a snap of His finger whereupon all His people will be in unity. If that be the case, we would be longing to be robots with our minds and feelings changed by an outside programmer. No, the Scripture is clear: God has given His people the life and nature; yes, all the tools necessary for oneness to take place naturally within each believer. They are all embedded in these three amazing gifts. If believers do not voluntarily enter into and enjoy these three gifts, then nothing more can be done by God.

Not everyone may agree how these three gifts were delineated and explained; nevertheless, at least bringing forth their awareness will stimulate discussion, knowledge, and further exploration of the same. I don't know of any other books expounding on these three gifts for the goal of God's eternal purpose in having His people in unity — the building up of His ekklesia. My hope is this trilogy will provoke more discussion and fellowship among Christians on this very important topic of God's eternal purpose.

Here are the highlights of the first two books for preparation in the reading of *One Life & Glory*:

One Ekklesia: The Vision and Practice of God's Eternal Purpose

- Opening both the Old and New Testament to unveil God's unique eternal purpose is His ekklesia.
- Exposing the conspiracy to purposely mistranslate the Greek word "ekklesia" to "church."
- Defining churches as a place belonging to ministries versus the Lord's ekklesia belonging to the Lord and His people.
- Explaining the similarities and differences between characteristics of secular ekklesia from the Lord's ekklesia.
- Defining the Lord's ekklesia using three words: constituents, reality and manifestation.
- Showing how ekklesia with diversity in unity is the expression of the Trinity.
- Expounding upon a perplexing verse, 1 Corinthians 11:19, where Paul said that factions are needed when the ekklesia comes together.
- Unlocking critical practices needed to crush Satan under the feet of believers as found in Romans 16
- Exposing Satan's strategy in spiritual warfare; whereby, God's people in division come under God's own judgment.
- Seeing the only description of the Lord's ekklesia in the epistles from a completely different light (1 Cor. 11:17 through to the end of 1 Corinthians 14).
- Many more points concerning the Lord's ekklesia

One Truth: Liberating—Nourishing—Unifying

- Dive into the unsearchable riches of Jesus Christ's person and work
- Consider each step of God's amazing salvation regarding how believers are being brought from sinners to mature sons of God in experiential stages.
- Addressing a rarely discussed topic, but it is the plan and way for God to accomplish His eternal purpose: the *oikonomia* of God
- Explaining a clear distinction between the first covenant and the new covenant

- A fresh look at the gospel of peace which has been neglected and is needed more than ever.
- A new expounding of Romans chapters 9-16 in its systematic development which results in glory to God and crushing of Satan.
- Proclaiming the completion gospel of Jesus Christ: the gospel of grace, the gospel of peace — which together constitute the gospel of the kingdom.

It is certain there are a number of new items unveiled in Scripture in these two books which have been hidden. In these later days, God is giving fresh revelation to His people for the accomplishing of His eternal purpose. May the Lord continue to speak and shine on His people.

2

MIRACULOUSLY
NORMAL LIVING

What is Miraculously normal? Everyone is in awe when a miracle truly takes place. It is supernatural. It cannot be explained. Five-thousand people got fed from five loaves and two fish with twelve baskets of food left over. That was supernatural, a miracle. After many decades, a person born blind could receive their sight without surgery. There is only one way to explain it — it's a miracle. A person who has been dead for four days, and then comes back to life? Science cannot offer an explanation. It's a miracle!

Well, "normal" is just mundane, dull, rather ordinary. Normal can be what happens every day to everyone. After not eating for a while people get hungry. They eat, they are full. That is normal. When tired, they go to sleep. When they wake up after resting, they are refreshed and ready to work — just normal. If people eat and don't exercise, they get fat; if they regularly lift weights, they will build muscle — again, normal. A male and female get married, the woman becomes pregnant and has a baby — once again, normal. Normal things of life are not newsworthy. No one will be surprised over normal occurrences.

Humanity is a good example of what is "miraculously normal." Dig a little deeper into human life and you will find many seemingly normal things are miracles. Life itself is a miracle. Where is it in the body? Doctors can locate every physical organ, but where is life? Yet it is normal to have life and live — miraculously normal. The formation of a baby is miraculously normal. Yes, science can explain the reproduction of cells and DNA, but what a miracle to have two cells joined; then, after trillions of cells have reproduced, the cells with the same DNA somehow become eyes, brain, heart, or fingers. These two cells joined eventually form a perfect being. A miracle! Yet, it is normal. Therefore, *miraculously normal*.

The miracle of life is so predictable and occurring to so many billions of people all over the earth — it is normal. It happens to everyone, everywhere, under just about any condition on earth. It is the same for rich, poor, educated and uneducated; it is the same for all races. All life is miraculously normal.

Working to get some things done with a purpose is also normal. People all over the globe get up and do things, to expand energy, do their part in a job. Billions of people: some do big things with grandiose ideas, others are just working in an office, a production line. Some are farming and others are raising their children. It's all normal and ordinary: everyone doing their small part to fulfill a variety of purposes. However, look again from afar. There is an amazing human civilization: the human kingdom. Everything works together: people can fly to every country, communicate with audio/video over the airwaves, powerful computers in the palm of their hands, travel to outer space, and much more. Billions of people doing their little part through life and the result is this miracle. If those who lived just 100 years ago were told what life would be like today, they would not believe it. If they could have seen some of the things today, they would no doubt think they were miraculous. Yet, to people living today it is normal. The advancement of technology is another example of miraculously normal.

Divine Life and Work

What was described above is miraculously normal for humanity. There is life and living, then there is working with a purpose. The result of this living and working is an amazing human race with its civilization — kingdom.

Now, let's consider the spiritual realm of God's divine life, which is the real miraculously normal being considered in this book. For the followers of the Lord Jesus Christ, the divine realm is more real than the physical world. Just as there is physical life and a human kingdom, there is a divine, spiritual life and God's kingdom. This book will attempt to correlate the examples of the physical world to that of the spiritual, from the human to the divine.

If it is purely God or divine, then it would be miraculous or supernatural all the time in every way. That, indeed, is the meaning of supernatural. It is not natural, it is beyond nature; therefore, it cannot be explained. Whoever God is and whatever He does is supernatural, miraculous, and extraordinary; not normal by human standards. God can be everywhere at the same time, all the time — that is miraculous. God creates the entire universe — truly a miracle.

However, God doesn't want to remain simply God, He purposed to become a man, to put on humanity — to become one with the pinnacle of His creation. His desire was to join Himself with humanity. The divine becomes human, expressed in humanity; and the human will be powered by divine life. It is amazing and inexplicable: The God of the universe desired to limit Himself within the confines of humanity. He did so to such an extend as to experience human birth, God was a human baby! He continued to experience life as a human from birth until a full-grown man of 30 years of age. During that period, there was no record or even a hint He did any miracles. Nothing supernatural, just an ordinary carpenter growing up in a normal family with parents, brothers and sisters.

> Let this mind be in you which was also in Christ Jesus, who, being in the form of God, did not consider it robbery to be equal with God, but made Himself of no reputation, taking the form of a bondservant, *and* coming in the likeness of men.
>
> – Phil. 2:5-7

> And Jesus increased in wisdom and stature, and in favor with God and men.
>
> – Luke 2:52

God the Spirit, the Divine, joined himself to physical humanity. He wanted to live a normal human life. He could have miraculously appeared in human form as He did in the Hebrew Scriptures; yet, He went through the helplessness and weaknesses of a baby and a toddler. He didn't just teleport Himself from one place to another; He had to walk to Jerusalem and back. He didn't speak furniture or houses into being; He had to take time, sweat and work to build them. This is normal and human, but what a miracle that was — the biggest miracle of the universe up till then: God joined and fused Himself to humanity and became a man. This is by far a bigger miracle than creating the universe out of nothing.

People are fascinated by the supernatural. Who wouldn't want to become rich without working? Who wouldn't want to be healthy and safe no matter the lifestyle or the risk taken? Superhero movies are popular because people can project themselves to have supernatural powers. However, God Himself is fascinated by being human, limited, weak, confined, and needy.

His desire was to be humanly normal; yet, it is one of the greatest and most daring or miracles. This is *miraculously normal*.

Many Believed in Jesus Due to His Miracles

Certainly, when Jesus was on earth, He did many miracles: He raised the dead, healed the crippled, restored the hearing to the deaf, opened the mouth of the mute and restored sight to the blind. Jesus healed a woman with a blood disease, and much more. He also sent His disciples to preach the gospel with the capabilities to heal and perform miraculous acts just as He did (Matt. 10:8; Mark 15:18).

Notwithstanding, Jesus didn't perform any miracles for His own benefit according to the records of the New Testament. Even His walking on water was for the benefit of His disciples. In fact, Satan did his best to tempt Jesus to take the position of God and perform miracles as God. The first temptation: "*If You are the Son of God, command that these stones become bread*" (Matt. 4:4). Second: "*If You are the Son of God, throw Yourself down*" and an angel will catch you (Matt. 4:6). Do something supernatural if you are the Son of God was Satan's temptation. To both, Jesus answered He was a man and as a man, He would not do anything supernatural. Even in the last temptation, Jesus committed Himself to be a man who worshiped God. While Adam fell by succumbing to Satan's temptation to be god, Jesus defeated Satan by becoming man — remaining in His humanity.

Yes, Jesus did perform miracles due to His compassion for those needing healing or hungry (Matt. 14:14). He also did it at times as a sign to show He was truly God in the flesh (John 10:38; 4:48) while delivering spiritual messages. However, He didn't become a man in order to perform miracles in the physical world. He could have easily performed miracles as God without putting on flesh. Many prophets performed miracles for centuries before Jesus came. Through His incarnation He was able to be an ordinary man; He was able to die on the cross for redemption; able to make His people one, and then resurrected in order for all His followers to live as He lived . . . divine life lived out through human flesh!

Moses and the prophets in the Old Testament time did many miracles, truly supernatural feats, including raising the dead. By accomplishing all these supernatural acts, did it change the trajectory of Israel? Not in the least! Israel was repeatedly rebellious before God during their wilderness journey — a time when miracles happened daily (e.g., manna and quail).

Israel, rejected God, turned to idols, and became devastatingly divided even after God brought them into the Good Land where they miraculously conquered all their enemies, established the kingdom of Israel and built God's temple. The Jews then were supernaturally returned to Jerusalem after their 70-years of captivity in Babylon to rebuild Jerusalem. However, after centuries of seeing God's miracles upon them, the result was opposition to God who came in the flesh. Jesus Christ was rejected by the Jewish leadership and subsequently crucified. This was the outcome of their journey after myriads of miracles performed for their benefit: They killed the Prince of Life, the One Who did the miracles on their behalf.

Therefore, although Jesus performed miracles, He didn't commit Himself to those who would follow Him due to miracles, because He didn't trust them. He knew what was in man.

> "... many believed in his name when they saw the signs that he was doing. But Jesus on his part did not entrust himself to them, because he knew all people and needed no one to bear witness about man, for he himself knew what was in man."
> – John 2:23-25 ESV

John said many people believed in Jesus due to the miraculous signs He did. Yet, Jesus did not trust them. He didn't trust the people who believed due to His miracles. He knew the reasons they believed was due to the supernatural; yet He wouldn't commit Himself to them. Later in John chapter 6, Jesus' prediction was correct. Those who wanted to make Him king due to His miracle of feeding them; yet, ultimately, they left Him.

In John 6 five-thousand people followed Jesus due to the miracles He did in healing the sick. Then afterwards, all 5,000, plus women and children, got fed by Jesus with only 5 loaves of bread and 2 fish; therefore, they wanted to make Jesus king by force. Isn't that wonderful? Shouldn't every preacher of the gospel rejoice with such a result? Isn't their goal of preaching to have people desirous for Jesus to be their king? However, Jesus didn't want to be their king; instead, He wanted to be their food and drink. He wanted them to eat Him and to drink Him; to have Him inside them. Not just inside them, but "digested" and become a part of them. Yes, "He that eats me, even he shall live by me" (John 6:57).

Surprisingly, many of those who wanted Him to be king turned away and stopped following Him. In fact, it seems as if everyone left except for the 12 disciples (John 6:66-67). All those who followed Jesus because of the miracles, couldn't be trusted. Jesus was correct, He couldn't commit Himself to those who were only interested in miracles. The problem was, and still is, those who follow Jesus because of miracles keep asking for even more miracles. They, like the disciples, become addicted to miracles. They follow Jesus because of all the miracles He did and still can do; but when Jesus asked them to believe "into" Him, to have a life relationship with Him, they reverted to asking for more miracles (John 6:29-30). They did not wish to have a relationship with Jesus, to believe into Jesus; they just wanted miracles from Jesus.

Yes, over the centuries until today, multitudes of people have been attracted to Jesus because of miracles. While many may have discontinued following due to various disappointments; yet, others have remained faithful. We thank God for all His miraculous acts which have caused many to believe; therefore, believers should pray the gospel will continue to go out with signs and wonders (Matt. 10:8, Mark 16:20). Those preaching the gospel of Jesus Christ should exercise their anointed authority to perform supernatural signs in order to attract people to hear the Word of the gospel of Jesus Christ and to demonstrate the authority of Jesus Christ through His members. However, even after resurrection, Jesus said to Thomas in John 21:29: *"Blessed are those who have not seen and yet have believed."* Thomas needed the physical evidence of resurrection; He needed to witness a miracle in order to believe. Nevertheless, those who believe without witnessing any evidence of a miracle are blessed. Instead of seeking and expecting miracles, it is more beneficial to consider being a *miraculously normal* believer of Jesus Christ.

The Ultimate Miracle

"Your fathers ate the manna in the wilderness, and they died. This is the bread that comes down from heaven, so that one may eat of it and not die. I am the living bread that came down from heaven. If anyone eats of this bread, he will live forever. And the bread that I will give for the life of the world is my flesh."
– John 6:49-51 ESV

Comparatively speaking, which was a greater miracle: bread coming down from heaven for 40 years, or Jesus Who is God in the flesh asking people to eat Him in order to have eternal and divine life within them? By far, the bigger and even the biggest miracle is the ability to ingest Jesus Christ wherein He becomes an integral part of the partaker's being. Certainly, it was miraculous when Peter, James, and John saw Jesus transfigured in His glory, but *"Christ in you the hope of glory"* (Col. 1:27) is far and away a bigger miracle. No matter how many outward miracles are witnessed by we humans, and no matter how we may marvel at God's greatness and supernatural abilities, our human nature remains the same with no hope of glory in and of ourselves.

God's desire is not for humanity to be in awe of Him — to prostrate and worship Him. He has angels to do just that 24/7 (Rev. 4:8-11). God's desire is to unite Himself with humanity, to be miraculously normal. He did so through the incarnation of His Son Jesus Christ Who became flesh and tabernacled among us (John 1:14). Jesus Christ then went through death and resurrection not only for redemption, for the forgiveness of sins, but to grant us eternal life by living His life in all His believers. Ultimately, those who "believe *into* the Son" become His "many brethren" — His one Body able to express God manifested in the flesh within a corporate humanity. This is the ultimate and consummate miraculously normal of the universe.

In the gospels while people were seeking the miraculous and the supernatural, the real miracle was standing right in front of them. Throughout the gospels people could not believe Jesus was God. He looked so dull with a common family. There was nothing physically desirable about Him (Isa. 53:2). Jesus Christ was so normal and mundane they missed Him. They missed the ultimate miracle — God in man.

Now, some 2,000 years later, people, including Christians, may still have their focus on the miraculous, hoping to witness more supernatural acts; but today an even greater miracle than God in the flesh of one man, Jesus, is God in millions upon millions of believers ready to live in and out of each of them. This is the enlargement of Jesus Christ. This is His corporate Body. This is today's miraculously normal.

When God lives His life within the humanity of each of the members of Christ's Body, He is fully living and serving through humanity — humanity filled with His divine life. This is the result of His salvation for humankind.

Glory to God, Satan is crushed, and the second advent, if you would, of Jesus Christ is here and now!

This third book in this trilogy (*One Ekklesia, One Truth,* and now, *One in Life and Glory*) is designed to explore and propel the miraculously normal living and service (the expression of His Life through us) capable to be lived out in every believer. It is normal for every believer to live and grow in God's divine-eternal life now living in them. It is also normal for each to do their small part in service so God's kingdom can be built, and God's eternal purpose fulfilled. It seems so ordinary; consequently, most have missed the miracle behind this most wondrous gift of divine life living in His people.

Genealogy of Jesus Christ

When Jesus Christ was born of Mary, He had a complete genealogy tracing Him back to Abraham making Him the rightful King of Israel (Matthew 1:1-17). In Luke His genealogy went all the way back to Adam showing He is a genuine man (Luke 3:23-38). His genealogy passed through all kinds of personalities including those who had a record of committing terrible sins.

Here is just a few examples of the colorful people who passed on their genetics to Jesus: One who played a prostitute in order to trick her father-in-law to have a child with her (Tamar); a prostitute (Rahab); one whose family line was cursed by God due to its origin from incest (Ruth); a man who committed adultery then murdered her husband (King David); a man who had 1000 wives and concubines (Solomon); one who slaughtered all his brothers (Joram); a leper (Uzziah); and others who worshipped idols and did many evil things. A person born of such a bloodline means that person has these characteristic traits in His genetic pool. The word "flesh" in the Scriptures is typically a negative term, a description of man's sinful condition. The flesh cannot please God (Rom. 8:8); in the flesh nothing good dwells (Rom. 7:18).

Jesus put on such a flesh. God did not come in the form of the original Adam before He fell into sin. He came in the form of *the flesh of sin* (Rom. 8:3); yet, without sin (Heb. 4:15). The flesh He put on came from a genetic pool replete with sinful people. What a miracle God would come in the "*likeness of the flesh of sin.*" It was in this flesh Jesus expressed the purity, sinlessness, love, patience, kindness, boldness, faithfulness, and all the goodness of divine life. Great is the mystery of godliness: God is manifested in the flesh (1 Tim. 3:16).

Today, all believers are still in their fallen flesh; yet, within each is the God of Glory with His divine-eternal life. It is normal to have st with sin in the flesh, but it is miraculous whereby through the dea Christ on the cross, God would view those having the faith of Jesus Chr to be righteous and justified. Being righteous before God while we are sti living in this flesh — susceptible to succumbing to various temptations of sin — is miraculously normal.

Just about all agree, Christians who walk with Christ do not find it unusual to fall into various kinds of sin: from inward disdain of others to lust of the flesh; from obvious forms of physical sins such as hurting others to blatant adultery. In the eyes of society there are gradients of sin resulting in a range of punishments: from monetary fines to capital offenses. However, in God's eyes, all sins are punishable by death before a righteous God. Whoever breaks just one of God's laws, that one is guilty of breaking all His laws (James 2:20). Therefore, the death of Jesus Christ for man's redemption resulted in the justification of humanity through faith in Jesus Christ — this is truly miraculous; yet, completely normal since it is the believers' daily experience.

Just about every day, we may be offending God with either inward thoughts and motives or outward actions; yet, for believers, we can continue living in fellowship with God and with other believers as wholly righteous in Christ (1 John 1:7; Rom. 5:17).

The Miraculous versus Miraculously Normal

Below are some examples highlighting the difference between a miracle and miraculously normal.

It is a miracle when medicine has failed, and a person is healed of a debilitating disease. It would be miraculously normal when one who has a debilitating sickness to rejoice in the Lord while continuing to live while struggling to get well.

It would be a miracle if the first lottery a person purchases wins a jackpot. It would be miraculously normal for one to give his hard-earned money to someone in need.

It would be a miracle if no one offends or hurts you. It is miraculously normal to forgive those who have offended and hurt you.

It would be a miracle if everyone around you is loveable. It would be miraculously normal to love those you naturally dislike and upset you.

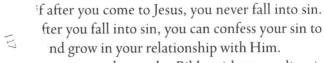

if after you come to Jesus, you never fall into sin. After you fall into sin, you can confess your sin to and grow in your relationship with Him.

for you to know the Bible without reading it teacher. It is miraculously normal for you to receive and spiritual supply daily as you read and study the Scriptures.

It would be a miracle if every time you preach the gospel thousands of people come to Jesus. It is miraculously normal for you to pray for, care for, and speak the good news of Jesus Christ to people around you, and then after months or years, they start coming to Jesus.

It would be a miracle if suddenly, all followers of Jesus Christ would come to the same understanding of doctrine and practice. It would be miraculously normal for believers to fellowship with each other while having different and conflicting understanding in their doctrines and practices.

It would be a miracle if all Christians wound up going to the same church. It would be miraculously normal for believers going to different churches; yet, coming together for worship and fellowshipping from house to house.

No doubt, miracles do happen, but if a person's relationship with God depends on one miracle to the next, then that person will regret it one day. Don't miss the biggest miracle of living normally by the power of His divine life abiding within every believer in Jesus Christ.

The Fruit of the Spirit Is Expressed in Miraculous Normality

Let's consider miraculously normal love. The definition of love is the willingness to sacrifice something of value for another person. The deeper the love, the greater the sacrifice. It is normal to witness people loving others. Billions of human parents sacrifice much for their children; it is normal to witness love even between men and women. However, what about the prolonged ability to love someone who is contradicting and wanting to cause you harm? For you to love such a person is miraculously normal, since only divine-eternal life within a believer can live such a life of loving his/ her enemy. We became God's enemy; yet, He loved us to such an extent He sacrificed His Only Begotten Son to die for us. To people observing a person's care and kindness for another is not extraordinary since those types of displays can be observed many times a day. However, when they find out the person being cared for by you is your enemy, then something of a miracle is manifested. They will not be able to understand how it is possible for you to love your enemy. They may even consider it a miracle; however, it is ordinarily expressed.

It is normal because this ability to love an enemy is within every single believer. People can witness such love and care within many followers of Jesus. Don't wait for an outward miracle to happen — the miracle is already within. It is Jesus living in you. It is His divine-eternal life empowering your love. It is your human love in action, but the source of the energy to love is God's. You have become a brother of Jesus on earth — God in the flesh. It seems nothing outward has changed, but your inside, your heart, your feelings, and thinking are changed by His divine life. This is miraculously normal.

The same can be described concerning patience, endurance, joy, forgiveness, faithfulness, self-control, and many other human virtues normally expressed by people; yet, for believers, there is more. The source of their human virtues cannot be depleted. They are powered by divine life, by God Himself indwelling His people. This is the fruit of the Spirit.

> "But the fruit of the Spirit is love, joy, peace, longsuffering, kindness, goodness, faithfulness, gentleness, self-control. Against such there is no law."
>
> – Gal 5:22-23

Consider the fruit of the Spirit on this list, there is nothing miraculous here. In fact, all items listed are quite ordinary. Every person on earth can claim they possess, experience and manifest each one of these items at various times. On this list, there is nothing about speaking in an unlearned dialect (tongues), about miraculous healing, or supernatural power; yet, it is called the fruit, the result of the Spirit, the very expression of the Spirit. How is the Spirit expressed? Through human virtues as listed in these verses. When they are expressed, there is something eternal and divine. Long after these characteristics would naturally run out, those living by this eternal life continue to express these virtues. Haven't we heard or uttered: "my patience ran out" - "my love ran out" - "this is the last straw" – "I'm at my wits end" or "I can't forgive anymore?" When love, joy and peace should have run out due to circumstances, those drawing from God's Spirit continue expressing and having love, joy and peace. This is both divine and human; "divinely human" – miraculously normal.

When there is no reason for joy; yet, by looking to Jesus, there is inner joy and rejoicing. During disturbing circumstances, when anxiety should rule the day, there is divine peace in God. No struggling or irritation when an antagonist is disrupting; rather, there is patience and an extension of peace. This too is miraculously normal.

A good illustration of the fruit of the Spirit is shown by a hand inside a glove. Consider a glove: it has four fingers and a thumb. A glove looks identical to a hand, it can even be mistaken as a hand. However, if a hand is not inside the glove, then the glove is not animated. It is just a lifeless glove that looks like a hand. However, if there is a hand in the glove then the two work as one. The glove would be powered by the hand.

The glove can be illustrated as man (male and female) was created in the image and likeness of God (Gen. 1:27); therefore, the glove with five digits can be likened to humanity with five virtues such as: love, joy, peace, self-control, and kindness. These can be likened to Jesus Christ with His divine-eternal attributes. Without Christ in humanity, humanity may have the same virtues as Christ; they may express many of His attributes, but there is no substance behind the "digits" of love, joy, peace, self-control, and kindness. The real "digits" showing the virtues of humanity is Christ. Without Christ in humanity, there can be the likeness of love, joy, peace, etc.; people do have such, but they lack power, endurance, and the sweetness of divine life behind their virtues. With Christ living in humanity, then Christ and humanity work together to have one manifestation. The virtues are the same, but now they last beyond what is normal – their intensity is amplified. They are expressed in circumstances where they are not expected to be found. This is the fruit of the Spirit. This is having Jesus to be life within His people – they become His life lived out through humanity. This is the "integrated life" and living between Jesus and His people, while still living in their flesh (body), they are manifesting this miraculously normal life.

Miraculously Normal Victories

Consider the human body; every day there are billions/trillions of pathogens (germs and viruses) within and outside the body. They are constantly seeking an opening to attack the body. Nevertheless, when the body is healthy, all the pathogens are contained, they are defeated and have little impact. This also is a good illustration of our miraculously normal life. In a way, it is a miracle how humanity can live and multiply over these thousands of years when the body is constantly being attacked from outside and from within the body.

With all the pathogens around and within, there are individuals who are constantly worrying about getting sick with various diseases. There is a name for these individuals: *hypochondriacs*. They can worry themselves sick due to being overtly anxious by becoming sick from of all the pathogens around them.[1]

In a general sense, if people would take care of their body by receiving proper nourishment; by keeping themselves well hydrated; by resting regularly and adequately; by exercising frequently; then they would be able to stay healthy despite the billions of pathogens in and around them. Even when they do get sick, typically, the best way to recover is to again eat well, drink, and get as much rest as possible. The body itself has a defense mechanism to combat and overcome all foreign germs and viruses seeking to destroy the body. This is another illustration of miraculously normal. As people live from day to day enjoying life and getting things done, the immune system within the blood stream in their bodies silently and effectively works to defeat the enemies of the body.

In the spiritual realm, there are also "pathogens" which include such things as sin within the flesh, as well as Satanic/demonic forces without. These conspire together to weaken and causing believers to become spiritually sick while manifesting such symptoms as: discouragement, depression, spiritual deadness, and loss of heart for God and people. However, if the physical body can fight off pathogens in a normally healthy body, then the spiritual being can certainly have victory over spiritual "pathogens" all the more.

> "These things I have spoken to you that in Me you may have peace. In the world you will have affliction but take courage; I have overcome the world."
>
> –John 16:33

> "Now is the judgment of this world; now will the ruler of this world be cast out."
>
> –John 12:31 ESV

---

1   https://www.sandiegouniontribune.com/sdut-ill-illusions-ailments-may-be-imaginary-but-2010mar23-htmlstory.html

"Since therefore the children share in flesh and blood, he himself likewise partook of the same things, that through death he might destroy the one who has the power of death, that is, the devil . . . ."
— Heb 2:14 ESV

"We know that our old self was crucified with him in order that the body of sin might be brought to nothing, so that we would no longer be enslaved to sin."
— Rom 6:6 ESV

"But if we walk in the light as He is in the light, we have fellowship with one another, and the blood of Jesus Christ His Son cleanses us from all sin."
— 1 John 1:7

There are Christians who are likened to spiritual hypochondriacs. They are hypersensitive to demonic forces and Satan's power. They are constantly aware of the sins and temptations within them and in others. Just like physical hypochondriacs who are afraid to touch things or come near people in their environment — being terrified of picking germs and viruses — these spiritual types can become manically fearful of being in various "worldly" environments and being close to those they consider as "sinners." They are afraid evil spirits will attack them or influence them in some way. To them, their environment is a constant battle against evil. It seems their focus is more on the negatives of evil and sin rather than looking at their victorious Christ.

One's spiritual being also needs to be healthy. To have spiritual vigor, there is also a corresponding need for nourishment, exercise, and rest. If believers recognized they are constantly in Christ, they can simply access spiritual food daily; they can easily exercise spiritually over the course of a given week, while resting in Christ for His purpose. By doing so they automatically become healthy. Instead of focusing on the negatives of evil around and within them, Christians should attend to the positive life of the indwelling Christ while providing service to both God and humanity. Doing so will keep them healthy. Experiencing such vigor will deplete the negativity of sins — defeating the devil and his wiles. Sin and Satan is no longer a barrier to all the benefits of grace constantly available to all of God's people.

No matter how healthy a person thinks he or she is, there still is occasional sickness. Similarly, a believer who is spiritually healthy does not mean he or she will never fall into sin anymore or have other failures. However, even in such negative occurrences, healthy believers with their focus on a positive relationship with Jesus Christ will learn and gain from every single failure. They will not be deterred. They will continue to run their spiritual course with resolve, while positively affecting their own humanity.

The Scripture clearly states the victories of Christ in all His followers (1 John 4:4). It is abundantly apparent the enemy, Satan, the ruler of this world, was overcome by Jesus. When Jesus died on the cross, He destroyed the one holding the power of death, the devil (Heb. 2:14). The word *destroy* in the Greek means *to made useless or ineffective*. Satan's power has been abolished.

Similarly, according to Romans 6:6, the body of sin was terminated on the cross of Christ. Sin is no more the master — believers are no longer slaves to sin. They are no longer enslaved; they cannot be destroyed by this "pathogen" of sin within. Just like the physical blood within the human body combats and subdues pathogens in the body, the blood of Jesus Christ is constantly cleansing believers of sin. As they stay in healthy fellowship with the Lord Jesus and with other believers, the blood of Jesus keeps on cleansing them from all sin.

Even after sundry occasions of falling into sin, every believer needs to continue their healthy spiritual practice by confessing their sins and restoring any loss of fellowship with the Lord and other believers. As Christians, we do not have a license to sin just because we are forgiven, but when we do, we have propitiation for our sins and an advocate with the Father (1 John 2:1-2). We can continue our journey forward.

Therefore, let's not become spiritual hypochondriacs living in anxiety and fear of the negative: Satan, evil spirits, and sin; rather, let's pursue Jesus. Keep our eyes fixed on Him by believing all negative things in the universe have been fully defeated and made harmless through the death of Jesus Christ Who took the penalty for our sin on the cross.

Did Miracles Ceased?

Certainly, there are still miracles done by God and there are clearly believers who are gifted with supernatural abilities (1 Cor. 12:9-10). In many instances, deliverance from demonic possession wrought by believers who walk in authority for this type of "deliverance ministry" are necessary within the Body of Christ. The goal of this book is not to depreciate such signs and wonders, but to uplift and call attention to the miraculously normal living and works of God. Yes, those gifted with such specific supernatural ability are needed in the Body of Christ; however, according to the apostle Paul, not every Christian is so gifted (1 Cor. 12:28-30). Nevertheless, the miraculously normal living and service can be activated and achievable by every single believer.

Consider all the epistles written after the book of Acts starting with Romans to Jude. Out of 121 chapters, only one chapter (1 Cor. 12), coupled with three other verses (Gal. 3:5; Heb. 2:4; James 5:16), speaks of miracles and supernatural healing. Paul's letter to the Romans can be considered his complete theology; his letters to the Ephesians, Colossians, and Philippians are considered the pinnacle in unveiling God's mysteries; His pastoral letters to Titus and Timothy are viewed as the most practical; yet, in all these letters, miracles, signs and wonders were not mentioned even once. Neither did Peter or John in their epistles mention such miracles. Additionally, there was not one mention throughout 121 chapters regarding deliverance from demonic spirits or possession. This is certainly surprising: Peter, John and Paul, who had witnessed and performed so many miracles themselves, only referenced this matter in a handful of verses. Though they had witnessed and cast out many evil spirits, they didn't mention this activity once in their epistles.

Instead, all the chapters are focused on helping distracted believers return to Jesus Christ — His person and work. Not simply Christ in the heavens, but the indwelling Christ and His corporate Body. While not all believers are gifted with supernatural abilities, every single believer can be expected to live and serve according to the riches of Christ they possess in order to build up God's ekklesia, which is the Lord's Body. These were the main items in their messages throughout the epistles: the person and work of Jesus Christ; the indwelling Christ received, lived, and flowing out of believers to others; and the building up of His ekklesia, His Body. In other words, the miraculously normal living and service of every Christian through the life, truth, and glory given by our Lord in John 17.

It is clear there is a distinct difference between the Gospels and the Acts when compared to the epistles in relation to the recording and referencing of miraculous signs and the casting out of demons. During the period of the gospels and Acts, it was the preaching and spreading of the good news of Jesus Christ. For this gospel work, not only did Jesus performed many miraculous signs, including the casting out many demonic spirits, but the Lord also gave His disciples authority to do the same. These supernatural actions demonstrated the divinity of Jesus Christ. People needed to believe in the divinity of Jesus in order to be saved. Therefore, according to the Lord's word, even today, Christians should exercise their authority in preaching Jesus Christ and expect signs and wonders to confirm the gospel of Jesus Christ (Acts 2:22, 43; 4:30).

On the other hand, the epistles were written to believers, those who are already following Jesus. They didn't need any signs (1 Cor. 14:22). What they needed was the full knowledge of the truth (1 Tim. 2:4); the maturity found in divine life (1 Cor. 3:1; Eph. 4:13); and the ministry of Christ for the building up of His Body (Eph. 4:16; 1 Cor. 14:26) through the empowering glory of Jesus Christ (2 Cor. 3:18).

> "And He said to me, 'My grace is sufficient for you, for My strength is made perfect in weakness.' Therefore, most gladly I will rather boast in my infirmities, that the power of Christ may rest upon me."
>
> – 2 Cor. 12:9

Paul Himself has supernaturally healed numerous people; even his handkerchief had the power to heal many (Acts 19:12). Paul delivered many from demonic possession in their flesh. However, when he was troubled with a thorn in his own flesh from Satan — while earnestly praying for its removal, the Lord said His grace was sufficient for Paul.

Here is a testimony of being miraculously normal: A person who is struggling with a thorn from Satan persists in the grace of the Lord. The word *grace* in the Greek literally means *joy, enjoyment, delight, and pleasure*. Here is Paul with this thorn which no amount of prayer can remove; yet, he remains in grace. The Lord's grace was sufficient for him to continue his journey in the joy and pleasure of the Lord.

Isn't that miraculous; yet, totally normal? From a human point of view, Paul remained in difficult circumstances, nothing changed. He is human like everyone else around him — normal. However, during such difficulties he maintained the enjoyment and delight of the Lord. No complaining, no blaming, and no discouragement; rather, he is able to boast in his weaknesses. This is miraculously normal.

Hearing this from the Lord and living in this grace, years later when Timothy, his young co-worker, was sickly, Paul didn't try to heal him. He told him to use a little wine for his stomach and for his frequent illnesses. Paul ended the letter to him with "grace be with you." Paul didn't exercise supernatural healing for Timothy; Paul simply told Timothy a typical remedy which people would normally take in those days for sicknesses: a little wine. Nevertheless, grace was with Timothy under such circumstances – miraculously normal.

Today numerous people are jaded by hyping up the "miraculous" with a large dose of skepticism. Clearly many are still fascinated with signs and wonders, but all people, no matter rich or poor, educated or uneducated, western or eastern are attracted to genuineness and authenticity of people who are kind, generous, loving, embracing, gentle, and magnanimous. These *divinely human* qualities are mysteriously pleasant and appealing to everyone.

> "But if the Spirit of Him who raised Jesus from the dead dwells in you, He who raised Christ from the dead will also give life to your mortal bodies through His Spirit who dwells in you."
> – Rom. 8:11

A hidden miracle is the Spirit indwelling all of God's people while they are still in their mortal bodies. Not only so, the Spirit is giving life, energizing, strengthening, and healing their mortal bodies. Believers may be going through life living normally as do all people, but very often, inexplicably, their mortal bodies are receiving a boost of life seemingly from nowhere. Many times, it can be in the form of healing, health, and strength in their mortal bodies. However, it doesn't seem particularly out of the ordinary, it is just normal. In other words, it may not be miraculous being healed from Stage 4 cancer; rather, it may be just keeping cancer cells in check, so it never multiplies and takes hold. So, who is to say whether it was natural or miraculous? It is a miracle to be miraculously healed of cancer; but isn't it a miracle not to have cancer in the first place? Receiving life in one's mortal body from the Spirit is also miraculously normal.

As believers live their lives in fellowship with the Spirit, with their minds focused on Jesus Christ being in them and on the throne in heaven – gradually, their spirit, and soul, and body are being sanctified (1 Thess. 5:23). They live and serve God as people living out the life and strength of the Lord. They are at peace bearing no anxiety. They can trust the Lord inwardly working His miracles in them in a way which seems regular and mundane. There is no weariness but only grace and rest. It is hard for people around them to understand because they are living a life which is miraculous, yet normal.

What Believers Need Today Are Not Miracles, but Normal Groth

The motivation for this book is not for the gospel's impact upon the unbelieving; rather, it is an encouragement for divided believers to mature and build up the Lord's ekklesia, His one Body. Today there are something like 2 billion professing to have the faith of Jesus Christ (including Catholics, Orthodox, Protestants, unaffiliated believers); yet, there are over 30,000 different kinds of churches and denominations with more independent churches starting every year. It is not simply an increase in ministries (which is acceptable), but most of these ministries become their own churches or groups where Christians in one group do not fellowship with those in another group. It seems the oneness Jesus prayed for in John 17 is still far from being answered. Where is the expression of different kinds of believers gathering as the Lord's ekklesia; yet, in one accord glorifying God (Rom. 15:6)? Where are believers arriving at the unity of the faith for the building up of His body through the equipping by differing ministers and pastors (Eph. 4:12-13)?

This book (including the other 2 books in this trilogy) is written with the express purpose to help believers to have the knowledge, vision, maturity and fruitfulness for the Lord's one ekklesia. It follows the same heart and emphasis as the epistles. There is little discussion in this text concerning matters which are purely miraculous, but there is extensive elaboration on the miraculously normal.

> ". . . so that you are not lacking in any gift, as you wait for the revealing of our Lord Jesus Christ. . . ."
>
> – 1 Cor. 1:7 ESV

> "But I, brothers, could not address you as spiritual people, but as people of the flesh, as infants in Christ."
>
> – 1 Cor. 3:1 ESV

Consider the saints in Corinth, they were not lacking in any gifts. They had all the gifts listed in 1 Corinthians 12 including healing, works or miracles, tongues and interpretations; however, Paul said they were not spiritual, but in the flesh — infants in Christ. Their divisiveness was the evidence of their being infants (1 Cor. 1:10). Divisions and factions (worse, divisiveness and being factious) among believers are due to spiritual immaturity; whereas, oneness and unity is a sign of maturity (Eph. 4:13). Spiritual maturity is the ability to love others who are contrary, to forgive those that are offensive, to be kind to the abrasive, and being a peace maker among those in various factions. These are the characteristics of mature believers who can be a catalyst for unity among divided believers. They are the "approved" ones among those who are in factions (1 Cor. 11:19).

This book and the other two books in the Trilogy are designed to highlight the Lord's prayer for the oneness of His people — while focusing upon equipping believers to grow and mature. My intention is not to criticize those practicing miraculous gifts; rather, it is to highlight the maturity of life needed for the building up of the one Body of Christ, His ekklesia.

In part 1 of this book, the four elements of life enabling growth, multiplication and maturity will be explored: nutrients, air, exercise, and rest. These four essentials are needed for the divine-eternal life to transform the followers of Jesus Christ. It is through the growth of God within believers the Body of Christ is built up (Col. 2:19). Practicing and enjoying these four essentials will enable all believers to live a daily life which is **miraculously normal**.

3

MIRACULOUSLY NORMAL SERVICE

Service can be considered as a job or work, a function to do something to benefit others. In the New Testament, the word *service* has the same meaning as *ministry*. There are two Greek words for *service* or *ministry*. One is *diakonia* which means *a servant*, one who executes the command of another, one who prepares and serves food (Strong's). The second word is *huperetes* which literally means an *under rower* (Thayer's), a person who does the rowing of a boat underneath the deck. This is like an invisible servant doing the work without recognition.

As believers, all of us are expected to be servants of God and man. The ultimate service to men is to serve or minister Jesus Christ as food for them to partake. Fallen humanity is devoid of God (Eph. 2:12). Not only so, they do not have a desire for God (Rom. 3:11). They have no hunger for God. When Jesus Christ is preached as the gospel, it is a description of Who He is and what He has accomplished for humanity. As the hearers listen, they come to appreciate Him; thus, an inward appetite is awakened to "*taste and see that the Lord is good.*"

Simultaneously, the minister of Christ then serves Jesus Christ as food – as sustenance – to fulfill the hunger in those listening. The hearer will receive Jesus Christ by faith in order to have eternal life. This is the meaning of preaching the gospel: to serve Jesus Christ as nourishment (John 6:51) to humanity.

Ministers should not stop there with the gospel of Jesus Christ just to unbelievers; no, they should continue to preach the gospel to saints (Rom. 1:7, 15). True preachers of the gospel will persist in presenting the truth of Jesus Christ to believers in order for them to grow, become fruitful, mature, and be built into the One Body of Christ. The apostle Paul as a minister of Jesus Christ (1 Cor. 4:1) continued to feed believers (1 Cor. 3:2) by announcing to them "Christ in you" until they would become mature in Christ (Col. 1:25-29).

This is the ultimate service to God: to build up the ekklesia which is His eternal purpose. Servants of God are to serve God by their participation and contribution into the building up of the one Body of Christ, God's Kingdom, the Temple, the Bride of Christ, and eventually, the New Jerusalem. Again, God's eternal purpose of His ekklesia is the subject of the first book of this Trilogy, *One Ekklesia*.

The building up of His ekklesia through the gospel of Jesus Christ depends on real spiritual food. This sustenance is simply Jesus Christ — the ingesting of the Trinity. Christian growth is completely centered on the understanding, appreciation, partaking, enjoyment, and having a daily relationship with Jesus Christ. Christian service in the building up of His ekklesia is based on the distribution of Jesus Christ as nourishment to others. This includes equipping or discipling more believers to become ministers of Christ. God needs a growing network of ministers, or distributors of the unsearchable riches of Christ. This is God's *oikonomia* (economy) which was fully explained in the book, *One Truth*.

What does God's ekklesia, His kingdom manifested on earth before His second advent, look like? It is unity between diverse and different kinds of believers. Christians who are normally contrary to each other — racially, socio-economically, culturally, doctrinally, and experientially — are loving, caring, being kind, forgiving, sharing meals, and serving one another. They can fellowship together anytime, anywhere. They can assemble as the Lord's ekklesia where there is complete freedom to express "spiritual democracy" — yet, they are one. They are one as the Father and the Son are one, that the world may believe in Jesus Christ (John 17:21). This is how ultimate service to God is manifested — this is what it looks like.

Every Believer Needed to Fulfill God's Eternal Purpose

"And he gave the apostles, the prophets, the evangelists, the shepherds and teachers, to equip the saints for the work of ministry, for building up the body of Christ, until we all attain to the unity of the faith and of the knowledge of the Son of God, to mature manhood, to the measure of the stature of the fullness of Christ. . . .."

– Eph. 4:11-13 ESV

"For as in one body we have many members, and the members do not all have the same function, so we, though many, are one body in Christ, and individually members one of another. Having gifts that differ according to the grace given to us, let us use them: if prophecy, in proportion to our faith. . . .."

~ Rom. 12:4-6 ESV

As pointed out earlier, the building up of human kingdoms or civilization necessitates contribution and participation of billions of people in every part of the earth doing their small part. Likewise, the building up of God's kingdom on earth cannot be accomplished by an elite group of gifted leaders, prophets, teachers, evangelists, ministers and pastors. In the human kingdom, it would be remiss to think since the Wright brothers invented airplanes, they would manufacture millions of planes with scores of airports around the earth. Instead, it took millions of people to do their small part from mining, fabricating, engineering, building, paving, communicating, to piloting in order for this complex network of airports and planes to be connected worldwide.

In comparison, most Christians over the centuries expect a clergy class of people to build up God's kingdom while they are simply the spectators. To be a "good" Christian, they merely pay tithes in support of their church and ministers while attending one or two services a week — obedient to the rules the best they can. That may be the extent of 99% of lay involvement (non-clergy class). Therefore, the development of God's kingdom on earth, the building up of the Lord's ekklesia, is greatly hampered.

Although, churches through the centuries with prominent men of God in leadership have accomplished much to spread the gospel of Jesus Christ; yet, due to their systematic and organizational nature, they also have intensely suppressed the innate spiritual participation and activities of individual Christians. The clergy long ago became the permanent and unceasing teachers and pastors delivering "services" to their congregants, while their "pew sitters" have largely remained as babes, always needing further nourishment and care. By grouping Christians into churches under their purview, Christians have become more and more segregated and divided from one another. No wonder the kingdom of God has little manifestation.

According to Ephesians 4:11-13, gifted minsters such as apostles, prophets, evangelists, pastors and teachers are to equip ordinary believers so that each Christian would be activated to minister — to replicate that for which they have been equipped. It is when each believer is exercising, then the Body of Christ is built up. The manifestation of the building up of His One Body is seen in diverse believers arriving at the unity of the faith. They become one in fellowship and expression while they are still on earth.

God has given each of His people at least one gift for them to use for the building up of His ekklesia. If those gifts are dormant — not utilized — then it will be impossible to build up His Body. Some gifted men of God can lead tens of thousands of people to salvation, but where's the building up of His Body? A person's thigh muscle can lift more weight than other muscles, but how dreadful it would be if a person's body had just two big thighs — the rest of his body would be emaciated!

The norm among gifted ministers today has become opposite to the clear speaking of Scriptures. Today, it is expected a gifted minister or pastor expands a group of Christians under his/her care, which becomes his/her church. Since there is a goal to grow membership (whether formal or informal), they become protective of their flock with a clear desire to guard them from conflicting influences outside their church, denomination or spiritual community. Therefore, Christians are manipulated not to wander off and freely have spiritual association with other believers who may have a different set of doctrines as their own. In other words, if you are in a once-saved-always-saved church don't be in fellowship with those who think believers can lose their salvation. This protectionism mindset among gifted ministers and pastors has divided and segregated Christians over the centuries. The sheep do not belong to ministers, they belong to the Great Shepherd of the sheep!

However, the clear teaching of Scripture encourages gifted minsters should equip and furnish believers; whereby, they can directly build up the Body of Christ. The gifted teachers do not directly build up the Body of Christ; only the common, regular/ordinary believer can do *"the work of the ministry."* The result of such building enables Christians to arrive at the oneness or unity of the faith. They are able to freely associate and fellowship with all those who have faith in Jesus Christ no matter the different and conflicting doctrines or spiritual practices among them. This is maturity, a full-grown man.

God Needs Man to Build His Kingdom Together.

"And I tell you, you are Peter, and on this rock I will build my church, and the gates of hell shall not prevail against it. I will give you the keys of the kingdom of heaven, and whatever you bind on earth shall be bound in heaven, and whatever you loose on earth shall be loosed in heaven."

– Mat. 16:18-19 ESV

". . . from whom the whole body, joined and held together by every joint with which it is equipped, when each part is working properly, makes the body grow so that it builds itself up in love."

– Eph. 4:16 ESV

"Now to him who is able to do far more abundantly than all that we ask or think, according to the power at work within us, to him be glory in the church and in Christ Jesus throughout all generations, forever and ever. Amen."

– Eph. 3:20-21 ESV

On the one hand, Jesus plainly said in Matthew 16 that He will build His ekklesia, His Body, which is also God's kingdom. On the other hand, in Ephesians 4 the Apostle Paul spoke of each and every believer building up the Body of Christ. Yes, Jesus Christ built by accomplishing crucifixion and resurrection, but now He abides in every believer. Each one who believes in Him needs to be activated to build up the Lord's Body. When Christians are participating in the building up of the Lord's ekklesia, then the Lord is the One building through them. If believers do not build, neither can the Lord build. In other words, when believers preach the gospel, teach the truth, visit and serve people, reach out to others for fellowship, and gather as the Lord's ekklesia for building, then Jesus Christ is doing all those activities through them. If believers are dormant whereby they become mute regarding the gospel and the truth of our oneness in Christ – while staying only within their own comfortable group by not fellowshipping with other Christians – then Jesus Christ is obstructed in the building up of His ekklesia, His kingdom.

God's desire from the very beginning was to work in cooperation – as co-workers together with humanity. His kingdom in the New Testament

ation with His people for their building up together. ...ke creation into being at an instant. Everything of ...ic creation was supernatural beyond comprehension. ...s formed by God Himself. However, when it came to ...is kingdom on earth, the Body of Christ, which is His ekklesia, He needed to team-up with man (male and female).

What, God needs man? Isn't that sacrilegious? Couldn't God be completely self-sufficient and accomplish all He desired by Himself? Yes, according to the revelation of Scripture, God needs man to build His kingdom. Not just a few gifted men, but every single one of His people in His ekklesia is needed to build up His kingdom. If Christians are enlightened to see such a revelation, then they will no longer be dormant. They can no longer be satisfied to relegate all their responsibilities to these gifted ministers and teachers. They will see they are required to contribute their portion no matter how insignificant they may think it to be.

Therefore, the human body is a suitable illustration used by Paul to highlight the Body of Christ (1 Cor. 12). Every member is necessary. It is when every part of the body, including the internal organs, in sync together, then a person is healthy and beautifully balanced.

When comparing the verses in Matthew 16 above, and Matthew 18:20, the ekklesia functions as God's kingdom on earth influencing the heavens. The concept most Christians have is this: God in heaven is directing matters on earth. Indeed, this was the case in Old Testament times. God, from the heavens, directedly manipulated various prophets and priests concerning their every move — what and how to carry out His dictums. However, God's eternal desire does not work in this manner; rather, He wants His kingdom on earth to directly influence the heavens: What the ekklesia on earth has bound or loosed is what shall be bound or loosed in the heavens. It is no longer God making decisions and doing what He wants all by Himself; instead, He is waiting for the members of His ekklesia, even 2 or 3 of her members in one accord, to make binding and loosing decisions on earth in order to effect divine change in the heavens.

As discussed in the book, *One Ekklesia*, ekklesia is a gathering of believers from "factions" (1 Cor. 11:19). Ekklesia is inclusive of all God's people no matter their differences in perspective, experience, or doctrinal understanding. Therefore, the two or three gathered in the Lord's name are not referring to two or three believers in harmony because they are from the same church, under the same ministry, with the same doctrinal mindset. Rather, these two or three are in the context of and within the Lord's ekklesia. These two or three have become one in the Lord's name though they are different or conflicting in practice and peripheral doctrines. They have dropped their concerns for their differences in order that they be gathered into the Lord's name. It is in this oneness they have the same authority as the ekklesia to bind and to loose.

For example, the two or three are not necessarily two or three from the same "Pentecostal" perspective; rather, one may be so oriented, but the other may consider such Pentecostal experience as strange or fake. Nevertheless, they would be willing to lay those differences aside and come together simply *into the name* of the Lord. It is in this fellowship of diversity in oneness, Jesus enters their midst. It is here they exercise their authority as the Lord's ekklesia to bind and to loose.

Ephesians 3:20-21 supports this reality. The phrase *"[God] is able to do far more abundantly above all that we ask or think"* is certainly acceptable to all Christians. This is, however, our understanding of the God of the Old Testament. Even any God-fearing person outside of Christianity can agree to such a statement. However, if such an awareness is taken in context, we discover the following: *God is able to do far above what we ask or think is according to the power at work within us*. He is not doing this on His own in the heavens; instead, He's working this out according to the power at work within the believer. If believers are activated, they will allow His power to work within them, then God is able to go far beyond our imagined efforts. Remember, today's human kingdom/civilization is beyond what men could have only imagined a hundred years ago. God's kingdom is the reality of Him being able to do above all we ask or think when His people are activated to do their small part.

Likewise, in Ephesians 3, God is working according to His power in each believer in relationship to the framework of His ekklesia. All kinds of believers are needed in order to apprehend the dimensions of Christ (Eph. 3:18). It is in the building up of the ekklesia where those normally in factions are fellowshipping together. This is where the glory of God is manifest. This is where the display of His wisdom to all principalities and powers, including Satan (Eph. 3:10), is on display. In other words, it is when diverse believers work together according to the "power which operates in them" toward the unity of Jesus Christ is when God will do above all what they ask or think. It takes the power of Christ's resurrection and ascension in His followers (Eph. 1:19-23) to break down the wall of division between them. Hence, the cooperation and activation of all believers are indispensable in their commission to preach the complete gospel of the kingdom, including the gospel of the grace of God and the gospel of peace.

The normal building up of God's kingdom is truly miraculous; yet, when it occurs normally to every believer, everywhere, every time they spiritually participate, then it becomes very ordinary. When a Christian presents the gospel of Jesus Christ while teaching the truth to another person, it may appear as hollow words, but behind this kind of speaking, God is working and giving the gift of faith to the hearer. At a certain point of hearing, the hearer will receive faith in Jesus Christ. They will repent and receive eternal life. Isn't that miraculous! Yet, it can normally happen every day throughout the earth. Similarly, when the truth of Jesus Christ is ministered, growth happens: A person can be transformed from weakness to strength, from discouragement to becoming energized, from passivity to motivation for God's purpose, from isolation to fellowship with others, and from division to gathering as the Lord's ekklesia.

Furthermore, consider the building up of the Lord's ekklesia as described in 1 Corinthians chapters 11-14. It seems so normal for believers holding different perspectives, who customarily would find themselves in different groups, to be gathered for a meal and break bread as the Lord's ekklesia. Over the course of their gathering they become united in the Gospel of Peace, loving one another, even though they still may have divergent doctrines and perspectives. Both diversity in unity and God Himself is now manifested among them whereby even the unbelieving will fall down to worship God. Isn't it a miracle for divided Christians to become one and for the unbelieving to see *God is among you of a truth*? Yes, and it should be the normal occurrence from house to house all over the earth. This is the building up — the manifestation of the kingdom of God in miraculous normality.

Those Who Know God Will Take Action

"With flattery he will corrupt those who act wickedly toward the covenant, but the people who know their God will be strong and take action."

– Dan. 11:32 CSB

"Go, therefore, and make disciples of all nations, baptizing them in the name of the Father and of the Son and of the Holy Spirit ...."
– Mat. 28:19 CSB

"So then, King Agrippa, I was not disobedient to the heavenly vision."
– Act 26:19 CSB

The need for God and man working together in order to fulfill His eternal purpose was alluded to in the Old Testament. At the very beginning of Genesis, it says: "God didn't send the rain and there was no man to till the ground." God sending rain which can be allegorized as the Spirit from God; while man tilling the ground is likened to man's labor and effort. God connected His outpouring with human effort. This is teamwork in action – this is a partnership between God and humanity. In relation to His purpose on earth, God wanted to be limited by man's efforts. If there is no human effort, God will also withhold His blessings. When there are humans working toward His purpose, He freely sends the Spirit.

This principle can be seen in major stories throughout the Old Testament. Noah needed to build the ark before God was able to judge evil on the earth. Abraham needed to leave his homeland and relatives for the promise land before God could abundantly bless him. God needed Moses to bring Israel out of Egypt. David was needed to fight in the Good Land before God could defeat all the enemies of Israel. Solomon was needed to build the temple before God could pour out His glory and fill the temple. Zerubbabel was needed to lead a return from Babylon back to Jerusalem for the rebuilding of the temple.

God easily spoke into being the creation of the entire universe, but He didn't speak into existence a little ark into being. He didn't recreate another people in the promise land. He didn't just blow upon and defeat Israel's enemies while the "armies of Israel" sat there and did nothing, nor did He speak the temple into being. No, each one of these momentous events of God's move on the earth needed God and man working in partnership. How limiting it is for the God of the universe to be constrained by lowly and weak men of flesh. Nevertheless, that is exactly what He did. This is miraculously normal.

Therefore, Daniel declared "*the people who know their God will be strong and take action.*" Those who know God and His way of working together with His people will know how to be strong and take action. Those who know God, which includes knowing His eternal purpose, do not wait; they move and act quickly and confidently.

In the New Testament, it is even more pronounced: Paul declared that ministers are co-workers together with God. They work as a team toward God's eternal purpose in the building up His ekklesia. Paul in 1 Corinthians 3 states: "*I have planted, Apollos watered, but God gives the growth.*" This sounds like what was pointed out in Genesis 2:5. Paul was needed to plant, and Apollos was required to water in order for God to give the growth. By logical deduction, He cannot cause His kingdom to grow without the working and efforts of men (male and female). Couldn't God do the planting and watering Himself, or couldn't He cause things to grow without the planting and watering? Apparently, the answer is *no*. He desires and mandates His coworkers to team up together for His kingdom to grow and be built up.

The Lord Jesus made it clear in Matthew 28:19: GO. All authority has been given to Me, now GO. There is no longer any need to wait. What is lacking is for Christians to go. For the establishing of God's kingdom: GO. The Lord Jesus has received all authority; He is now in believers as their life. He has clothed His followers with power; therefore: GO. If His people do not go to baptize and make disciples, then the kingdom of God would remain only with Jesus Christ and the 12 or the 120, at best, in the upper room.

Fortunately, the 120 in the upper room came out from the room after being equipped by the baptism of the Holy Spirit and went. Although Paul was not in that number; yet afterwards, he was called to follow Jesus. Paul saw the heavenly vision of the Lord's one Body; he was faithful to that vision until the end of his life.

How was Paul faithful to the heavenly vision? After his conversion to faith in Jesus Christ, "*immediately he proclaimed Jesus*" (Acts 9:20). Even before Paul was sent out by the brothers in Antioch, he was already preaching the gospel of the kingdom. Christians do not become activated due to some form of appointment; rather, every Christian should already be activated from the moment of faith in Jesus Christ. Any official appointment as an apostle, prophet, evangelist, pastor or teacher is not necessary. It is in the activation and utilization of the gift of the Spirit of Grace (Heb. 10:29) whereby a believer's spiritual endowment is recognized – then, fellow believers will recognize this person's role in the Body.

Before Paul's baptism, he was told by God to wait at a certain place for Ananias. After baptism, there was no more record of Paul waiting for God to tell him where to go or what to do. He took action, initiative, to go about doing extensive activities in the spreading of God's kingdom, the building up of His ekklesia. While it was typical in the Old Testament for God to tell the prophets where to go and what to speak, there was only one such record in the book of Acts where God supernaturally told Paul to go to Macedonia in a dream. However, even in such a case, he was in the midst of taking action by going to Bithynia. It was God diverting His going rather than initiating his going. He was not idly waiting for God to lead him.

Although Paul took initiative while being very resourceful for the spreading of the gospel, God teamed-up with him all along the way. Where Paul went; God went. What Paul spoke; God spoke. God was led by a man, because this man knew God's heart and God's eternal purpose. He saw the heavenly vision; he took action to fulfill this vision.

When Paul wanted to go to Jerusalem the last time, he was told by the Holy Spirit through a prophet of God he would be bound if he went to Jerusalem. Believers then told Paul not to go to Jerusalem. Regardless, Paul went anyway. He would not listen to the warning of the Holy Spirit nor the restraining of the saints. In typical Christian logic, Paul was on his own because the Lord would have left him to his own demise for not listening to "God and man." Nevertheless, the Lord went with Paul. Not only did the Lord sustained him through his persecution in Jerusalem, but bore with him through his seeming disobedience; Paul was able to write epistles with the highest revelation concerning Christ as the Head of His One Body (Colossians), and the ekklesia as the Lord's Body (Ephesians). Therefore, God was able to unveil more revelation when he became a prisoner due to his taking action purely on his own initiative against the warning of the Spirit and the counsel of the saints.

In 1 Kings chapter 13, a story was told of a prophet who was killed due to his disobedience to God. Furthermore, his disobedience was not to do something sinful; rather, he simply went back to the city where God told him not to go. Moreover, in Old Testament times, a prophet could only speak what God had told him what to speak. Speaking anything more or less than what God spoke would put the prophet in danger of God's judgment.

Today, most Christians are still living under the concept of Old Testament times. They feel they shouldn't do anything for God unless they have a clear leading from God. They consider doing something without God's leading is to act presumptuously. They speak in terms like "God told me" or "I'm waiting on a word from the Lord." They need to wait on the Lord and have confidence in His guidance before any actions should be taken. They will not preach the gospel if God is not leading. They will not visit people unless the Lord told them to do so. They should not speak for the Lord unless the Holy Spirit is charging them. Therefore, most Christians are idle, with little confidence in building up God's kingdom. They may know God for their personal salvation, but they do not know God in His eternal purpose. They are not driven by a heavenly vision. They are "waiting on the Lord" — not taking initiative with the Lord.

The apostle Paul tells the followers of Jesus to imitate him. He said: "*become imitators of me*" (1 Cor. 4:16). Certainly, this is a characteristic of Paul in which believers should imitate him. His relentless pursuit of the vision he received is manifested in his own initiative to fulfill God's eternal purpose embedded in that heavenly vision received from God.

What was the heavenly vision Paul saw (Acts 26:13-19)? In short, He saw believers of Jesus on earth are just Jesus Himself. He was persecuting the Lord's followers, but the Lord Jesus in heaven said, "*Why are you persecuting ME?*" Immediately Paul understood the people he was persecuting on earth were simply Jesus Himself. Therefore, he came up with the phrase: "*the Body of Christ*" to identify the Lord's people. They are Christ on earth. Based on this vision, Paul was called to build up the Body of Christ, His ekklesia. He endeavored to accomplish this in His ministry for the rest of His life.

Every Believer Is Qualified to Be a Servant

"To me, who am less than the least of all the saints, this grace was given, that I should preach among the Gentiles the unsearchable riches of Christ . . . .."

– Eph. 3:8

"This [is] a faithful saying and worthy of all acceptance, that Christ Jesus came into the world to save sinners, of whom I [Paul] am chief. However, for this reason I obtained mercy, that in me first Jesus Christ might show all longsuffering, as a pattern to those who are going to believe on Him for everlasting life."

– 1 Tim. 1:15-16

Clearly there are some qualifications laid out in Scripture concerning a person who is to be pointed out as an "elder" or a "deacon." These qualifications are clearly laid out in 1 Timothy 5 and Titus 1. If one is to be appointed in having a certain recognition among believers as an elder (Gr. *Presbyteros*) — one who is providing oversight (Gr. *Episkopos*) to believers — that person should possess certain qualifications. With those qualifications, believers may be supporting them materially (1 Tim. 5:17). In many churches today that person may be considered as a "pastor." If one is going to be recognized as a pattern for believers to respect and follow as examples (1 Pet. 5:3), then certainly there are some qualifications for such a person as laid out in the New Testament.

On the other hand, as far as preaching the gospel of Jesus Christ, loving and serving people, no requirements are given. Every single believer, no matter their spiritual condition is qualified to preach Jesus Christ and present Him to others for their salvation. Wouldn't it be ludicrous if a person starts considering whether he is worthy to throw a drowning person a floatation device? What if you see someone drowning and you begin to consider you are not worthy to help because you have just committed a sin, or you are not holy enough. No, you will throw that person a lifeline no matter what you think of your spiritual condition. The salvation of Jesus Christ is much more than a floatation device to save a person from drowning. It is to save people from eternal judgment and give them eternal life.

It is not your qualifications that save others. It is Jesus Christ. He is the qualified Savior. However, Jesus needs His people to speak and present Him to those drowning and spiritually dying. No matter what your spiritual condition is, you have the responsibility and privilege to be one who preaches the gospel of Jesus Christ to those in the grip of death.

Too often, believers become self-centered while considering their own spiritual condition before they will speak about Jesus to others. Most may feel unqualified to speak due to their self-condemnation due to their failures, sins or worldliness. Satan's accusations have silenced them from speaking about Jesus Christ. Those who may consider themselves qualified due to some level of holiness may come across with their own confidence and self-righteousness, tarnishing the good news of Jesus Christ.

Another example: Does a person have to be a good basketball player before he can point to the winning moves of his favorite basketball star? It would be ridiculous to say to a person: since you can't play basketball, I don't want to hear about how good your star player is. No, just because a person is not sinless and perfect as Jesus Christ, does not mean he cannot show his appreciation to the One who is sinless and perfect; Who died for humankind and resurrected and ascended as Lord and King. In fact, it is precisely when a person recognizes he is not perfect and sinless, he can be thankful and speak about His appreciation for Jesus Christ.

Therefore, qualifications are needed for one desiring the good work of having a status or recognition among the brethren as an overseer. However, no requirements are needed to speak the good news of Jesus Christ. All are qualified anytime, anywhere, just as they are. The only thing needed is a love for the lost and those needing to be fed with spiritual food.

Consider the apostle Paul. He said he is less than the least of all believers. He considered Himself the least qualified. Paul was given grace to preach the unsearchable riches of Christ. All the riches of Christ comprise the message Paul was given grace to speak. If he were given grace to speak the things of Christ, then every other believer has received the same grace to distribute the riches of Christ. According to Paul, no one is less qualified than he is.

Even nearing the end of his life, he considered himself the chief of sinners. It is through him as the worst sinner, we can see a pattern displayed of the effectiveness of God's eternal salvation. He never forgot his failures and his struggles with the thorn from Satan troubling him. If Paul can speak and preach Jesus Christ as the chief of sinners, certainly everyone else who has received this wonderful salvation can speak the same gospel of Jesus Christ to people all around.

As was discussed in the book *One Truth*, the gospel of Jesus Christ has two major impacts: The gospel of grace which saves individual sinners by grace through faith, and the gospel of peace which brings divided believers into one fellowship in Jesus Christ, i.e., into His One Body. The complete blessing of the gospel of Jesus Christ is grace and peace resulting in the building up of the Lord's ekklesia, which is His eternal kingdom.

Satan is the accuser of the brethren with an intention to shut up the words of their testimony concerning Jesus Christ (Rev. 12:10-11). Joining with him are the Pharisees and the religious leaders of their day who charged the disciples not to speak and teach in the name of Jesus (Acts 4:18). God needs everyone to speak up concerning His Son, Jesus Christ. Satan wants everyone to shut up and not speak anything concerning Jesus Christ. Which side would you pick?

Believers need to come into the understanding each of their small contributions is necessary. No matter their condition and level of spirituality, all are needed to do their tiny part in the building up of God's kingdom. Everyone needs to understand God's eternal purpose and come to know His ordained way of building up His one ekklesia, the Body of Christ.

Serving Faithfully When It Seems Impossible

Going back to the illustration of human civilizations being built up by so many people all over the earth doing seemingly insignificant jobs – these people, who are doing mining or working in a production line, produce products which become components which in turn provide humanity with a global flight system.

When Christians look at the darkness of this world and the rampant factions and divisions among God's people, a logical person no matter the amount of faith in God, might consider it impossible for the Lord's prayer for the oneness of His people to be a reality before the second advent of Jesus Christ. To these folks, the Lord's prayer in John 17 is simply rhetorical, at best a long shot, just an optimum expression of His good will never to be achieved – the "heavenly ideal" or simply idealistic; at best, something to shoot for but unattainable until His Second Coming.

If we look at the history of Christianity, it is much easier to bring a person to faith in Christ and be converted than to witness the building up of the Lord's ekklesia for which He prayed. Today, over 2 billion people consider themselves to have faith in Jesus Christ. In fact, there are numerous, credible stories of miraculous conversions in Moslem nations directly through dreams. Even in African nations such as Nigeria, 50% of the population consider themselves Christian out of 220 million. The point is the gospel of the grace of God is reaching people all over the earth; this will continue. Conversely, unity among God's people seems more and more difficult and remote since divisions or factions among Christians continue to increase – the more believers, the more factions!

However, it is clear the Lord's prayer for the oneness of His people must happen before His second advent, before the kingdom of this world becomes His kingdom. He specifically prayed in John 17 for His people in this world to become one in order that the world may believe in Him (John 17: 15, 21). The Bride, which is the Lord's ekklesia, has to make herself ready before the return of the Lord Jesus as the Bridegroom (Rev. 19:7).

The Lamb, Bridegroom, is not coming back to an immature infant who is divided in her defeat.

What glory is there for God, even after sending His Son to die and putting His Spirit in His people, clothing them with power; yet, they are divided, striving, and deprecating each other. What glory is there to the Father if His children remain infants and cannot mature.

Jesus is coming back to marry His Glorious Bride. It is the Father's will to find mature sons ready to inherit His Kingdom. It is the Spirit's will to have a Body coordinated under His bidding; God will have His Temple (dwelling place) built to express the oneness His people (Mount Zion), and the United Kingdom of David will no longer be scattered but gathered together for all eternity. This is the very glory of the Lord; this is shame to His enemy, Satan.

> "... the LORD and set me down in the middle of the valley; it was full of bones . . . and behold, they were very dry. And he said to me, 'Son of man, can these bones live?' And I answered, 'O Lord GOD, you know.' Then he said to me, 'Prophesy over these bones, and say to them, O dry bones, hear the word of the LORD . . . .' So I prophesied as I was commanded. And as I prophesied, there was a sound, and behold, a rattling, and the bones came together, bone to its bone . . . . So I prophesied as he commanded me, and the breath came into them, and they lived and stood on their feet, an exceedingly great army."
>
> – Ezek. 37:1-4, 7, 10 ESV

These bones that were dried and scattered were not referring to the world of unsaved people. Rather, it was the house of Israel, God's people — ALL Israel. Today's condition in Christendom is this Valley of Dry Bones. They are scattered, divided, dry and spiritually deadened. Ezekiel didn't have faith to answer in the affirmative when God asked him: "Can these bones live?" He could only answer: "Lord God, You know." He didn't want to say "no" because he knew God could do anything, but on the other hand, it was so depressing and devasting he couldn't muster the confidence to say "yes" either.

Can Christians really become one and arise as one army against the enemy, Satan? Anyone who is realistic, having followed Christian history, will have to demur and say to God "you know." Christians can believe just about everything in the Bible, but when it comes to the manifested oneness of the Body among diverse and contrary believers, their faith is truly challenged. It's just too ethereal. New believers will enthusiastically proclaim: "Yes, all believers are one." However, as they continue their Christian journey and join the ranks of older Christians, their enthusiasm begins to wane. Eventually, they too can only say: "Lord God, You know."

Let's witness real prophetic ministry — for this is a major vision of the latter days: Speak to the bones. Speak Christ and His one ekklesia to the bones. When the prophets speak according to the revelation of God's eternal purpose, God joins in to work. A human is doing the speaking and God is behind the scenes doing His job: joining the bones together, putting sinews on them, and breathing the breath of life into them so they rise up as one army.

No matter the division and spiritual deadness among God's people today, more and more prophets are needed to speak the entire revelation of God. More are needed to preach not just the gospel of grace, but the gospel of peace. Such speaking by God's people will cause God to work. He will make the bones come together and live. Humans have no such ability, but *we can speak and prophesy*. Again, we find ourselves cooperating with God; even when we question God's ability to bring them to life. God needs us to do the prophesying and we need God to bring these bones to life — that's His part. We are truly co-workers needing each other. This is miraculously normal service.

Keep Speaking Even When Nothing Seems to Be Happening

There is a story concerning Joseph in the Hebrew Scriptures. He was one of the sons of Jacob. He was one who interpreted dreams. God revealed to him the meaning of dreams. He dreamt there were eleven sheaves bowing down to him and the sun, moon and stars bowing down to him. He told his brothers his interpretations that they were all to bow down to him. By speaking forth this interpretation, his brothers detested him. They wanted to kill him. Instead they sold him into slavery. Joseph eventually wound up in an Egyptian prison.

He spoke concerning his being the ruler over his family — that they would bow to him. Instead, he was languishing in prison. This was the result of his interpreting his own dream. Maybe he misinterpreted his dream? Maybe his dream was a deception? It was such a dreadful reversal of his interpretation; he must have questioned his dream and interpretation every step of his journey of descending into prison with no hope of being released. At this point he should have lost all faith in dreams and their interpretations.

While in prison he met the baker and the cupbearer for Pharaoh. Both had a dream and they came to Joseph to seek understanding. One would think, based on his dismal track record, he would give up interpreting dreams. He didn't; rather, he kept his faith in what God had shown him. He interpreted their dreams – both dreams quickly came to pass in three days. That could have been depressing for Joseph: The interpretation of his own dream got him into prison without any fulfillment for over a decade; while these other people in prison with him got their dreams fulfilled in just three days.

Nevertheless, it was through the continuing use of his gift he was given a chance to analyze Pharaoh's dream. It was through the interpretation of Pharaoh's dream he became the governor over all of Egypt. Eventually, his original dream of the shaves bowing down to him was fulfilled when his entire family bowed down to him when they came to him for food in Egypt. In typology, Joseph ruling over the kingdom in Egypt can be likened to Jesus Christ becoming the King in God's kingdom. The New Testament's dream is for the kingdom of this world to become the kingdom of Jesus Christ where He will reign forever (Rev. 11:15).

The point is this, even when his interpretation of his own dream got him into trouble and eventually landed him in prison, he didn't waver, he didn't give up. He continued to use the gift God gave him toward others. Eventually, it was due to his enduring faith in God's gift, he was able to fulfill his own dream.

This can be applied to us today. Don't be discouraged and give up when you don't see the results of your service and ministry. You may speak God's vision concerning His eternal purpose of the one ekklesia. You may see relationship among those hearing these things getting worse instead of better. Don't despair! Continue in the ministry of the gospel of peace which the Lord has given to His people. Continue to speak the dream of believers participating and expressing the oneness of the Body of Christ. Continue to proclaim the good news of the kingdom where believers can remain with their distinctions, their different ways of expressing Christ — yet united under Him alone. All Christians should share this dream. They have hope! Be like Joseph — endure in service and ministry

God Working Behind the Scene

God's work in the New Testament for the building up of His ekklesia, His Kingdom, is akin to being miraculously normal. Certainly, God is working, but He likes to work in a way that is hidden. His working is in coordination with human effort; therefore, often it becomes indistinguishable whether it is a human or God working. The miraculously normal is manifested in many ways as we serve and minister to both God and others. Here are some examples:

- Inexplicable coincidences of being at the right place at the right time
- Open doors for ministry in people, places, and under circumstances beyond imagination
- The hearts and minds being prepared and ready to receive the gospel of grace and the gospel of peace
- Funding made available for service and support when needed
- People made happy and encouraged when the situation is dire
- The right people coming along side to support unexpectedly
- More people responding to the gospel of peace for the oneness of the Body than anticipated
- The spreading of a ministry much more effective than efforts expended
- Being kept safe during dangerous environments
- A mysterious source of physical strength and endurance when laboring

There are many more ways God is working than those seen above. All we ask or think according to the power operating within believers — that's miraculously normal. As believers labor toward the building up of His ekklesia, they will witness more and more how God is supporting, performing miracles in a way that seems ordinary and normal. However, God's work is hampered by Christians who appear dormant — not doing their part in service. They may be stuck in the "Lord, You know" syndrome.

In part 2 of this book, very practical steps are described for every believer to serve God and humanity according to God's economy. These activities are begetting, cherishing, nourishing, discipling, and building.

It is the gift of the Lord's glory which enables each Christian to perform these services faithfully. These activities may seem insignificant, but when believers do their small part, then taken aggregately all over the earth it is the **miraculously normal** building up and fulfillment of God's eternal purpose.

4

LOVE AND ONENESS

The night before the Lord Jesus went to be crucified on the cross was the most significant evening of His entire journey on earth before His death. Many crucial matters took place that evening. Without diving into and understanding this last evening, Christians can miss the entire counsel of God, His eternal purpose, and the way given to achieve God's eternal will.

Washing the Disciples' Feet

> ". . . rose from supper and laid aside His garments, took a towel and girded Himself. After that, He poured water into a basin and began to wash the disciples' feet, and to wipe [them] with the towel with which He was girded . . . .. " If I then, [your] Lord and Teacher, have washed your feet, you also ought to wash one another's feet."
>
> – John 13:4-5, 14

That evening Jesus being the Lord and master washed the disciples' feet. The washing of feet in those days was usually done by the lowliest of slaves since it was one of the most demeaning of chores. Due to dirty roads, feet needed to be regularly washed. It was also a sign of respect and hospitality to have the feet of guests washed.

If this event of Jesus washing his followers' feet was not recorded in the Scriptures, it would almost be impossible to believe such an act took place. Jesus is the God and the Creator of the universe. He is the Lord and Master; yet, He is the One washing the disciples' feet. Moreover, there is no record of any of the twelve washing Jesus' feet. In order to wash their feet, Jesus laid aside His position, dignity, splendor, and His divine glory to put on true humility and meekness. He became a slave to serve His followers.

Even more incredible was Judas Iscariot who was included with the twelve – Jesus washed the feet of Judas. Jesus had foreknowledge Judas' betrayal; yet, Jesus still washed His feet. What humility, love, care, and selflessness to wash the feet of someone who would deliver Him to death via betrayal. Jesus is the true pattern of loving your enemy.

Jesus commanded His disciples to do the same, to wash each other's feet. Dishonoring and humbling oneself to wash another person's feet, and especially one who is an enemy, is too much to ask of any person. People with the sin of pride simply are not capable of doing such a thing — and doing so, genuinely from the heart. Hallelujah, for believers in Jesus Christ who have Christ in them, His divine life enabling them to serve others in this way.

For Christians today, it may not be literally washing another person's physical feet. However, there are many other ways of serving and honoring others which requires the utmost in humility which only the miraculously normal life of Jesus Christ can do. It takes an amazing amount of divine power to be in and function under such humility. A typical reaction when someone is disrespected sounds something like this (although it may not be verbalized): "Who are you? Don't you know who I am?" It is so easy to write off and avoid an offending person when one gets insulted. A Christian in such a state will not be able to serve such an offending person. However, Jesus can!

A New Commandment: Love One Another as I Have Loved You

> "A new commandment I give to you, that you love one another; as I have loved you, that you also love one another. By this all will know that you are My disciples, if you have love for one another."
> – John 13:34-35

If asked "what is the greatest commandment?" — most Christians will quote: "*Love the Lord your God with all your heart and love your neighbor as yourself*" (Matt. 22:37-39). However, that was Jesus answering the question "*which is the great commandment in the law*" (Matt. 22:36). The law was given in the Hebrew Scriptures. Jesus summarized the requirements of the Old Testament: "*Love God with all your heart and love your neighbor as yourself*" (Deut. 6:4-5). This is the law of Moses related in the First Covenant, but this is not the commandment propounded by Jesus in the New Commandment, which is based upon the New Covenant, found in John 13:34-35.

Jesus gave a New Commandment. This New Commandment is embedded in the New Covenant. Jesus singled out only one commandment to be His commandment: *love one another as I have loved you*. He didn't give any other "commandment." He only gave one — He owned this one. He re-emphasized the New Commandment and said: "*This is MY Commandment, that you love one another as I loved you*" (John 15:12).

One may say, isn't this commandment the same as love your neighbor as yourself? It may sound about the same, but the source is completely different. The "original commandment" regarding "love" was to love God and to love your neighbor. The predicate of this old commandment was based upon the First Covenant (Heb. 8:7) with a requirement for humanity to fulfill this on their own. The source and energy to generate this love in the First Covenant has as its basis within man's capabilities, which has proven to be an impossible task. No one can be justified based on their ability to fulfill God's laws (Gal. 3:11). Indeed, "*For whoever shall keep the whole law and shall offend in one point, he has come under the guilt of breaking all*" (James 2:10 – Darby Version).

Whereas, the source of the New Commandment is Jesus Christ Himself being the love and life in the believer. A Christian can love others because they are tasting and enjoying the love of Christ within themselves. One can only love as Christ loves if Christ is the one doing the loving. "*. . . As I have loved you*" can only be accomplished if Christ is the source. Since Christians are receiving Christ's love as the source, they can in turn love others as Christ loves them. They have become conduits of Christ's love in life, nature, and expression. This is miraculously normal.

Christ loved and died for people when they were sinners and enemies (Rom. 5:5-11). They were against Him. They hated Him. They condemned and crucified Him. Nevertheless, Jesus Christ loved them and died for them in order to save them. Jesus is the embodiment and expression of God's eternal, divine love which is full of compassion and mercy. God is love. Jesus came to express that love by His death on the cross for all those who hated and killed Him.

This is the love believers have indwelling them with which they can love one another. While the "great commandment of the law" depends entirely on one's human effort predicated on their fallen nature – the New Commandment is totally dependent on the indwelling Spirit of Christ as the source within them.

Indeed, *"For the law was given through Moses, but grace and truth came through Jesus Christ"* (John 1:16). Yes, *"Noah found grace in the eyes of the Lord"* (Gen. 6:8); however, it is one thing to find favor (viz., "grace") in God's eyes, but it is quite another matter to have Christ as your grace, the supply in you, to fulfill the Law of Moses. Again, one thing for you to love God but altogether another matter to have the love of God abiding in you to love God and others as He loved us!

Yes, God Almighty gave the "great commandment of the law" — knowing full well that man was incapable of performing such a task in and of himself . . . therefore, He came and became our justification, our righteousness, our life so that we would be able to love one another as He loved us — this is wholly different; this is the New Commandment.

The current usage of "love" in society has cheapened this word. "Love" today it is akin to passionately "liking" something. Instead of *I like to play basketball*, it is *I love to play basketball*. Instead of *I like those shoes and purse* — it's *I love those shoes and purse*. Love has lost its meaning, especially as defined and expressed by God. God is love. God's love is sacrificial. When the Bible speaks of God's love, it is typically in connection to Him sending His Son to die for humanity (1 John 4:9). This sacrificial love produces many other actions such as kindness, mercy, forgiveness and much more.

Therefore, the one commandment Jesus gave to "love one another" is expressed in many facets. Out of this spawned many other "one anothers." All the other "one anothers" are the various expressions of "love one another." Below are just a few of the verses showing the expressions manifesting love based upon the Lord's New Commandment. These can be considered as love's ancillary instructions:

> "Therefore, let us not judge one another anymore, but rather resolve this, not to put a stumbling block or a cause to fall in [our] brother's way."
>
> – Rom. 4:13

> "And be kind to one another, tenderhearted, forgiving one another, even as God in Christ forgave you."
>
> – Eph. 4:32

"That there may be no division in the body, but that the members may have the same care for one another."

— 1 Cor. 12:25, ESV

"But whoever has this world's goods, and sees his brother in need, and shuts up his heart from him, how does the love of God abide in him?"

— 1 John 3:17

The entire chapter of 1 Corinthians 13 was dedicated to describing the characteristics of God's love. Spurgeon, a famous and well-respected preacher, spoke concerning 1 Corinthians 13:7: *"love bears all things, believes all things, hopes all things, endures all things"*. . .

"The love which is spoken of in this chapter is absolutely essential to true godliness. So essential is it that if we have everything else but do not have this love, it profits us nothing. This love is not the prerogative of a few, but it must be the possession of all believers. This love has four sweet companions. They are: tenderness that 'bears all things.' Faith that 'believes all things,' hope that 'hopes all things' and patience that 'endures all things.'

"The word rendered 'bear' might as correctly have been translated 'covers.' This love both covers and bears all things. It never proclaims the errors of others. It refuses to see faults unless it may kindly help in their removal. It stands in the presence of a fault with a finger on its lips. It does not attempt to make a catalog of provocations.

"Love 'believes all things.' In reference to our fellow Christians, love always believes the best of them. This love believes good of others as long as it can, and when it is forced to fear that wrong has been done, love will not readily yield to evidence but will give the accused brother or sister the benefit of many doubts. Some persons habitually believe everything that is bad about others, they are not the children of love.

"Love 'hopes all things.' Love never despairs. We should never despair of our fellow Christians. As to the unconverted, we will never do anything with them unless we hope great things about them. We need to cultivate great hopefulness about sinners.

"Love 'endures all things.' This refers to patient perseverance in loving. This is, perhaps, the hardest work of all, for many people can be affectionate and patient for a time, but the task is to hold on year after year. In reference to our fellow Christians, love holds out under all rebuffs. We endure not some things but all things for Christ's sake. As to the unconverted, they may shut their ears and refuse to hear us — never mind, we can endure all things."

Truly this New Commandment from the Lord Jesus is all-inclusive. This love includes every positive attribute and characteristic of divinity and humanity. This is the love with which Jesus loves His people, whereby they are to love others.

Accomplishing "As I Have Loved You"

The first part of the New Commandment: "*love one another*" is straight forward in our understanding. It is very similar to "*love your neighbor as yourself.*" Such a concept is easy to grasp. However, the phrase: ". . . *as I have loved you*" is difficult to explain. Does it mean believers are willing to die for each other? How is it possible to love as He loved us since He is the eternal God? Do Christians simply mimic Him as best they can, while trying to do as He does . . . WWJD (What Would Jesus Do)?

After Jesus gave His New Commandment in John 13, He proceeded to explain in detail how His people can fulfill: "*love one another as I have loved you.*" Remember "love" in God's definition is sacrificial. Therefore, in John 14, Jesus spoke of His imminent death by saying He is going away (John 14:3-4). Though the disciples were confused by the meaning of His going away, Jesus explained it in this manner: By His going, He would send the Spirit of Truth, the Helper or Paraclete (i.e. Comforter). The Spirit will come to indwell them, and He Himself would be coming to indwell them (John 14:17-18). That is not all, even the Father Himself who is the very embodiment of love would also indwell them (John 14:23). Through Jesus' death and resurrection, the entire Trinity came into His disciples. Not One was left out. They can love in truth, in reality. Now they could love as Jesus loved them. They can love with the love of God. Unlike the "first covenant" with its "Greatest Commandment" – which relied on self-effort – now in the New Covenant, the Lord made the way for believers to love one another as He loved them by living in them as the God of love. This is "empowering love."

In John 15, Jesus said He is the vine while His disciples are the branches of this vine. A vine is the sum of all the branches. A vine is not a vine without branches. At best it would just be a stump, but not a vine. By this one description, Jesus opened a heavenly and mysterious reality for through His death and resurrection all believers became a part of Him, His Body. He expanded and increased Himself from one person domiciled in the man, Christ Jesus, to millions as this universal vine. God's ekklesia is this vine: full of life, growth, duplication and multiplication. The branches are constantly bearing fruit: multiplying into an ever-increasing number of believers while displaying all the attributes of God. When the universe looks at this vine, what is seen is the vibrant, eternal, divine life coursing through all the branches – extending, life transforming, displaying love, joy, peace with other attributes of the Spirit expressed in humanity (Gal. 5:22). Jesus repeated His New Commandment again in this chapter (John 15:12) showing Christians can love one another as He loves, because they are as He: an integral part of the vine which is the increase of Himself.

Jesus continues in John 16:7 to encouraged His sorrowful disciples by declaring: *"Nevertheless, I tell you the truth: it is to your advantage that I go away, for if I do not go away, the Helper will not come to you. But if I go, I will send him to you."* This Helper is the Spirit of Truth who will guide believers into everything real concerning the Trinity. Everything that the Father is, and all that Jesus Christ has accomplished, will be declared and made real to all believers through the Spirit. All His followers become the recipients of the unsearchable riches of the entire Trinity expressed to all the universe. How awesome!

John 14 to 16 show His New Commandment was not an empty command without the provision needed for Christians to fulfill His commandment. Rather, after giving His New Commandment, He went to the cross to accomplish crucifixion and resurrection in order to enact the New Covenant; thus, fulfilling His New Commandment by living and being the very source of love in them to love one another. Unlike being under the First Covenant where humanity was condemned and cursed for their inability to fulfill the law, Jesus enacted the New Covenant so that they would be able to perform, thereby fulfilling the requirements of the New Commandment (Rom. 8:4). The New Covenant proclaims it is the Spirit of God within believers which causes them to "*walk in My statutes, and you will keep My judgments and do them*" because "*I will put My spirit within you*" (Ezk. 36:27).[2]

From Individuals to One New Man

> ". . . you will be sorrowful, but your sorrow will be turned into joy. A woman, when she is in labor, has sorrow because her hour has come; but as soon as she has given birth to the child, she no longer remembers the anguish, for joy that a human being has been born into the world. Therefore you now have sorrow; but I will see you again and your heart will rejoice, and your joy no one will take from you."
>
> – John 16:20-22

> "God has fulfilled this for us their children, in that He has raised up Jesus. As it is also written in the second Psalm: 'You are My Son, Today I have begotten You.'"
>
> – Act 13:33

> "For He Himself is our peace, who has made both one, and has broken down the middle wall of separation, having abolished in His flesh the enmity, [that is], the law of commandments [contained] in ordinances, so as to create in Himself one new man [from] the two, [thus] making peace . . . .."
>
> – Eph. 2:14-15

Continuing in John 16 Jesus likened the disciples' sorrow to giving birth: when a human being is born, all the sorrows are exchanged for joy and rejoicing. Jesus compared His going to death and resurrection as a birth of a new person, a man. Something wonderful took place when Jesus

---

2   One of the astounding discoveries of the "Love Commandment" has been made by Gaylord Enns in his text: *The Love Revolution*. In his research, Gaylord found that virtually all Early Church Fathers omitted any discussion of the New Commandment – God's love through believers was virtually obfuscated from their writings. Is it any wonder then, that the Lord chided the Church in Ephesus for having "lost their first [viz., "best"] love"? (Rev. 2:4)

resurrected. In Acts 13:33 it declares the day of His resurrection to be the birth of the Son of God. Jesus was already the Son of God in His divinity, but His humanity – the nature of His birth through Mary – needed glorification whereby His humanity would be glorified as the Son of God. The humanity of Jesus Christ became the Son of God at His resurrection. His entire being with dual nature, divinity and humanity, is declared to be the Son of God. He brought His humanity into the Godhead – He resurrected with a transfigured human body. It is in this manner that divinity and humanity merged into the Godhead – there is a "Man in the Glory!" He is now "the glorified Man."

May the majesty of this reality of the "Man in the Glory" seize upon us – for it is His goal in *"bringing many sons to glory"* (Heb. 2:10) as the fullness of glorified humanity! This happened at His resurrection, all His believers were included – He became *"the first born of many brethren"* (Rom. 8:29). All His people were instantaneously regenerated and made sons of God with Him. When Jesus resurrected, we were all there with Him. God being in eternity doesn't have to look through the lens of time; therefore, all Christians were there with Him in death, resurrection and ascension (Gal. 2:2; Eph. 2:5-6). While as humans, we come to experience Him and His salvation in our "confined time."

His people didn't simply resurrect with Him as many individuals. It was the birth of a corporate person. All His believers became members of His One Body through His resurrection. They became One New Man. A corporate New Man was birthed. Before His death and resurrection, His chosen people were from every tribe, tongue, people, and nation – yet, they were divided (Rev. 5:9). This was especially true between the Jews and the Gentiles – there was enmity between them. One essential reason for His death was to break down *"the middle wall of separation"* (Eph. 2:14) between the Jews and the Nations (aka, "Gentiles"). Now, *"He might reconcile them both to God in one body through the cross"* (Eph. 2:16). Any barrier separating His people from each other has been demolished. His death and resurrection brought peace – freedom from the hostility that divided people enabling them to become one new man (Eph. 2:15). This was the New Man brought forth in His resurrection. How mysteriously wonderful. All His people rejoice. Sorrow truly has turned to rejoicing.

> "... and have put on the new [man] who is renewed in knowledge according to the image of Him who created him, where there is neither Greek nor Jew, circumcised nor uncircumcised, barbarian, Scythian, slave [nor] free, but Christ [is] all and in all."
>
> – Col. 3:10-11

At the cross, Jesus broke down the thickest and tallest divisive wall between Jews and Gentiles. This barrier was *"the law of commandments contained in ordinances"* (Eph. 2:15); all other kinds of walls separating peoples are easy in comparison. "Greek and Jew" can include all racial and ethnic differences. "Circumcised or uncircumcised" can be in reference to religious walls due to the ***interpretation of various Biblical teachings*** (viz., these can be considered *"the law of commandments contained in ordinances"* – i.e., "laws" derived from various interpretations made by human understanding of the text). "Barbarian, Scythian" can refer to educational, cultural, and political segregation. "Slave or free" can include the various levels of socio-economic inequalities. Believers are enjoined to put on the new man where all these walls are broken down. Yes, the differences are still there. No one must conform to another or force another to change – the focus now is simply Jesus Christ. All these diverse individuals are in Christ: They are in Him, and Christ is in all these different individuals. This is the New Man birthed at the Lord's resurrection after breaking down the middle wall through His death on the cross.

Becoming ONE Is the Building Up of the Ekklesia

When Jesus said "I will build my *ekklesia*" in Matthew 16:18, it was the first time this word was used in Scripture. It was mistranslated to "church" in most of the English versions of the Bible. The word "church" literally means the physical building for worship. However, Jesus appropriated the word "ekklesia" from the Greeks. The Greeks were having ekklesia in their cities starting from about 600 years before Christ. The Romans continued this practice through the New Testament period. The Greeks invented democracy. Ekklesia was how they practiced democracy. Every citizen in a city were called together periodically for discussions, debate, and finally voting concerning affairs of the city brought forth. In their democracy, there was not a king, emperor, or any person ruling, but every citizen had a voice and a vote no matter if he were rich, poor, a tradesman, or a farmer. Each person was equal and could vote according to their own preferences.

Democracy may be a good form of government, but as witnessed around the globe, it is messy, divisive, and contentious. All the diverse sub-groups in a society usually look out for "#1", each person's own interest. They vote for what benefits themselves, their group. A democratic society may not be righteous since a majority may well be swayed by unrighteousness — Jesus was crucified because the people raised their voices to "vote" in unison: "Crucify Him."

Jesus came with a mission to build God's ekklesia. His Kingdom is not to be ruled by an objective king outside the people; rather, it would flourish as a "democracy" — a spiritual democracy. His ekklesia would be the most diverse; it would include people from every imaginable stratum of society: poor to rich, educated to illiterates, slaves to masters, from all different ethnicities, and especially from the most divided factions in history, the Jews and the Gentiles. In a secular society, individuals identify with conflicting factions — factions which, taken to the extreme, might wish to kill each other. Notwithstanding, in the Lord's ekklesia they love one another, and they are one. It is this true oneness among diverse peoples which testifies of God's eternal life, divine nature, and sacrificial love indwelling His people. This oneness is impossible among divided people of the world. But now they become genuine, pure and real in His ekklesia because God's people are in Christ and Christ is in them.

Finally, in John 17 Jesus ended the supper with a monumental and wonderful prayer to the Father. This prayer is the conclusion of that evening as described above prior to His interrogation and trials later that evening, and crucifixion the next morning. This is Jesus' outpouring from the deepest part of His heart for His followers according to the eternal purpose of God. This prayer unveils what He was sent to accomplish as the Anointed One. The focus of His prayer: His people would become ONE. He declared this three times: "*That they may be ONE.*" Petitioning three times in the Scripture signifies Jesus was desperate and persistent. This was the ultimate reason He was going to the cross: not just for redemption and forgiveness of sins, but to gather into one His scattered and divided people (John 11:52).

In His prayer, He revealed such oneness would come through His death and resurrection; therefore, He gave His people three gifts to accomplish this oneness. The result of each gift is that "*they may be ONE*" — even as one as the Father and the Son are ONE. What a mysterious and extraordinary oneness! God is eternally one, though He is distinctly three: The Father, Son, and Spirit. The building up of the ekklesia occurs when millions of distinct individual believers are brought into oneness, just as the Father and the Son are one.

Jesus' mission to build His ekklesia is consummated in the oneness or unity of God's redeemed and regenerated people. It is the ultimate manifestation of diversity in unity. Though different and distinct, God will use His ekklesia to show His wisdom and His glory to the entire universe (Eph. 3:10, 21). His ekklesia is ONE. His people are individuals with a free will sourced from divergent and different backgrounds; yet, they are one, they are unified.

In the secular world today, it seems the more diversity is celebrated the more divided and antagonistic occurs among these groups. This is the strategy of the evil one: divide and conquer. However, in the ekklesia, Christians can truly enjoy the diversity in the Body because no matter the differences, they are one Body in Christ. Moreover, this oneness must be manifested not in the heavens, not in the "sweet by and by" in some future Kingdom of God, but squarely in this divided world. In the Lord's prayer for oneness, He specifically prayed His followers not to be taken out of this world. They would stay within the world but be kept from the evil one (John 17:15). Thus, within this divided world of hate and antagonism God would have His ekklesia of oneness and love. It is seeing the diversity in oneness that the world would believe in Jesus Christ (John 17:20-21).

The Trinity Himself is the pattern for diversity in unity — He is the three-one. He is three: distinctly Father, Son, and Spirit; yet, He is literally one. There is no conformity nor uniformity within the Triune God. The Father, Son, and Spirit continued their distinctiveness from eternity to eternity, but are also eternally one. Therefore, the one ekklesia manifests God's life and nature within each of the members. She has uniquely His eternal life and partakes of His divine nature which allows each believer to be who they are as individuals; yet, loving one another and manifesting oneness in Christ.

Relationship between Love and Oneness

Simply put: Love is the source which is God Himself and oneness is the manifestation of God. God works as three: The love of God, the grace of the Lord Jesus Christ, and the fellowship of the Holy Spirit. However, in the entire record of the Bible both testaments, God never appeared as three. Whenever God appeared in a bodily form, He manifested Himself in one person. God is one sitting on one throne. In Revelation 22:3, in describing aspects of the New Jerusalem, the throne is called "*The throne of God and the Lamb*." The entire three of the Godhead dwells in one body (Col. 2:9).

The relationship between the three is love and fellowship. God is love. The Son is the Father's beloved — the Father loves the Son (John 3:35). The Son abides in the love of the Father; and, the Son loves the Father (John 14:31; 15:10). The fellowship of the Spirit between all three is constant and eternal. Fellowship (Gk. *Koinonia*) defined: Share which one has in anything (Thayer's). Not only do they share the same love, but also the same honor (John 5:23), the same will (John 5:30), the same glory (John 17:50 and they speak the same things (John 12:50). Therefore, all that is of the Father belongs to the Son and all that the Son has accomplished belongs to the Spirit (John 16:14-15), which means they have all things common, and they do not withhold anything as their own domain. This is the fellowship within the Three.

"*Love one another*" means His eternal ekklesia is made up of many individuals with personalities, characteristics, diversities, variance, and divergence — many individual members in one Body. It is critical to appreciate the distinctiveness and uniqueness of others; otherwise, who are the "others" to love? By commanding "*love one another as I have loved you*" all the various individuals and personalities are included since the Lord Himself has loved every single person no matter what their differences may be. Without recognizing and experiencing the "one another" aspect and only focusing on "one," this will misguide Christians to seek and force uniformity in Christian assemblies and communities. Many teachers and "church" movements in history have focused on the aspect of "one" without seeing the diversity of individuals needed to comprise this one; therefore, unwittingly, they have become homogeneous where members are expected to "toe the line" of standards whether written or implied. This has resulted in the formation of more separate and well-defined groups of Christians; whereby, the Lord's ekklesia is no longer visible or represented. They compound their error by becoming more divisive than former divisions wrought by Christian groups who were not promoting the "unity of the Body."

On the other hand, the Lord's prayer for His people to be one points to unity, harmony, and accord among divergent individuals. God's eternal purpose mandates this oneness. There are those ministers speaking forth a sorely needed message of "loving one another." Many who promote this commandment or those who are hearing this message may only apply this loving relationship to those within their own church community or defined group. "Brothers and sisters, we need to obey the Lord's New Commandment to '*love one another*.'" This charge may only be relevant in the context of people in the same church loving one another. Their consideration and practice may rarely extend beyond those outside their group. Even in the same church, it may shrink more by isolating itself to the same home group. "In our home group, we really experience loving one another."

The reason for this declining love or constricting sphere of love can be due to the lack of vision concerning God's eternal purpose of His one ekklesia. The sphere of the Lord's ekklesia includes people of all stripes. This accurate understanding concerning the Body of Christ, His ekklesia, which requires Christians from every faction should motivate believers to expand the realm and sphere of their fellowship to include different kinds of believers whom they need to love. Christians will need to draw from the eternal source of love within them in order to enlarge their love to include more and more people . . . including those who are contrary to their peripheral doctrines and practices. They will need to proactively seek those outside their comfort zone to love.

The Lord Jesus rhetorically asked: "*If you love those who love you, what reward have you?*" However, it is entirely a different kind of love when you love your enemies, do good and bless them (Matt. 5:44-46). Therefore, oneness of God's people is not simply a motivating vision. It is a testing or proving ground for the genuineness of the love for one another . . . whether it is the same love as the Lord's. Remember, the New Commandment is "*love one another as I have loved you*." How do we know whether we are truly sharing the love with which Jesus loves? It is in the experience and environment of His ekklesia where the Lord's New Commandment was intended to flourish and the environment in which it is tested. It is among diverse believers of equal standing where the genuine love of the Lord Jesus is proved and tested.

Churches and ministries are generally homogenous in nature in one form or another. It can be ethnically, doctrinally, similar Christian lifestyles, or even politically compatible. Therefore, the New Commandment in its purpose must leap over any and all dividing walls in order to love those dissimilar to our "Christian experience."

Love without oneness is seeking for experiences without God's purpose as the goal and lacking in testing of its genuineness. Oneness without divine love becomes theoretical or academic lacking both power and beauty. Love and oneness are equally needed as the Alpha and Omega of the last supper.

The New Commandment is the Alpha, the beginning of the Lord's supper. The prayer for the manifestation of oneness is the Omega, the conclusion of the Lord's Supper.

Eventually, the reality of loving one another results in the one ekklesia which in its basic definition and practice is an assembly of inclusion and freedom of expression. Loving one another is clearly a benefit for all believers; but oneness of the Lord's ekklesia benefits God Himself. It is in the ekklesia in whom He is glorified. It is through the ekklesia Satan is crushed and defeated. Without coming to the point of the manifestation of the Lord's ekklesia, then loving one another is still short of the goal. Loving one another is the means by which the Lord's ekklesia can be realized and manifested — however, it is not (per se) the goal.

The overarching message by Paul in 1 Corinthians 11:17 through 1 Corinthians 14 concerns the gathering and building up of the Lord's ekklesia. In 1 Corinthians 13 the focus on love is embedded in the practical and physical gathering of the Lord's ekklesia. Likewise, in Romans 9 through 16, where Paul's goal was to bring two divided groups of believers into the same physical space to have meals and glorify God with one mouth, the need for love was embedded in Romans 13. Therefore, from this and other biblical portions, it is clear the Lord's ekklesia is the ultimate focus of the Almighty. Loving one another is an indispensable ingredient or relationship needed to arrive at God's goal: His ekklesia.

Loving one another must result in the manifestation of the ekklesia where dissimilar believers are gathered for fellowship in order to "wash one another's feet" in their care and humility in serving one another. Where each one is to lift up Jesus in one accord in their speaking, singing, and praying; whereby, the world believes, Satan is crushed, and God is glorified.

The Many Descriptions of God's One Ekklesia

Oneness or becoming one as prayed for by Jesus is the consummate definition and description of what He is building: the ekklesia. The ultimate expression of God's eternal purpose is His ekklesia: *Many-One in Christ*. The Scriptures have described the Lord's ekklesia in many ways. Here are a few major ones:

- The kingdom of God (Matt. 16:19)
- The bride of Christ (Eph. 5:31-32)
- The body of Christ (Eph. 1:22-23)

Ministers who have received insight into these different aspects will highlight and attempt to inspire believers to seek and experience that particular trait. For example: those inspired by the kingdom of God will speak of having authority to influence this world. The kingdom of God means God is reigning through His people; therefore, Christians need to establish their authority as the kingdom of God and impact various marketplaces of the world such as politics, entertainment, education, etc. Those who have gained insight into the Bride of Christ will focus on having a loving relationship with the bridegroom, Jesus. Their ministry is to motivate Christians to love Jesus and spend time with Jesus since they are the bride espoused to Jesus. Those with an appreciation of the Body of Christ will lay emphasis upon the various gifts in the Body according to 1 Corinthians 12; and how every member needs to function – the body ministry. Each one of these emphases is not wrong in and of themselves; however, giving priority to these various aspects outside the understanding of ekklesia has also divided God's people. For example: This church is really for God's kingdom; whereas this other church is into the gifts for the Body; and this other group really loves the Lord with a deep relationship with Him.

The reason for these positive elements becoming divisive or deficient has to do with the focus being placed on the outcome of what the built up ekklesia is; rather than on the ekklesia itself. In other words, the Lord's ekklesia is the foundational item – not a miscellaneous outcome. It is the ekklesia Jesus was commissioned to build up. "*I will build my ekklesia*" (Matt. 16:18). He never said, "I will build my Kingdom." It is when the Lord's ekklesia is built-up that the Kingdom of God has authority on earth. Paul said it is the ekklesia which is the Lord's Body and not the other way around (Eph. 1:22-23). The great mystery of the universe is "*Christ and the ekklesia*" and not Christ and the Bride (Eph. 5:32). It is when God's ekklesia is built up, the Kingdom is manifested, then the Bride of Christ is made ready, the Body of Christ is functioning while many other aspects are expressed; such as, the New Man, the Household (family) of God, the Temple, the United Kingdom of David, the New Jerusalem.

Ministers cannot build up the Kingdom of God as a separate item without building up the ekklesia. Neither can the Bride or the Body be a separate experience or expression apart from the ekklesia. All ministers share the same anointing and commission as Jesus Christ: to build up His ekklesia.

It is critical to have sound fundamental understanding regarding the Lord's ekklesia: His distinctly diverse believers are one. Certainly, the various descriptions of ekklesia can be discussed, but if there is no ekklesia, then the reality of those items are absent. When the ekklesia is built up according to the clear revelation of Scripture, then all the various descriptions of God's ekklesia become real and activated. When believers are one and loving one another, there is harmony to bind and loose (Matt. 18:19); there is the function of each member in one accord (1 Cor. 14:23-26); God receives glory (Rom. 15:6); and Satan is defeated (Rom. 16:20).

The Amazing Three Gifts Given in Order to Have Oneness

In John 17 in the Lord's prayer, He distinctly gave three gifts for His believers to be one as the Father and He are one. The first gift was eternal *life* (v. 2), the second was God's Word which is *truth* (v. 14, 17), and the third is His *glory* (v. 22). It was after each gift Jesus asked for His followers to be one. This clearly shows that these are the gifts given to believers which enable them to be one, in unity — He gave us these gifts to facilitate His goal of oneness.

John Lennon's song "imagine" was all about the people of the world becoming one — it would be utopia. The music was beautiful, and the imagery of the lyrics was captivating and inspiring to an entire generation in the '70s. Almost 50 years later, it is still a dream in people's imagination. It is not to be. It can easily be argued people today are more divided than ever. Divisions in Christianity are just as bad, if not worse, than those of the secular world. The number of denominations and independent churches continues to grow around the earth. Christians belonging to one church often do not fellowship with those belonging to another church.

Jesus prayed specifically and desperately for His disciples to be one. This is not a minor matter found in the teachings of the New Testament; rather, this is at the nexus upon the Lord's heart. This was His motivation in His inexorable march to the cross. It was through His death, resurrection and ascension He would give these three gifts to all His people that they would be one. Therefore, without seeing, understanding, and experiencing these three gifts, it is impossible for people to love one another to the point of oneness among disparate believers. Especially, when this oneness is divine: as the Father and the Son are one.

It is critical to prayerfully consider and study these three gifts if believers are serious concerning God's eternal purpose. It is possible to recognize and see God's eternal purpose concerning the building up of His one ekklesia in love; yet, continuing in the way of division. These three gifts are the provisions needed to achieve love and oneness. If even one is omitted or diminished, the stability of the building up of His ekklesia will not have a good foundation. Can any chair have only one leg or two legs? No, three are needed to have stability.

The three gifts correspond to the three of the Godhead: Father, Son, and Holy Spirit. Oneness due to the first gift of eternal *life* is realized by being kept in the *Father's* name. The source of Eternal life is God the Father. The second gift of God's Word is God the *Son* reaching humanity. Jesus is the Word of God, the **truth**, who reached man. He brought the reality of the entire universe to people. It is through this sanctifying truth Christians are made one. Finally, the third gift of *glory* which Jesus received through death, resurrection and ascension was related to the *Spirit*. The Spirit of glory empowers believers to lay aside any dignity in order to serve people in humility.

A Summary of the Gift of Truth

Since this book's emphasis is to explore the first and third gift of *life* and *glory* — a short summary of *truth* will be helpful. The entire subject of the second gift of Truth (God's Word) was the focus of the books: *One Ekklesia* and *One Truth*.

According to the unveiling of Scriptures, the Truth liberates, nourishes and unifies. In the Lord's prayer (John 17:17), sanctification can be identified as the entire process relating to these three experiences. Satan, the evil one, has used both the Scriptures and the focus on holiness (sanctification) to divide believers. Just about all divisions among Christians are based on various emphases from the Bible. Christians will not use the Koran to cause a division. Typically, only the Bible is cited by ministers seeking to start another church more "correct" than others.

Out of all the topics in the Bible, holiness or sanctification has perhaps caused more division among Christians than any other doctrine. Factions have been created based on what holiness should look like, the various methods of sanctification, how to treat other Christians deemed unholy, and defining and confronting sins and worldliness. Somehow, Christians have used something only God possesses — holiness, to be a factor of much divisiveness when according to the Lord's prayer sanctification should unify His followers. Those being made holy by Truth are those able to be one with other believers. God in Jesus Christ is uniquely the Holy One; yet, He is the most loving and accepting of all people including those unholy. Through the blood of Jesus Christ, God became the most approachable. Likewise, the sanctified ones are those who can receive and love all of God's people in the oneness of the Lord.

John 17:17 states, "*Your word is truth.*" The "word" in this verse does not refer to the actual words in Scripture (the Bible). The Bible contains and conveys the Word; however, people can read and study the Scriptures, yet *miss* the Word. In John 1:1 it says, "*In the beginning was the Word and the Word was with God and the Word was God.*" This verse alone shows that "word" in John 17:17 is not referring to the Bible since the Bible was not written in the beginning of eternity! Then, in John 1:14 he writes, "*The Word became flesh . . . .*" This "Word" is God Himself, incarnate. God became man, in the form of Jesus Christ. *The* Word is Jesus. Jesus confirmed this in John 5:39–40 when He said, "*You search the Scriptures, for in them you think you have eternal life. But you are not willing to come to Me that you may have life.*" Here, Jesus clearly separated Himself from the Scriptures. One can read and study the Scriptures without coming to Jesus. Life is in Jesus, not in mere Scripture absent of Jesus.

The Greek word for "word" is *logos*. It means "a speech, something said, and reasoning." It is the root word for "logical" (Gr. *logikos*). Jesus being the "Word" is the expression of God as speech, and that Word comes in a way that is reasonable and can be understood logically. John 1:18 reveals God is hidden and no one can see or perceive Him but the Son, Who is the Word and Who declares (or manifests) God. It is through the Word — Jesus Christ — man can see and know God. Words can be written down, passed on and reproduced in an accurate manner; this is how the Word has been recorded in the Scriptures. God will be manifested to those who seek Jesus as the Word in the Scriptures, through understanding and reasoning. Believers need to do more than simply read and study the Bible because it contains the Word; they should simultaneously come to Jesus, seek Him, see Him, speak to Him, know Him, handle Him, and have fellowship with Him; otherwise, they will miss the words of eternal life (1 John 1:1–2).

According to Vine's Expository Dictionary, truth, as used in the New Testament, is "the reality lying at the basis of appearance and manifestation." According to this definition, truth is much more than not telling a lie or saying something factual; it is the reality of the universe. When a person realizes what is hidden behind what appears and what is manifested, *that is truth*. No wonder "truth" has such prominence! It is one of the two items that came through Jesus Christ. It is important to elevate the understanding of the word "truth" to a high and spiritual level, and not relegate it to a simple secular concept such as, "Tell me the truth! Did you take a cookie?"

John says that Jesus Christ is *full of grace and truth*. He continued to say that grace and truth came through Jesus Christ (John 1:17). Based on the above definition, when a person receives Jesus Christ, they possess *the* truth, *the* reality. They will know and discern what is real, what is behind the entire "shadow" of the universe (Col. 2:16–17). Without Jesus Christ, men are stuck knowing only what they can see and what is physically manifested. Men's lives and all that they strive for — money, fame, material gain — are all vanity. Even the physical universe is not reality! Receiving and believing into Jesus Christ brings people out of the pit of vanity, emptiness, and false reality — into truth, veracity, and something substantial that is eternal.

The more a believer stands in truth alone, the more open and receptive in fellowship that believer will be with all other believers. When a believer is established in the truth, that person is not blown about by various doctrines (Gk. *didaskalia*) and practices. Neither will there be objections to or insistence on any non-essential doctrines, nor the wide array of Christian practices. This is because that person will be peaceful, comfortable, confident and grounded in the truth which is the doctrine (Gk. *didache*) of Jesus Christ.

ONE in Life, Truth, and Glory

The three gifts given are not independent of each other; rather, they are interconnected. When believers consider and focus on these three gifts as factors or elements to becoming one, they will be brought into the heart of God's purpose and pleasure, and in turn they will be full of the joy of the Lord having purpose and eternal value in their lives. The following is a general sketch concerning how these three gifts are related with truth being the connector:

1. The Eternal life, the Father's Name

Believers were born anew with God's life at the time of receiving the Truth which is the gospel. Through faith, they are regenerated with the Father's divine life and partook of the Father's divine nature. There are two innate functions defining life on earth: metabolism and reproduction. In fact, without these two items, life cannot be classified as life. Scriptures have also unveiled spiritual life in similar terms: the need for daily spiritual food (Truth) – to reproduce and bear fruit. Additionally, all life needs four elements to survive and thrive: nutrients, air (environment), exercise, and sleep. If these four elements are present, life will spontaneously thrive, reproduce, and mature. When these four essentials are applied to the spiritual life within believers, their lives will be healthy and fruitful; they will be able to go through the day-to-day challenges with contentment, joy and purpose.

2. The Truth (His Word)

The truth is the "nutrient" for spiritual life and knowledge to inspire believers to live and serve God in His ordained way. To partake of Jesus Christ from day to day, it is through Truth. The Truth, unveiling the person of Jesus Christ and His work, is the daily bread for believers whereby they may grow in Christ. The Truth is also spiritual food to serve and feed others. The goal of every ministry should be to feed God's people in order for them to come to salvation and the full knowledge of the truth. Therefore, truth is central for believers to express miraculously normal lives and service. Truth is what every believer needs to ingest and dispense as food to others.

3. His Glory

The glory the Lord received at His resurrection and ascension He gave to all His followers. It is through this glory Christians are empowered to serve God and people as ministers of Christ. The "food" they are to serve people, to both unbeliever and believer, is the truth of Jesus Christ. In order to be a servant, there is the need to endure suffering in humility. The Lord's glory is needed to be exemplified in such faithful ministers. God is truly served when His ekklesia, His house, is built up. All believers have the privilege and responsibility to build up the Lord's ekklesia through their own ministry. They will be able to fulfill their calling for the ministry of the Spirit during their regular daily living with the people who surround them.

PART 1

LIFE FOR LIVING

(Chapters 5–8)

> "... that He should give eternal life to as many as You have given
> Him. And this is eternal life, that they may know You, the only
> true God, and Jesus Christ whom You have sent."
>
> "Now I am no longer in the world, but these are in the world,
> and I come to You. Holy Father, keep through Your name those
> whom You have given Me, that they may be one as We [are]."
> —John 17:2-3, 11

Eternal life is the first gift, which is the result of being born of God in order to become God's child. This is how God becomes every believer's Father, and, in turn, all believers receive the Father's name. John 17:3 states: knowing the Father and the Son is eternal life. This is what it means to be "born of God" (John 1:13). Being born of God is not just a metaphor; it is a reality. God is now the believer's Father, not just Creator. In addition to receiving God's eternal life, believers now partake of His divine nature (2 Pet. 1:4). The reality of God as the believer's Father is all the more real than their earthly (biological) fathers from their "first" birth, because God is eternally their Father. Christians have actually received the Spirit of the Son by which they can call out to God in the most intimate way, "Abba, Father" or "Daddy, Father" (Gal. 4:6). This is knowing the Father and the Son.

To most Christians, the concept of eternal life means everlasting life — they will live forever. Before they die and before eternity, they should strive with their best efforts to follow the example of Jesus and the laws in the Bible in order to properly live before God and man. After they die, they imagine they will go to heaven and live forever in a wonderful environment of celestial mansions with God and loved ones for eternity. A typical unbeliever has a similar concept concerning the Christian faith.

It is atypical for Christians to consider eternal life begins the very moment a person believes in the Lord Jesus Christ. However, the very meaning of "born again," means to receive a new life . . . *another* life. This new life is the eternal-divine life. At the time of faith, believers literally receive God's divine-eternal life into them.

It is by being kept in this life of the Father, enjoying the Father's name, believers are made one. Christians are one because they have the same eternal life and participate in His divine nature — they have the same Father. They all originate from the same source; they become genuine brothers and sisters within the same family. In many cultures, those who are born from the same earthly father have the same name — their family (last/surname) name. Similarly, Christians bear the same "name" as their heavenly Father because they are born of Him. So being kept in the Father's name is to remain in the enjoyment of the reality where all believers are in one family with the same Father, having the same name. If believers are not kept in the enjoyment of this divine life, then they will gravitate back to their divisive old nature.

The Father and the Son, though distinct, are one in life and nature; therefore, they are both eternally one. Thus, all believers who abide in this life and nature of God are automatically one in Christ. This is the most basic factor of the believer's oneness. In 1 John 3:14 it states, *"We know that we have passed from death to life, because we love the brethren."* This new life causes them to love one another; this divinely supernatural love is proof they are no longer in death, but in the Father's life.

Every believer, upon receiving Jesus Christ as their Savior, being born anew, immediately feels a connection with other believers. They don't know much, if at all, concerning various Christian doctrines, practices, or denominational affinities, but are just happy to meet any other believer. Their first thought when they meet a fellow believer is not to what denomination a person belongs, but simply: "You believe in Jesus Christ. Praise the Lord! Let me tell you, I just found Jesus! Let's fellowship." This is real, spontaneous, unadulterated love for other believers. There is immediate oneness in His eternal life.

Instead of being kept in that life, in the Father's name, many Christians over the centuries picked up assorted doctrines (Gr. *Didaskalia*) and practices making them their own. Sitting under the tutelage of various Bible teachers, they began to align themselves with certain schools of theology — a *way* of practicing baptism, a *method* for holy living, or *steps* to receiving miraculous gifts. It may have seemed they were learning a lot of Christian and scriptural "truths," but the more they learned, the more they began to separate themselves from other believers. They began to identify themselves with a certain type or group of Christians. They may have taken on an identifying name such as Baptist, Catholic, or Methodist. Soon, Christians were labeled: he is a Pentecostal; she is a reformed Christian; he is a dispensationalist — the labels are endless.

This is not being kept in the Father's name. This is leaving the Father's name to take on other names.

Oh, how believers need to be kept uniquely in the Father's name! This is the first and most basic element of believers being brought into one. Those who are kept in the Father's name will not bring about problems with other believers by promoting anything which would cause other believers to be distracted from eternal life, the Father's name.

Those who are kept in the Father's name will receive all fellow believers as true brothers and sisters into His one fellowship of the divine life. They will seek to grow in His eternal life and desire to help other believers to grow in His life as well. They will not want to remain as babes but will strive to reach maturity.

A babe in this life is a person who is easily carried away from the Father's name. These Christians are easily distracted by the world — by political or social causes, law keeping, doctrinal debates, various Christian practices, or personalities. In Ephesians 4:14, Paul said believers should no longer be like babies, tossed and carried about by every wind of teaching (Gr. *Didaskalia*). Men use both secular and biblical teachings with craftiness, carrying off the "babes" into their schemes or systematized error — that is, a system in error. The enemy's schemes cause divisions and eventually sects or factions in the Body of Christ, resulting in separation and hostility among believers.

Conversely, mature believers who share in God's divine life are immovable from the Father's name. They are no longer diverted or confused by various doctrines or practices. They are guarded to remain in the Father's life. Such followers of Christ can fellowship easily with all believers, even with distracted babes. Mature believers can bring those confused by diverse doctrines and Christian practices back to the enjoyment of the Father's name. The more His divine life grows in a believer, the more this "oneness" toward other diverse believers will naturally grow, widen, and deepen. The ability to be one with other followers of Christ in receiving, accepting, honoring, fellowshipping, and caring for them is the sign of spiritual maturity, the maturity of His eternal-divine life in the believer.

Fruit of the Spirit

"But the fruit of the Spirit is love, joy, peace, longsuffering, kindness, goodness, faithfulness, gentleness, self-control. . . .."
— Galatians 5:22–23

Most Christians, after accepting Jesus Christ, spend a lot of effort trying to behave according to what is portrayed in the Bible. They focus on overcoming their sins and failures. They do their best to be holy in order to have a "good" testimony. Though these efforts seem admirable, they can all become a distraction from doing the things that will actually help them spiritually grow (Gal. 3:1–5). If they are not growing, then trying to live the Christian life becomes a very frustrating endeavor. Consider the fruit of the Spirit: that is what the Christian life should be. Fruit is just the product of life and growth, not self-effort and work. If believers will focus on these four essentials for life and growth, then the resultant fruit will make a believer a duplicate (the "same image") of Jesus Christ (Rom. 8:29). A believer with the fruit of the Spirit, as listed, is certainly united with all believers in the Body — that believer is a joy for people to be around. This is the result of the eternal-divine life lived and expressed in those growing in life.

Four Essentials for Growth

Part 1 in this book will explore how followers of Jesus can grow in God's life. This new life may be likened to a newborn baby who needs to grow. A believer's spiritual growth should take place while they are still living in this world, raising families, and doing a job to make a living. This divine-eternal life needs to progress, develop, bear fruit and mature. This should take place while a believer is still on earth; notwithstanding, this thinking is foreign to most Christians.

Each living being, whether animal or human, needs four items to live and thrive. These four essential items include: nutrients (eating and drinking), breath (environment), exercise, and sleep. Life will not continue if even one of these items is missing. When these things are present, life spontaneously and innately grows. There is no need to be anxious about whether one will grow spiritually, because a person's spiritual life will automatically grow and function well under these conditions. Nevertheless, these things need full cooperation with a believer's physical and psychological being.

The next four chapters will cover these four items:

1. Nutrients (eating and drinking)
2. Environment for breathing
3. Exercise
4. Sleep (rest)

It is critical to understand these four essentials for life and stay in them day by day. Anyone who does this will spontaneously grow over time in the speed of life, however long it takes God's life in them to grow. Growing is itself miraculously normal. A baby through growth becomes mature to its life potential encoded in its DNA. Miraculous! Yet, normal.

5

EATING THE WORD; DRINKING THE SPIRIT

The Real Food and Drink!

Who or what are the spiritual nutrients for eternal life in believers? It is Jesus Christ. Jesus said in John 6:54, *"Whoever eats My flesh and drinks My blood has eternal life. . .."* It is amazing that Jesus Christ came to be food and drink, asking men to eat and drink Him. Eating and drinking are not only essential for life, they are also two of the most enjoyable activities for man. Additionally, what human beings eat and drink becomes their body's composition. Not only do food and drink provide energy to live, they also become part of a person's physical constitution. There is oneness between the physical body and the food or drink we consume. By Jesus aligning "food and drink" or "eating and drinking" Him in this manner, He purposefully sought to take the most essential items in maintaining human life and relating them to the reality of spiritual sustenance, superseding the physical realm.

Consequently, *real* food and drink is Jesus Christ. He came to have such an amazing relationship with man! Eating and drinking Him is the beginning of this new life. It is also how believers continue their Christian journey. In order to maintain following Jesus through the rest of their time on earth, they need to be kept nourished by eating and drinking Jesus. Not only so but eating and drinking Him is what they will continue to enjoy for eternity.

"Eating" or ingesting Jesus Christ occurs when a person comes to know Jesus. When a person is inspired by the knowledge of Jesus — that knowledge makes sense, and is appreciated — namely, receiving spiritual nourishment. This is the purpose of reading and studying the Scriptures — to know Him. "Drinking" occurs when there is a response in faith, receiving what is understood concerning Jesus Christ. When Jesus is revealed in the Word of God, there should be a response. Speaking to Him with thanksgiving, praise, or a request applying to life's situations should be our response. Upon believing the Word, the Spirit transfers into the person or operates within them, joy, peace and love, and makes the words spoken and accomplished 2000 years ago real and tangible. This continual transmission of the Spirit through faith while "hearing" the Word is drinking.

The simplicity of this is eating and drinking Jesus.

Generation, Continuation, and Destination

Jesus Christ came that man may eat and drink Him, to generate life in man:

> "'This is the bread which comes down from heaven, that one may eat of it and not die. I am the living bread which came down from heaven. If anyone eats of this bread, he will live forever; and the bread that I shall give is My flesh, which I shall give for the life of the world.' The Jews therefore quarreled among themselves, saying, 'How can this Man give us His flesh to eat?' Then Jesus said to them, 'Most assuredly, I say to you, unless you eat the flesh of the Son of Man and drink His blood, you have no life in you. Whoever eats My flesh and drinks My blood has eternal life, and I will raise him up at the last day. For My flesh is food indeed, and My blood is drink indeed. He who eats My flesh and drinks My blood abides in Me, and I in him. As the living Father sent Me, and I live because of the Father, so he who feeds on Me will live because of Me.'"
>
> – John 6:50–57

These verses by some can be considered both repugnant and wonderful; they declare believers are to eat and drink Jesus Christ in order to have life and live. This is the purpose for which Jesus came down from heaven. He entered the world as "bread" for man to partake in order to have life. In God's eyes, only *eternal life* is life. John 6:53 states that unless a person eats and drinks Jesus, no life is in them. However, the very first time a person eats and drinks Him, they receive His eternal-divine life, which is the new birth.

To continue to live after the new birth, Christians need to regularly eat. Just like people need to physically eat, believers need to spiritually eat in order to live and grow. These verses in John 6:50–57 show the generation of a believer's life in Christ begins with eating and drinking of Jesus Christ, followed by a continual "eating" throughout life. He is true food and true drink. By eating and drinking Him, a believer's relationship with Jesus Christ is as intimate and as one as the relationship between Jesus and the Father. Jesus is unique nourishment for believers.

God is not looking for worshipers in the way of bowing before Him to sing His praise. He is looking for people to eat and drink Him, to ingest Him. How absurd it would be if people bowed before a plate of food, worshipping it, while they were starving? God does not want to be outside of man for man to worship. He wants to be food and drink for man to enjoy and partake so the two may become one.

Consider this example further: What if a person was weak from hunger; therefore, he couldn't get out of bed to help his daughter move furniture. A plate of food is available for him to eat every day, but instead of eating the food, he prays: "Oh food, please help my daughter to move, you know I can't do it. I am so weak, please strengthen me. Oh food, I beg you to send someone to help her move." This sounds so bizarre, but this is exactly what most religions teach when praying to God for help. Now, what if this dad simply gave thanks, then would eat and enjoy the food available to him? The food would become energy in him to strengthen him, so he could get up and help his daughter move furniture.

Was it the man who helped move his daughter, or was it the food he ate and digested? The fact is, it was *both*: The food in him, together with his physical body, helped his daughter move. The food could not get up from the plate to move his daughter, nor could the father get up from bed to help his daughter. However, together, by eating the food for energy, he rose up and the job was done. God does not want to be outside of man to do things externally for him; rather, He wants to be *in* man to live and work together with him. He wants a relationship with humanity such that it will be hard to know whether it is God working or man working — it would be impossible to know whether it is human or divine love, patience, or joy, because God and man become one through eating and drinking.

This is the meaning of John 6:57, where Jesus said, "*I live because of the Father. He who eats Me shall live because of Me.*" The only way a believer can live as Jesus lived, like the way Jesus lived by the Father is through eating Jesus. This is the wonder and mystery of God in Jesus Christ, being food to man. It is utterly different from any religious concept concerning worshipping and praying for help from an external God.

How can believers love others as Jesus loves? Eat Jesus. How can believers forgive others the way Jesus forgives? Eat Jesus. How can believers be one with all other believers? Eat the Bread of Life. How can believers live like Jesus? The only way is to eat Jesus. This is miraculously normal.

Christ Knocking at the Door: Continue to Dine with Him

The apostle John wrote in his Revelation describing Christ knocking at the door, desiring those in His ekklesia would continue to dine with Him:

> "Because you say, 'I am rich, have become wealthy, and have need of nothing' — and do not know that you are wretched, miserable, poor, blind, and naked — Behold, I stand at the door and knock. If anyone hears My voice and opens the door, I will come into him and dine with him, and he with Me."
>
> – Revelation 3:17, 20

The ekklesia in ancient Laodicea was made up of believers, but they began to decay; they became degraded, wretched, miserable, poor, naked and blind. The worst part is they thought they were rich and wealthy — and had need of nothing. While these believers imagined everything was fine, the Lord Jesus was knocking outside their door. They had gained a wealth of Bible knowledge and spiritual experience in the past, but were blinded; thus, by extension they were not aware of their true condition. They replaced the living Christ, Who can be experienced *now,* with old knowledge and good memories. They thought they had everything, but Christ was not in their midst; He was outside knocking.

The people in this type of assembly believed their experience and knowledge made them rich, but they missed out on the Christ Who could have been so rich to them in the "here and now" — sadly, they were poor and miserable. They stopped enjoying Christ Who is always new and available. They lived life in a religious shell, going through the motions, while the Lord was outside their door knocking — shut out. He desired to be brought back inside the assembly in Laodicea. Although the knocking is on the door of the ekklesia, it is the responsibility of each believer to open the door and let the Lord inside in order to eat and drink together.

These believers were missing something profound: dining with the Lord. They were not enjoying Him. They held on to the past but missed

His present nourishment. Believers in this kind of degraded situation miss the reality of the Lord. However, Jesus is not seeking to condemn and judge His children. He wants to dine with them and to feast with them. In this way the saints in Laodicea would be recovered from spiritual degradation. He deeply desires Christians to eat of Him and drink of Him.

To continue as a believer, no matter how much a person may already know about the Bible or how much they have experienced Christ, they can never "graduate" from eating and drinking of the Lord. This is the only way to progress as a believer for His ekklesia: through daily partaking of the nourishment found in Christ alone. Once a believer stops receiving daily nourishment, degradation (or deterioration) kicks in — it only gets worse over time. Sadly, believers are often oblivious or unable to process this diminishing in their spiritual lives. It is critical for believers to hear the Lord knocking and open the door to Him when they are malnourished.

The Reward Is to Eat and Drink More of Christ

Eating and drinking Christ is a reward for those who overcome. This is the believer's portion for eternity:

> "He that has an ear, let him hear what the Spirit says to the assemblies [ekklesia]. To him that overcomes, I will give to him to eat of the tree of life which is in the paradise of God . . . He that has an ear, let him hear what the Spirit says to the assemblies. To him that overcomes, to him will I give of the hidden manna. . . .."
> – Revelation 2:7, 17, DBY

Most of the seven ekklesias described in Revelation 2 and 3 were not in a good spiritual condition. They had become religious, which brought deadness, worldliness, hierarchy, heresies and many other negative things into the Lord's ekklesia. To be *religious* means to stray from focusing on the Lord Himself, and instead establish rules for what is "right and wrong," or what is okay or not okay to do — making formalities, ordinances, and regulations the center of the assembly.

Degradation started with the very first ekklesia: Ephesus. Jesus said the Ephesians had "*left* [their] *first love*" (Rev. 2:4). They had not kept Him preeminent. They stopped feeding on Him as their unique source of spiritual nourishment. To each assembly in Revelation 2 and 3, even to

Philadelphia (the only one Jesus spoke of positively), the Lord called for overcomers. Believers are to triumph over all religious distractions and come back to Jesus alone — to enjoy Him as their food and drink. The reward for those who overcome is more enjoyment of Jesus. Therefore, believers eat to overcome and overcome to eat.

The Tree of Life first made its appearance at the creation of humanity. In Genesis 2:9 and 16, God told our original parents: *"You may freely eat"* of the Tree of Life positioned in the center of the garden. The tree of life in Genesis appeared again in Jesus Christ being the real Tree of Life. Jesus declared He is the vine tree in John 15. He also declared He is the life (John 11:25); therefore, *He is the Tree of Life.* He is the Tree of Life and reality of which humanity was privileged to partake. Now, believers need to overcome all distractions to eat of the Tree of Life — Jesus. When a believer's life begins to deteriorate, the way to recovery is to eat and drink Jesus.

In John 6:22–40, Jesus referred to Himself as the manna from heaven, the living bread. Today, Jesus as the "bread of life" (John 6:35) is "hidden" in heaven and in all His followers. He is not seen by the people of the world, but believers can be sustained and nourished by this invisible Bread if they overcome to eat Him every day. Revelation 2:7, 17 reveal the reward for overcoming degradation is the blessing of eating from the Tree of Life, and the hidden manna.

Eating and Drinking Christ Is Our Eternal Destiny

> "Then the angel showed me the river of the water of life, bright as crystal, flowing from the throne of God and of the Lamb through the middle of the street of the city; also, on either side of the river, the tree of life with its twelve kinds of fruit, yielding its fruit each month. The leaves of the tree were for the healing of the nations."
>
> – Revelation 22:1–2, ESV

These verses describe a couple of the major features of the New Jerusalem in eternity. This city is a sign showing the composition of all of God's people throughout time and space in perfect union with God. God and His people are one for eternity. At the center of the city, which is likened to the peak of a mountain, is the throne of the God-Man, Jesus, from which flows the river of the water of life; this is the Spirit flowing throughout the city. In the middle of the river, easily accessible from the street, is the Tree of Life producing new fruit every month. This imagery reveals that for eternity God's people will continue to eat and drink of Him. He will be fresh and new forevermore. Believers will never grow tired or bored of participating in Him, being nourished by Him, and enjoying Him as their source. This is the believer's destiny.

Eat and Drink to Remember Jesus

The most important symbol established by the Lord Himself is for believers is to eat and drink in remembrance of Him.

> "And when He had given thanks, He broke *it* and said, 'Take, eat; this is My body which is broken for you; do this in remembrance of Me.' In the same manner *He* also *took* the cup after supper, saying, 'This cup is the new covenant in My blood. This do, as often as you drink *it*, in remembrance of Me.'"
> – 1 Corinthians 11:24–25

What is commonly known as communion (or the Lord's table), initiated by Jesus the night He went to be crucified, is a continual reminder that Jesus is the real food and drink. This was practiced every day among early believers. Perhaps, this had everything to do with partaking of physical food; they were being reminded: *Jesus is the real food*. Eating and drinking is truly the most amazing example of the intimate relationship and oneness between Christians and the Lord Jesus.

Physically, what people eat and drink actually becomes part of their being. The Lord Jesus was outside His believers, but through "eating" and "drinking" Him, He became intrinsically a part of them. Eating and drinking Jesus is the way to remember Him. Just as the source of a person's physical energy comes from eating and drinking, in the New Covenant, the believer's source of vigor comes from enjoying Jesus by partaking of Him. Jesus is doing everything necessary to supply, energize, and fulfill His eternal purpose in those who ingest Him.

The Word Is Tangible Food to Assimilate Christ

The Word of God is the Bread — the nourishment by which believers live:

> "But He answered and said, 'It is written, 'Man shall not live by bread alone, but by every word that proceeds from the mouth of God.'"
>
> — Matthew 4:4

> "Your words were found, and I ate them, And Your word was to me the joy and rejoicing of my heart; For I am called by Your name, O LORD God of hosts."
>
> — Jeremiah 15:16

The Word of God, truth, conveyed in the Bible is tangible for His people to receive food. His Word is the provision which sustains and nourishes a believer's inner man. When children of God eat the Word, the result is joy and rejoicing — a satisfaction continually available to them regardless of their environment.

The Lord's Word Is Spirit and Life

> "It is the Spirit who gives life; the flesh profits nothing. The words that I speak to you are spirit, and *they* are life."
>
> — John 6:63

Earlier in John 6, Jesus spoke of eating His flesh and drinking His blood in order to have life. Many who heard this proclamation were offended. It sounded like cannibalism! The Lord explained He was not speaking of His physical body, since "*the flesh profits nothing*" (John 6:63). He was speaking of the Spirit. Eating His flesh and drinking His blood means partaking of and ingesting His Spirit. His Spirit is living and real, yet mysterious, intangible, and difficult for people to apprehend. Therefore, Jesus made eating of Him much more practical by referring to His words as Spirit and life. His words are substantial and understandable. When a person receives His words by faith, they are filled with the Spirit, who is life. Therefore, it is paramount for believers to ingest His Spirit through His words, in order to have life.

> "And receive the helmet of salvation and the sword of the Spirit, which *[Spirit]* is the word of God."
>
> – Ephesians 6:17

Paul shows clearly in Ephesians 6:17 that the Word of God is His Spirit. The Spirit and His Word are like "two sides of the same coin." To possess the Spirit the believer needs His Word; but to take in His Word, the believer needs to utilize the human spirit to fellowship with the Spirit in His Word. Ephesians 6:18 continues on to say the way to take in the Spirit in the Word is by praying in the Spirit; therefore, whenever believers come to the Word, they need to utilize their praying spirit to fellowship with the Lord – for "*that which is born of the Spirit is spirit* (i.e., the human spirit – John 3:6).

Tasting and Eating through Knowledge

The way to eat the Word and drink the Spirit is through understanding and tasting of Christ.

> "As newborn babes desire earnestly the pure mental milk of the word, that by it ye may grow up to salvation, if indeed ye have tasted that the Lord is good."
>
> – 1 Peter 2:2-3, DBY

The Greek word for *word* here is *logikos*, which is where the English word for *logic* or *logical* is derived. Therefore, the "*milk of the word*" is nourishment from something of reason or logic. God's Word is full of logic, enabling His children's understanding. Read the Scriptures concerning Jesus Christ, Who He is, what He has done, His purpose, and His relationship to humanity; consider it, and follow its logic. When the Scriptures unveil Jesus Christ to a sensible person with understanding, it becomes milk or nourishment for the mind, soul, and one's inner being. The milk of the Word, relating to the knowledge of Jesus Christ the Lord, causes spiritual growth. Peter writes in 1 Peter 2:3 when ingesting this nourishing milk, it means to "*taste the Lord.*" The way to receive nourishment from the milk of the Word is to focus on Jesus Christ when reading the Scriptures. The Lord is sweet, and He is so good when He is tasted. People simply do not know how good the Lord is until they've tasted Him. When they do, they will desire more of this milk of the Word. A person knows they have received nourishment when they come to appreciate anew the goodness and loveliness of Jesus Christ.

This happens through proper studying, consideration, and retention of the knowledge of God and Jesus the Lord.

> "Grace and peace be multiplied to you in [the] knowledge of God and of Jesus our Lord."
>
> ~ 2 Peter 1:2, DBY

The knowledge of God and of Jesus Christ as Lord will cause grace and peace to multiply. Many believers who study the Bible focus on countless other topics such as end times, miraculous gifts, or settling various socio-political controversies such as inequalities and abortion. They strive to answer the "how to's" — how to pray, how to tithe, how to live or how to become holy, to name but a few. The number of topics one can pick from the Bible is endless, but only the knowledge of God and Jesus Christ can multiply grace and peace. The entire Bible unveils who God is, His Son Jesus Christ, and His eternal plan. Read, study, and understand the Bible by focusing on living knowledge to gain what is profitable!

> "That the God of our Lord Jesus Christ, the Father of glory, would give you [the] spirit of wisdom and revelation in the full knowledge of him."
>
> ~ Ephesians 1:17, DBY

> "Until we all arrive at the unity [or oneness] of the faith and of the knowledge of the Son of God, at the full-grown man, at the measure of the stature of the fullness of the Christ."
>
> ~ Ephesians 4:13, DBY

In order to have this knowledge of Jesus Christ, it is necessary to be of a sober mind to consider and understand His words. Nevertheless, a spirit of wisdom and revelation is also needed, which is received through prayer. Believers who possess an increasing knowledge of the Son of God will grow and mature resulting in love wherein they will be receiving all believers in oneness without disputations and judgment. Possessing and pursuing mere scriptural knowledge (on any topic) without a focus on Jesus Christ's person and work (in that topic/doctrine) can lead to friction and disputes among believers. Therefore, it is critical to center on Jesus Christ and let His knowledge saturate the Christian's mind.

Use and Apply the Word to Teach and Admonish One Another

For the Word to dwell in believers richly, they must use and apply the Word to teach and admonish one another.

> "Let the word of Christ dwell in you richly in all wisdom, teaching and admonishing one another in psalms and hymns and spiritual songs, singing with grace in your hearts to the Lord."
> — Colossians 3:16

Teaching, admonishing, and singing are all words modifying the verb "dwell." This indicates the way for the Lord's Word to "dwell in you richly" (Col. 3:16a) is by teaching, admonishing, and singing. The more a person teaches the Word of Christ to others, the richer His Word will dwell in them. Before the New Testament was penned and canonized, much of the Word of Christ and the apostles' teachings were formulated into various spiritual songs — from long ones to short ones. As believers would "sing" these songs, they also would teach and admonish. By singing and teaching the content of these songs, the Word of Christ would richly dwell in believers, in all wisdom.

> "And how from childhood you have been acquainted with the sacred writings, which are able to make you wise for salvation through faith in Christ Jesus. All Scripture is breathed out by God and profitable for teaching, for reproof, for correction, and for training in righteousness, that the man of God may be complete, equipped for every good work."
> — 2 Timothy 3:15–17, ESV

It is crucial for believers to know Scripture specifically in the knowledge of Jesus Christ, the Son of God. Not only does it contain the way to salvation, but it is also "breathed out" by God (2 Tim. 3:16). Therefore, when Christians read the Word via prayer and praise, they are breathing in the breath of God, the Spirit. Believers who come to know the Scripture in such a living way in both knowledge and Spirit can, in turn, use this Word to minister to people around them. Being filled with Scripture, both in understanding and in breath, equips people to be men and women of God in order to minister Christ in every work they do. Without such knowledge and Spirit sourced in the Scripture, they will not be adequately equipped to serve the Lord according to *His* purpose.

The Spirit of God Is the Living Water for Drinking

> "In the last, the great day of the feast [Feast of Tabernacles], Jesus stood and cried saying: If any one thirst, let him come to me and drink. He that believes into me, as the scripture has said, out of his belly [innermost being] shall flow rivers of living water. But this he said concerning the Spirit, which they that believed into him were about to receive; for the Spirit was not yet, because Jesus had not yet been glorified."
>
> – John 7:37–39, DBY

There were three major feasts of Israel in which God required His people to physically eat and drink for seven days as a worship to Him (Ex. 23:14; Deut. 16:16 – Feasts of Unleavened Bread; Weeks/Pentecost; Tabernacles). By the time Jesus Christ came on the scene, these corporate festival times had degenerated to a mere religious observance, even though the feasting continued. Knowing man (male and female) was still thirsty in their inner being after practicing their religion where they were filled up physically, Jesus called people on the last day of the feast to *come to Him* to drink spiritually (John 7:37). The unique way of drinking Jesus was to believe into Him. Upon belief in Christ, spiritual thirst is quenched and satisfied. Jesus becomes the source of the water of life in the believer's innermost being. A "river" flows out from their spirit and soul. Not only are they filled, but they can also quench the thirst of others. This drinkable out-flowing water is the coming Spirit of Promise. God's Spirit is eternal, but the drinkable Spirit *"was not yet"* and could not enter into men and women until after Jesus Christ died for their redemption and was resurrected in victory; only then did He become the life-giving Spirit (1 Cor. 15:45) in order to enter and indwell humanity – when He became the "Glorified Man" then, and then only, could He become the life-giving Spirit.

"For in one Spirit we were all baptized into one body — Jews or Greeks, slaves or free — and all were made to drink of one Spirit."

– 1 Corinthians 12:13, ESV

Drinking of the Spirit by believing into Jesus Christ immerses the believer into the one Body of Christ. Before drinking of the Spirit, people can be from various nationalities and social statuses, which can be in conflict with each other. Paul stated, for example, that there was enmity between Jews and Gentiles (Eph. 2:14–15); moreover, that "slaves and free" were a world apart (Col. 3:10–11). But when people drink of the one Spirit, then they are baptized into one body where all the separation and hostility between peoples are eliminated. Therefore, it is important to keep drinking the Spirit for a person's inner being to be satisfied, and to become one with all His believers. This powerful verse supports the Lord's Prayer in John 17 and connects with drinking Jesus as an essential item for life, making diverse believers one.

Drinking the Spirit by Believing

"This only I want to learn from you: Did you receive the Spirit by the works of the law, or by the hearing of faith? Are you so foolish? Having begun in the Spirit, are you now being made perfect by the flesh? Therefore He who supplies the Spirit to you and works miracles among you, does He do it by the works of the law, or by the hearing of faith?"

– Galatians 3:2–3, 5

The Galatian believers were being deceived. Some Christian teachers were telling them they needed to go back to keeping the law in order to please God — trying to perfect themselves by the flesh — the fallen man operating under his own efforts independent from God. Because of this, the apostle Paul reminded them of what they already had: they had previously received salvation by faith. They should continue their spiritual journey in the same way — through faith. The supply of the Spirit is by faith as well. Believers recognize their life in Christ began with simply believing into Jesus Christ; unfortunately, many foolishly labor to keep God's laws by the efforts of their flesh *after* becoming a Christian. Paul encourages Christians to turn back to their simple faith, no matter how far along they have progressed as believers.

Some have advocated that keeping the "law of commandments contained in ordinances" (Eph. 2:15) is not necessary for salvation, but it is needful or helpful for sanctification, or to make a Christian whole. This is yet another way of enticing Christians to practice the law for spiritual advancement. However, since authentic spirituality is from the Holy Spirit, the verses above are clear: Believers who begin by faith, should continue to receive the supply of the Spirit by faith. On-going spiritual growth is by receiving the Spirit by faith and not by the works of the law.

> "That the blessing of Abraham might come upon the Gentiles in Christ Jesus, that we might receive the promise of the Spirit through faith."
>
> – Galatians 3:14

The blessing of Abraham in the Old Testament was the Almighty's commitment to Abraham and his descendants to possess the Good Land; but in the New Testament, the reality of the promise of Abraham is found in the Spirit of Christ – the real Good Land. Entering Christ is likened to entering His Rest – Christ Himself (Heb. 4:1-10). God wants people to receive the Spirit, through believing into the Lord Jesus Christ. It is only through faith anyone can receive the Spirit as the "Good Land" of God into their inner being.

> "In Him you also trusted, after you heard the word of truth, the gospel of your salvation; in whom also, having believed, you were sealed with the Holy Spirit of promise."
>
> – Ephesians 1:13

In Ephesians 1:13, Paul reveals it is through believing in the good news of Jesus Christ the Holy Spirit is received. The Holy Spirit becomes a seal upon believers. A seal is a permanent mark placed on an object to verify ownership and authenticity; this permanent mark is the Holy Spirit. Upon belief, the Spirit is permanently sealed into the believer's inner being.

Blending the Word with Faith

> "For indeed the gospel was preached to us as well as to them; but the word which they heard did not profit them, not being mixed with faith in those who heard *it*."
>
> – Hebrews 4:2

In the Hebrew Scriptures, the Israelites heard the good news concerning God bestowing upon them the Good Land, but when they saw obstacles in the way, they didn't believe God's Word. Because of their unbelief, they didn't enter the Good Land, but wandered in the wilderness for forty years. Today, the good news of the reality of the Good Land — Jesus Christ and the Spirit of Promise — is extended to all those wanting to hear. If this good news is going to profit the hearer, faith must be actively mixed, blended, or united with the gospel heard. There is much to learn concerning Who Jesus Christ is and what He has accomplished for humanity; but these eternal truths are only profitable and made real through believing this full and wonderful gospel.

> "Jesus said to him, 'If you can believe, all things are possible to him who believes.' Immediately the father of the child cried out and said with tears, 'Lord, I believe; help my unbelief!'"
>
> – Mark 9:23–24

Since faith is essential in receiving all God has done and provided for humanity, every man (male and female) needs to ask for faith. Does a person believe enough to *ask* for help? What a simple and honest prayer from this man in Mark 9:23! A believer should pray the same upon hearing difficult things concerning whom the Lord is and what He has accomplished: "Lord, I believe; help my unbelief!" This is the way to receive more faith . . . *simply ask.*

Take the Spirit–Word through Prayer, Praise and Thanksgiving

> "And take the helmet of salvation, and the sword of the Spirit, which [Spirit] is the word of God. With all prayer and petition pray at all times in the Spirit, and with this in view, be on the alert with all perseverance and petition for all the saints."
> – Ephesians 6:17–18, NASB

Paul tells his readers in Ephesians 6:17–18 the Spirit is the Word of God. The way to receive this Word is with all kinds of prayers. On one hand, logic and reasoning is needed when reading the Bible, and on the other hand, a praying spirit is necessary in order to enter fellowship with God's Spirit by faith. It is important to turn what is read and understood into prayer — drinking the Spirit.

Conversing with the Lord concerning the wonders in His Word will lead to petition. "Petition" means asking specifically for something in relation to anyone the Lord brings up in the believer's heart while praying. The things that are read together with prayer can then be applied to others. For example, as you are encouraged by the above Scripture, you may petition the Lord to strengthen struggling brethren by energizing them to take "*the helmet of salvation*" and "*the sword of the Spirit*" to slay their enemy.

> "In God will I praise [his] word; in Jehovah will I praise his word. In God have I put my confidence: I will not fear; what can man do unto me? Thy vows are upon me, O God: I will render thanks unto thee."
> – Psalm 56:10–12, DBY

The psalmist praises God's Word. He turned God's Word into praise. Praising should be accompanied with reading and understanding. Praising as one reads and understands His Word activates faith. Additionally, for all God's vows (His promises), which are now fulfilled in the New Testament, thanksgiving should be offered. Believers should thank Him for all His fulfilled promises. As believers praise and give thanks, all things promised by God in Scripture are made real in Christ — each one is "yes and amen" (2 Cor. 1:20).

Practice: Prayer and Praise with the Word

Now, it is time to practice! There is no "right" way to do this; any way is fine! Begin by reading a verse or two. Then, turn those verses into prayer, praise, and thanksgiving. Converse with the Lord using the content of these verses. Personalize the verses by changing the pronouns from "*the* Lord" or "*your* people," to "*my* Lord" or "to *me*." In other words: Personalize the Word. Apply the verses to others which the Spirit recalls: pray and praise God for them.

Here is an example using one of the verses above for prayer, praise, and thanksgiving:

> "Grace and peace be multiplied to you in [the] knowledge of God and of Jesus our Lord."
>
> – 2 Peter 1:2, DBY

"Lord Jesus, thank You for grace and peace. Lord, multiply grace and peace to me. Praise You for making grace and peace so available. I love You Lord. Open me to receive more knowledge of You. Grant me more understanding concerning Your Person, dear God, and all You have accomplished so that grace and peace will multiply more to me. Lord Jesus, I also pray for _____ (insert a name). I pray he/she will know You and receive grace and peace. Thank You for unveiling Yourself to him. I praise and pray in Your name, Amen."

Now try a verse and practice yourself.

6

Breathing – Living in Christ, the Good Land

Breathing is another requirement for life. However, in order to breathe, there must be an environment of air. Breathing is a nonstop function which continues throughout a person's walk each day; wherever anyone goes, whatever they do — they need to breathe!

This chapter will explore the environment believers live in, and the function of "spiritual breathing" as they go about their daily living. For believers, the environment in which they live is Christ; it is full of "living air" for breathing as they live and work each day.

Every believer should ask themselves two questions relevant to this topic of spiritual breathing: How "big" is Christ in their life, and how can they "breathe" Him in? God has given a blessing to every believer: the vast and unsearchable riches of Christ, or the "Good Land." Believers who lift their eyes to see Christ as the Good Land will enjoy Him wherever they journey from day to day. Continuously, Christ is the Spirit Who dwells in believers and surrounds them in a way it is impossible to be separated from Him. The Spirit supplies believers abundantly as they continue in fellowship through the practice of unceasing prayer.

An Overview of This Chapter

A believer's experience of Christ should progress from the Passover Lamb to daily manna; finally, arriving at God's chosen destination: the Good Land. This land is so rich and vast that whatever the believer sees and wherever they walk, 24/7, is Christ Himself. The key for a believer to possess and enjoy such a rich and vast land is to lift up their eyes to see Christ as the reality in everything.

The promised blessing to Abraham was the Good Land, a physical piece of land. The reality of the Good Land for Christians, however, is the Spirit. After crucifixion, Jesus Christ, in resurrection, took the form of the Spirit.

Therefore, through faith, a believer's spirit and the Spirit of the Lord are joined as one – impossible to separate. Because of this, followers of Jesus are not only in the *real* Good Land, but the Good Land is in them.

The Spirit a believer has received in their spirit is also the praying Spirit. Just like a person's lungs continually breathe, the believer's spirit unceasingly *prays*. Having constant fellowship with the Lord in prayer is innate and normal for every believer. Seeing Christ in everything reminds Christians to pray, to give thanks, and to make requests on the behalf of others.

Believers should practice unceasing prayer by turning everything – activities and situations – to prayers of fellowship. Seeing Jesus Christ as the reality of everything positive reminds believers to pray and give thanks. They can do this at work, at home, at play, in everything – as they walk and live through daily life.

Typology – the Shadow of Things Depicting Jesus Christ

The "Good Land" in the Old Testament is a type of Christ for believers in which to live and walk. He's the good and spacious land.

> "So let no one judge you in food or in drink, or regarding a festival or a new moon or sabbaths, which are a shadow of things to come, but the substance is of Christ."
> – Colossians 2:16–17

The writers of the Hebrew Scriptures described key people and events such as: Moses, David, crossing the Red Sea, building the temple, and numerous other items. They also foretold of things to come and painted pictures through the instructions of sacrifices and offerings. Many of these things including diet, festivals, and Sabbaths were part of God's law; people were judged by whether they practiced such instructions or not. Paul alluded to these things in Colossians 2:16–17, calling them "shadows" (or "types") of Christ.

Typology is symbolism seen throughout the Old Testament (OT) – something that represents something else. When a person in the OT is identified as a "type of Christ," it means the person behaved in a way corresponding to Jesus' character or actions in the New Testament. An object or even an event in the OT can also represent some quality or characteristic of Jesus.

In the verses above, several rituals and practices are mentioned: eating, drinking, festivals, new moon celebrations, and Sabbaths. These items were given meticulous detail in the OT. They instructed Israel how to live: what rules the nation was to abide by concerning what to do and what not to eat and drink, how to conduct their annual festivals, and what each Israelite could and could not do during the Sabbath day. There were judgments upon those breaking laws relating to these items. In Colossians 2:16–17 Paul told believers they were no longer judged by rules governing these practices, because these rituals were merely a shadow of things to come. The substance or the reality, the solid object, which cast these shadows is Jesus Christ. Believers are freed from performing these religious rituals since all these OT practices are just shadows. These rituals or shadows were never the reality; they were *types* pointing to the reality: Christ.

The reality of eating and drinking is Jesus Christ; the true substance of food and drink. He is the "clean" food for all to eat and drink. He satisfies man's inner hunger and thirst. The reality of each feast of enjoyment is Jesus Christ. He brings God's people together for a celebration in the building up of the Body rendering worship to God. Jesus is the reality of a new moon. In Christ everything is new; old things have passed away. Failures of the past should be forgotten. Every time a believer turns to Jesus Christ, they receive a new start. Finally, He is the true Sabbath rest. Jesus finished all His work – He is resting. Believers now come to Him to rest and should abide in Him and rest in Him for eternity. Resting means believers are filled, satisfied, and peacefully enjoying Him – we are to "enter into the rest" (Heb. 4:11)

The Passover Lamb in Egypt—the Feast of Redemption

Just before the Israelites escaped Egypt and crossed the Red Sea, God gave specific instructions for what they were to do:

> "Speak to all the congregation of Israel, saying: 'On the tenth of this month every man shall take for himself a lamb, according to the house of his father, a lamb for a household.
>
> 'Now you shall keep it until the fourteenth day of the same month. Then the whole assembly of the congregation of Israel shall kill it at twilight. And they shall take some of the blood and

put it on the two doorposts and on the lintel of the houses where they eat it.

'And thus you shall eat it [the lamb]: with a belt on your waist, your sandals on your feet, and your staff in your hand. So you shall eat it in haste. It is the LORD's Passover. For I will pass through the land of Egypt on that night, and will strike all the firstborn in the land of Egypt, both man and beast; and against all the gods of Egypt I will execute judgment: I *am* the LORD. Now the blood shall be a sign for you on the houses where you are. And when I see the blood, I will pass over you; and the plague shall not be on you to destroy you when I strike the land of Egypt.'"

– Exodus 12:3, 6–7, 11–13

Passover was the last of the ten plagues which afflicted Egypt before Moses was to lead the children of Israel out from under slavery. God was about to judge Egypt by sentencing all the firstborn sons of each family to death. For the Israelites' firstborn to be saved from death, each family was to kill a lamb, put the blood on the outside doorposts of the house, and eat the lamb inside. God passed over the houses where He saw the lamb's blood, delivering those inside the house from the judgment of the plague of death. While inside the house, God's people enjoyed eating the lamb, which would provide them the energy needed to leave Egypt later that night. From that point on, Passover became an annual feast which God's people were to enjoy as a memorial.

"The next day John saw Jesus coming toward him, and said, 'Behold! The Lamb of God who takes away the sin of the world!'"

– John 1:29

"Therefore purge out the old leaven, that you may be a new lump, since you truly are unleavened. For indeed Christ, our Passover, was sacrificed for us. Therefore let us keep the feast, not with old leaven, nor with the leaven of malice and wickedness, but with the unleavened bread of sincerity and truth."

– 1 Corinthians 5:7

The first introduction of Jesus Christ to the world came from John the Baptist, who said, "Behold, the Lamb of God!" (John 1:29) Jesus is the true Lamb Who was to shed His blood so the world would be freed from sin and God's judgment. Jesus, the reality of the shadow of the annual sacrifice of a Passover lamb, perfectly fulfilled this "type" at His crucifixion. Paul made it clear in 1 Corinthians 5: Jesus is the real Passover Lamb sacrificed for the world. As a result of faith in Jesus Christ, believers are freed from God's wrath, which is the penalty for sin: Death. Our pardon is secured through the death of Jesus on the cross.

Once freed from spiritual death – pardoned by God because of our Passover Lamb, it is important to keep feasting on Him as *the* Passover Lamb who provides life, and the means to escape corruption and sin. Jesus is both the Lamb believers should continue to eat for the rest of their journey on earth.

Manna—the Living Heavenly Bread for Daily Eating

God provided the Israelites with bread (or "manna") while they were in the wilderness for sustenance; manna is another beautiful picture or type of Christ.

> "And when the layer of dew lifted, there, on the surface of the wilderness, was a small round substance, as fine as frost on the ground. So when the children of Israel saw it, they said to one another, 'What is it?' For they did not know what it was. And Moses said to them, 'This is the bread which the LORD has given you to eat.'"
>
> – Exodus 16:14–15

> "And the house of Israel called its name Manna. . . . that they may see the bread with which I fed you in the wilderness, when I brought you out of the land of Egypt.'"
>
> – Exodus 16:31–32

> "And the children of Israel ate manna forty years, until they came to an inhabited land; they ate manna until they came to the border of the land of Canaan."
>
> – Exodus 16:35

After the Israelites left Egypt, they wandered in the wilderness for forty years because they didn't believe God could bring them into the Good Land. During their wandering, their food was bread from heaven — called manna. God provided this bread six days a week, and it sustained the Israelites for forty years.

> "Our fathers ate the manna in the desert; as it is written, 'He gave them bread from heaven to eat.' Then Jesus said to them, 'Most assuredly, I say to you, Moses did not give you the bread from heaven, but My Father gives you the true bread from heaven. For the bread of God is He who comes down from heaven and gives life to the world.' Then they said to Him, 'Lord, give us this bread always.' And Jesus said to them, 'I am the bread of life. He who comes to Me shall never hunger, and he who believes in Me shall never thirst.'"
>
> ~ John 6:31–35

Jesus referenced the Israelites eating manna in the wilderness when responding to the people's questions in Capernaum. He proclaimed what their forefathers ate in the wilderness was not the *true* bread from heaven. It was only a type. Jesus told them He is the real living Bread from heaven. Though God miraculously gave manna to Israel, it was still only physical bread; those who ate manna, nonetheless, died. But Jesus Christ — the real Bread of Life — is for all men to eat. Whoever eats of Jesus, the living Bread from heaven, shall have eternal life. The actual ingesting of Jesus is to believe into Him.

The Good Land—the Unsearchable Riches of Christ

The "Good Land" with all of its produce is the most beautiful picture of the all-inclusive and expansive Christ.

> "And they ate of the produce of the land on the day after the Passover, unleavened bread and parched grain, on the very same day. Then the manna ceased on the day after they had eaten the produce of the land; and the children of Israel no longer had manna, but they ate the food of the land of Canaan that year."
>
> ~ Joshua 5:11–12

The Israelites were called to fulfill God's purpose. Their journey was in three stages: in Egypt, in the wilderness, and finally when they reached the Good Land. Notice in each stage, eating was prominently mentioned. In Egypt, the Israelites ate the Passover lamb; moreover, the lamb was their salvation. In the wilderness, they ate manna which sustained them for forty years. In the Good Land, which God promised to give them, they began eating the produce of the land. Manna continued for about four days after entering the Good Land before it stopped

Scripture reveals manna stopped the day after the Israelites began eating the produce of the land. The food from the Promised Land not only replaced manna, but their diet was greatly enhanced. While manna never changed – it was the same bread for forty years – the food in Canaan was varied, assorted, and abundant. The significance of this will become evident later in this chapter.

Just as the lamb and the manna are types of Jesus Christ, the following verses reveal He is also the land and the produce for His people to enjoy.

> "For the LORD your God is bringing you into a good land, a land of brooks of water, of fountains and springs, that flow out of valleys and hills; a land of wheat and barley, of vines and fig trees and pomegranates, a land of olive oil and honey; a land in which you will eat bread without scarcity, in which you will lack nothing; a land whose stones are iron and out of whose hills you can dig copper. When you have eaten and are full, then you shall bless the LORD your God for the good land which He has given you."
>
> – Deuteronomy 8:7–10

From these verses, one can appreciate the beauty and riches in the Good Land. Canaan was an expansive land open for exploration and abounding in resources, food, and minerals. There was no scarcity; in this land, God promised the Israelites "*you will lack nothing*" (Deut. 8:9).

Jesus Christ is truly the reality of this Good Land. It is an elaborate description of Who He is. The Passover lamb was enjoyed just once a year. Manna was eaten daily. It was minuscule in comparison to a piece of land. Manna never varied in flavor or amount for forty years. However, the Good Land of Christ is immense. Believers are surrounded with all kinds of enjoyment in Him. As believers spiritually progress, their enjoyment of Christ increases more and more.

Interestingly, Deuteronomy 8:10 was the first time in the entire OT the Israelites were told they would "bless the Lord." Man had never blessed God until this point in history; this blessing is connected to man's satisfaction from partaking of the food produced in the Good Land. This is a further indication their diet in the Good Land is the finality of the three archetypes of eating Jesus Christ.

God's purpose was fulfilled by eating the produce of *this land*.

> "As you therefore have received Christ Jesus the Lord, so walk in Him, rooted and built up in Him and established in the faith, as you have been taught, abounding in it with thanksgiving."
> – Colossians 2:6–7
>
> "To me, who am less than the least of all the saints, this grace was given, that I should preach among the Gentiles the unsearchable riches of Christ."
> – Ephesians 3:8

Paul declared believers need to walk in Christ Jesus — to be rooted in Him. Both of these descriptions provide beautiful images of the land. Firstly, believers are to take root in Jesus; secondarily, they are to walk in Him as this vast land. This is the "unsearchable riches" Paul spoke about in Ephesians 3:8.

The root system of a plant draws all its nourishment from the land. The root firmly establishes the plant. Plants taking root downward will grow upward. Likewise, believers are to dig down and take root in Jesus Christ, in order to grow and be built-up.

Like a firmly established plant, believers need to be continuously drawing nourishment from Christ (the land). The growing up of the plant is the building up of the Body of Christ. The building up of believers into one and functioning as the Body of Christ are the results of drawing nourishment from Jesus. Believers are not built up through negotiation, compromise, or some sort of human coordination. These things can never produce genuine oneness among all kinds of believers. The way for true building up of the Body is when individual believers are rooted in Christ — the land — and grow from the nourishment derived from Him.

Then in Ephesians 3:8, Paul said Gentiles should come to know and enjoy the "unsearchable riches of Christ." This clearly speaks of the vastness of Jesus, and the diversity of His riches. He is not limited to being the Lamb and manna. His unsearchable riches far exceed what can be described of the Good Land. Throughout the Scriptures, Jesus Christ can be surveyed as the Good Land: the real water for His children to drink, the real sun to provide growth and warmth, the true Sabbath rest, and the real house to dwell in. He is the real husband, door, light, shepherd, rock, lion, lamb, and bread. Hundreds of physical items in the Scriptures describe the reality of Jesus. This reality runs deeper than the human mind can comprehend; He is the reality of every positive thing in this universe. By applying His reality today, we can say Jesus is the real electricity providing energy for His people; the real car transporting people; the real rocket bringing people to the heavens; and the real mobile phone keeping people connected to Him anywhere. The unsearchable riches of Christ can be infinitely explored and enjoyed!

Possessing the Good Land

Possessing the Good Land depends on seeing and walking *in* the Good Land. Believers need to appreciate the immensity of Jesus Christ.

> "And the LORD said to Abram, after Lot had separated from him: 'Lift your eyes now and look from the place where you are — northward, southward, eastward, and westward; for all the land which you see I give to you and your descendants forever. Arise, walk in the land through its length and its width, for I give it to you.'"
>
> – Genesis 13:14–17

In order to see the spaciousness of the Good Land, believers need to lift up their eyes. Focusing downward on personal situations results in missing Christ; believers who do so forget how big He is.

The experience of Christ in Egypt is His being the Passover Lamb. It is through the blood of His cross, believers are saved from the wrath of God (i.e., the penalty for sin, death). That experience is only needed once. When a person believes in His redemptive death, that person is justified before God and delivered from God's eternal condemnation.

Some believers progress forward to the point of spending daily time in the Bible, in pursuit of feeding on Christ as the manna in their "quiet time." However, when they face challenges at work or frustrations at home, they become anxious or angry. Christ disappears from their realization and experience. This is a sign such believers are not yet enjoying the "Good Land" of Christ. Though they are being sustained by Christ with seeking hearts in the morning, it seems Christ disappears for the rest of the day in their lives. A person in his daily living is stuck looking down at himself and his situation. When this happens, it is critical for him to lift up his eyes to see in all four directions, as far as he can see, Jesus Christ is available to experience and enjoy. The writer of Hebrews exhorts believers to *"[look] unto Jesus, the author and finisher of our faith"* (Heb. 12:2). When believers see Jesus, they will be released from bondage while being supplied with the unsearchable riches of Christ (Heb. 2:9).

When God's children see Jesus Christ as this vast and rich land, they will rise up and walk through its length and breadth. He is for the taking! Yes, Christ is big enough to include everything — at work, at home, with friends, even in recreation. He is so vast one can never step outside of Him, no matter where they walk. He is the rich supply Who satisfies all our needs. Jesus Christ is truly the Good Land!

> "In order that you may be fully able to apprehend with all the saints what is the breadth and length and depth and height; and to know the love of the Christ which surpasses knowledge; that you may be filled even to all the fullness of God."
> ~ Ephesians 3:18–19, DBY

In an attempt to describe the vastness of Christ, Paul points out Jesus' four dimensions without being able to give an actual measurement . . . because Jesus is immeasurably spacious. Though His vastness and depth surpass knowledge, believers can still know and experientially apprehend Him. As they explore the Good Land — Christ — they are filled and become a more complete expression of God. The experiences of the Passover lamb in Egypt and the manna in the wilderness have huge limitations; additionally, neither can fulfill God's goal.

In the OT, God commanded the temple only to be built in the Good Land; it could not be built anywhere else. The building up of the temple was a type of the building up of the ekklesia in the New Testament. It is not until believers enjoy the unlimited Christ as the reality of everything around them and indiscriminately share their Christ with all kinds of believers can they be satisfied, and God's purpose be fulfilled: the building up of His Body.

To apprehend the dimension of this immense Christ, Paul instructs "*all the saints*" are needed (Eph.3:18). The word "all" in the original Greek does not emphasize quantity (meaning every single person), but "types" or "kinds." Thus, this phrase means a variety of saints are needed to capture the depths of the love of Christ. Therefore, the sheer number of believers gathered is not what enables them to grasp the vast dimensions of Christ. It is the fellowship in the ekklesia which occurs with believers from all kinds of diverse backgrounds and environments which empowers them to apprehend the immeasurable scope of Christ.

As individuals, believers can only enjoy Christ based on the environment in which they find themselves. For example, a stay-at-home mom's environment includes caring for her children, her house, and her interactions with other moms. Christ exists to be rich in such an environment for her to enjoy; however, she will not know Christ in an environment she never enters — such as a global business operation. However, a believer who engages in a global business environment will also find Christ there to enjoy and experience. If these two believers are isolated from each other and never fellowship, each will not know Christ in the other person's environment; their apprehension of Christ is limited and one-dimensional.

This same concept can be applied in a spiritual sense to an entire category of people. Let's say that a person only fellowships with believers in their own church consisting of a particular ethnic group, a particular political leaning, or a particular doctrinal understanding. This, then, remains the only environment in which they experience Christ, which is limited to one track. One day they begin to fellowship with believers of other ethnicities — perhaps with opposing political views. They will find those believers are experiencing Christ as well. As they enter into the fellowship of Jesus Christ with them, then what they receive is not their political viewpoint, but their Christ. They are able to enjoy Him in a way they may have never before considered, since that is not their normal environment. They will begin to realize Christ is just as enjoyable in their new environment, as in their own. Their "apprehension" of Christ expands! Therefore, the more kinds or types of believers with whom a Christian is in fellowship, the more he or she will lay hold of this vast all-inclusive Christ. It is the enjoyment of Christ as the vastness of the Good Land which brings believers into oneness for God's building.

Thus, the building up of the temple — His ekklesia, which is the one fellowship of Jesus Christ — can only take place when believers explore the vast and diverse Christ as the Good Land in fellowshipping with all kinds and type of believers. This is the corporate aspect of enjoying Christ as the Good Land.

Believers Cannot Get Out of Christ; Learn to Walk in Him

"Moses My servant is dead. Now therefore, arise, go over this Jordan, you and all this people, to the land which I am giving to them — the children of Israel. Every place that the sole of your foot will tread upon I have given you, as I said to Moses."

— Joshua 1:2–3

"Where can I go from Your Spirit? Or where can I flee from Your presence? If I ascend into heaven, You *are* there; if I make my bed in hell, behold, You are *there*. If I take the wings of the morning, *and* dwell in the uttermost parts of the sea, even there Your hand shall lead me, and Your right hand shall hold me. If I say, 'Surely the darkness shall fall on me,' even the night shall be light about me."

— Psalm 139:7–11

"As you therefore have received Christ Jesus the Lord, so walk in Him. . . .."

— Colossians 2:6

Is it hard to believe once a person receives the faith of Jesus Christ they cannot be removed or detached from Him, no matter what happens? Many believers have such a small Christ they think if they do certain things, socialize at certain places, or behave in a certain way they will find themselves outside of Christ and miss Him. Psalm 139 contradicts this idea. No matter where believers go or what they do, they cannot get away from Christ. Christians must stand firm in this assurance, and boldly declare even when failures bring the weight of hell and darkness upon them, they still can never get out of Him! Believers can go anywhere in this universe and never be outside of Christ. It is not proper behavior which keeps believers in Him; it is the realization they are already in Him which experientially *keeps* them in Him. They simply need to walk in Him according to their seeing of this vast Christ.

Wherever believers go, wherever they tread, Christ is the land for them to possess. It is simply not possible to be outside of Christ! This is what it means to learn how to explore the vastness of Christ — to consider and enjoy His riches, no matter what situations and challenges impact one's daily life.

Most Christians may consider whether they are in Christ in order to enjoy Him based on a set of criteria or behaviors. If they behave in a certain way, then they are in Christ; if they misbehave, they are excluded from the pleasure of being in Christ. Whether a believer can enjoy Him — whether they are in the right condition to delight in Him or not — depends on faith in God's Word. In 2 Corinthians 5:7, Paul says, "*We walk by faith and not by sight*." The word "sight" in this verse refers to an individual's own perception, which can be very deceptive. Faith, however, is the ability to spiritually see the real situation in God's realm. The reality is believers are in Christ as a vast land out of which they cannot escape. It is by this faith believers need to walk in Christ. The faith of permanently being in Christ allows believers to turn their focus away from their behavior and criteria, to behold Jesus Christ in their daily living. This is the individual aspect of enjoying Christ as the Good Land.

The Good Land in the Believer's Spirit

Now Christ is the Spirit; thus, the all-inclusive Christ as the Spirit *is* the Good Land in the believer's spirit.

> "Now the Lord [Jesus] is the Spirit; and where the Spirit of the Lord *is*, there *is* liberty."
>
> ~ 2 Corinthians 3:17

> "And so it is written, 'The first man Adam became a living being.' The last Adam [Jesus Christ] became a life-giving spirit."
>
> ~ 1 Corinthians 15:45

In both verses, Paul declared Jesus Christ, *today*, is the Spirit. The God who became man, died on the cross and resurrected, is now, as well, in a spiritual form. Because He is the Spirit, believers can be in Him and He in them.

The Greek word for "spirit" is *pneuma* meaning, "breath" or "wind." It is the origin of the word "pneumatic." Air is in people, but air also surrounds them. The air in a person is their life. The air surrounding a person, regardless of where they are or what they are doing, is the environment of their daily living. This is the Spirit intermingling with believers: The Spirit is in them and they are in the Spirit. They are completely joined and integrated together with the Spirit, within and without. Therefore, a believer does not have to fulfill certain laws in order to enjoy Jesus as the Spirit; rather, they are liberated and free to live in Him just as they are.

The Good Land for the Believer's Enjoyment

The all-inclusive Christ is the Good Land for the believer's enjoyment.

> "That the blessing of Abraham might come upon the Gentiles in Christ Jesus, that we might receive the promise of the Spirit through faith."
>
> – Galatians 3:14

According to the OT (Gen. 12:7; 13:15; 17:8), what was promised to Abraham was a piece of land called the "Good Land." That was the physical blessing Abraham's seed was to receive. Today the blessing of Abraham, which is available to all believers, even the Gentiles, is the Spirit. This is the reality (or the archetype) of the Good Land for believers today. The Spirit is the real, vast, and abundantly rich land for believers to enjoy and in which to live. No matter where the believer walks, what he or she does, or what time of day it is, the Spirit is available for enjoyment as the all-inclusive blessing.

> "For I know that this shall turn out for me to salvation, through your supplication and the [bountiful] supply of the Spirit of Jesus Christ."
>
> – Philippians 1:19, DBY

The root word for "supply" in the Greek is the word *epichorēgia*, which means "to supply bountifully, abundantly; to supply all things necessary." While Paul (the writer of Philippians) was a prisoner chained to a guard, the Spirit of Jesus Christ was abundantly supplying all he needed. The Spirit was ministering to him. Surely Paul experienced the "Good Land," even while in chains. Regardless of the challenging situations facing believers, they can find themselves in the Spirit — the vast and rich land which supplies, saves, and delivers them.

> "So then, those who are in the flesh cannot please God. But you are not in the flesh but in the Spirit, if indeed the Spirit of God dwells in you. Now if anyone does not have the Spirit of Christ, he is not His."
>
> – Romans 8:8

The word "flesh" in Romans 8:8 refers to the fallen old self, without Christ. A person devoid of Christ cannot please God. However, believers are no longer in the flesh but in the Spirit. The Spirit is now their land, realm, even their universe. The Spirit of God and Christ dwells in the believer and the believer is dwelling in the Spirit. There is nothing more a believer needs to do in order to be "in." They are to simply rest and enjoy the reality they are *already* in the Spirit.

One Spirit

Through faith in Jesus Christ, believers are joined to Him in perfect union. Thus, the Spirit with the believer's spirit is one spirit.

> "But he who is joined to the Lord is one spirit."
>
> – 1 Corinthians 6:17

> "You received the Spirit of [sonship] adoption by whom we cry out, 'Abba, Father.' The Spirit Himself bears witness with our spirit that we are children of God."
>
> – Romans 8:15b–16

Once believers are joined to the Lord, they become one spirit. His Spirit and their spirit together become one. There is no more separation or even the possibility of becoming separated again.

The physical act of eating food is a good illustration. When a person ingests food, the food and the person's body become one. It is no longer possible to separate digested food from the body. This is how believers become children of God: by *their* spirit and *God's* Spirit being joined as one.

That is the meaning of being "born again," "born anew," or regeneration. How is it possible for believers to "come out of" the Good Land, if the Good Land is now part of their very being?

> "The Lord Jesus Christ be with your spirit. Grace be with you. Amen."
>
> – 2 Timothy 4:22

The Lord Jesus became the life-giving Spirit after resurrection. The Spirit is now indwelling the spirit of His believers; therefore, the Lord Jesus Christ is with their spirits. Today, believers are in the Good Land and the Good Land is in them; their response should be to lift up their eyes and see Christ in everything around them, and in all they are doing!

The Mind-Set of the Spirit and Breathing Prayer

First, to live according to the Spirit is to have the mind-set of the Spirit:

> ". . . in order that the law's requirement would be accomplished in us who do not walk according to the flesh but according to the Spirit. For those who live according to the flesh think about the things of the flesh, but those who live according to the Spirit, about the things of the Spirit. For the mind-set of the flesh is death, but the mind-set of the Spirit is life and peace."
>
> – Romans 8:4–6, HCSB

The requirements of the law set a high standard. In fact, it is so high only God can fulfill His own law. How can believers fulfill this law with such extreme requirements? It is by walking according to the Spirit. For example, the way to fulfill the requirement to love and forgive one another as Christ is not by self-effort; it can only be done by walking according to the Spirit. Paul says in Romans 8:5 the unique characteristic of one living according to the Spirit is when they constantly think about the things of the Spirit. To live according to the Spirit is to consider the things of the Spirit. So then, *what are the things of the Spirit?*

Those in the Good Land experience the Spirit in everything around them. Everywhere they look, and whatever they do can be things of the Spirit for their contemplation, consideration, and appreciation. This is the mind-set of the Spirit which gives life and peace and leads to constant fellowship with the Lord. Believers can switch from the mind-set of the flesh to the mind-set of the Spirit in a split second. It is that quick to embrace life and peace and to fulfill the requirement of the law.

For example, think of commuting to work. Believers can experience Christ as the car providing transportation, the gas which powers, the air conditioning which cools, and when driving by an emergency call box — Christ is the person to call when in need. This kind of thinking concerning the things of the Spirit will spontaneously lead the believer to fellowship with the Lord resulting in an outpouring of thanksgiving — for the Lord is so many things! In such enjoyment of the Good Land, believers will also experience Christ as their patience and love. When another driver cuts a person off who is in such fellowship with Christ, their spontaneous reaction will be one of understanding and forgiveness because they are enjoying while resting in the Good Land.

Let's say upon arriving home from work after a long day, a husband finds his spouse has forgotten to do something important she promised to do. Before reacting, the husband prays inwardly and thinks on how Christ is the real husband and how He came to give His life in love on behalf of His people — He is the faithful servant. Instead of reacting in anger resulting in a deadened situation, the husband's mind-set is now full of appreciation for all the blessings of Christ around him. The result: he will not only remain in life and peace but will minister the same life and peace to his spouse.

Breathing in the Believer's Spirit

Living in the Good Land is to continuously breathe the Spirit — this is unceasing prayer in the believer's spirit.

> "And I will pour on the house of David and on the inhabitants of Jerusalem the Spirit of grace and supplication [prayer]."
> – Zechariah 12:10

The key to enjoying the Good Land is having the mind-set of the Spirit who is joined to the believer's spirit. The key to being in the fellowship of the Spirit is supplication.

"Supplication" in this verse means *prayer*. Prayer means speaking to God in fellowship and making requests of Him. Any time believers turn their heart to speak to the Lord Jesus, they are praying. There is no "right" way to pray. Just start talking to Him, have a conversation — make any requests known to Him.

The Spirit Who has been given to every believer is the Spirit of grace and prayer. The Spirit Christians have received in their spirit and joined as one is a praying spirit. Grace and prayer go together. Grace is related to all Who the Lord Jesus is and has accomplished and has given freely for the believer's enjoyment. The way to realize this grace is through fellowship in prayer. When believers are in fellowship with the Lord, grace is their reality. Wonderfully, the Spirit within believers is constantly praying to bring them into continual fellowship and grace.

> "Pray without ceasing, in everything give thanks; for this is the will of God in Christ Jesus for you."
> — 1 Thessalonians 5:17–18

There is only one thing human beings do without ceasing: breathe. A person can be very aware of their breathing; sometimes they may even need to stop and breathe deeply, to calm down or muster up energy to do something. However, most of the time people breathe subconsciously. Praying is like breathing for believers. God's Spirit joined with the believer's spirit is unceasingly praying. However, believers need to recognize and enter this constant connection of prayer. Yes, sometimes people need to stop everything to pray, but Christians can be constantly praying as they walk and live in their daily lives.

Many believers consider prayer to be an event; they may even feel they need to go through a certain process before praying. If that is the case, it will be impossible to pray without ceasing. Since Christians already have the Spirit in them praying incessantly, whether they are aware of it or not, it is simple to "join in" and pray as the Spirit makes one aware. A believer's praying spirit is independent of their behavior and actions. A person may be upright and respectable or morally deficient. They may be about to fall (or have fallen) into sin. It doesn't matter; any believer can immediately enter into prayer because the Spirit Who resides in them is still praying, even when they are not.

Just as it is physically hard for people to hold their breath, it is actually more difficult to have broken fellowship with the Lord. Once a person realizes praying is like spiritual breathing, they will find it is easier to pray and have fellowship, than not having either prayer or fellowship!

Paul also exhorts believers in 1 Thessalonians 5:17 to give thanks in everything. A believer who realizes God has done everything and given everything to them, naturally responds in thanksgiving and praise. Throughout the day, consider all the items which can be enjoyed through prayer and thanksgiving in Christ as the Good Land.

For example, as I sit at my desk and glance at the various items on it, I might be able to realize: "Lord Jesus, You are my real money. You are all the riches I need in the world. Lord, You are my reading glasses; with You I can see clearly. Lord, as I see this bill, I thank You for paying off all my debt of sin. I am free from debt because of Your death on the cross. Lord, You are my real headphones! I want to hear You and not be distracted by the noise of the world. Lord, as I am writing, You are writing in me. Write Your letters by Your Spirit on the tablets of my heart."

In the Good Land, the believer never becomes exhausted from exploring and enjoying the riches of Christ. This is the will of God.

> ". . . praying always with all prayer and supplication in the Spirit, being watchful to this end with all perseverance and supplication for all the saints."
>
> – Ephesians 6:18

> "I desire therefore that the men pray everywhere."
>
> – 1 Timothy 2:8

Believers are to pray always and everywhere; this is what it means to be joined with the Spirit. Through prayer, believers will also make requests concerning others. Prayer is never self-centered because the Spirit cares for *all* people. When believers are joined with God's Spirit, they spontaneously pray for the needs of others. Praying is one of the most powerful ways to care for other people; the love of God will instill believers with a love for others as they pray for them.

Practice: Turning Everything into Prayer

Take time to practice turning everything in life into prayer and thanksgiving, enjoying the all-inclusive Christ as the Good Land. This should be as easy as breathing! At home, take pleasure in Christ while completing daily chores — when cooking, washing, or relaxing. Enjoy Him as the Good Land when together with a spouse, friends, relatives, or taking care of children. Enjoy Jesus as the Good Land while at school or work, when solving problems, when interacting with others, when deadlines are approaching, and when working on the computer!

Jesus, the Good Land, can be experienced when exercising, commuting, and entering various environments (good and bad). This can continue even during accidental or willful failures.

Take five minutes right now and look around you. Start applying what you see into a fellowship prayer with the Lord Jesus. Talk to Him and allow the things surrounding you to prompt you to see Jesus as the reality. Let them be an opening for you to enjoy Him in prayer.

Write down the items you see and write down how they remind you of Christ:

Item 1:
How applied:

Item 2:
How applied:

Item 3:
How applied:

Item 4:
How applied:

7

EXERCISING: TEACHING AND A GOOD CONSCIENCE

A ll life needs activities, or exercise. If a person lies in bed day after day without any physical movement, their muscles will soon atrophy. Eventually they will die from the absence of activity. Exercise involves pushing against an opposite force – it requires effort. Sadly, that is the reason why most people don't like to exercise; consequently, they are unhealthy. Healthy people are active and regularly exercise; the more they are willing to physically push themselves, the more their health will improve over time. They will become physically stronger. Even though effort is required, exercising can also be fun and enjoyable. Certainly, regular exercise will improve a person's quality of life; their efforts will be well rewarded! Paul affirmed this by saying: "*For **bodily exercise has some value**, but godliness has value in all things, having the promise of the life which is now, and of that which is to come*" (1 Tim. 4:8).

What *spiritual* exercise should every believer engage? Firstly, it is ministering and teaching the Word of Jesus Christ to others. The effort put forth to help others understand the Word concerning Jesus Christ and ministering spiritual food and drink to others is "exercise" for believers. There are all sorts of forces inside and outside of believers which oppose this ministry of the Word and the Spirit. Therefore, believers must put forth effort to push through these contrary forces, and why it is considered exercise.

Secondly, living a life without offense – keeping a clear conscience toward God and man – is also an exercise. Without these activities, believers will feel unfulfilled and without purpose.

Most believers today passively listen to the teaching of members of the clergy; because of this, there is a lack of growth. A baby is physically active immediately at birth; moreover, this person needs to continue to be active until death. New believers need to start learning to teach others and live according to their conscience — immediately. This exercise will cause them to grow, enjoy more of Jesus Christ, and fulfill what God intended for them.

What Is Spiritual Exercise?

Spiritual exercise is teaching and ministering what has been eaten — learned and enjoyed — of Christ. The writer of Hebrews 5-6 says exercise means participating in the priesthood of Melchizedek. God commanded the Aaronic priesthood to make sacrifices for sinners, whereas the priesthood of Melchizedek ministered bread and wine to victorious fighters.

> "He [Aaron] can have compassion on those who are ignorant and going astray, since he himself is also subject to weakness. Because of this he is required as for the people, so also for himself, to offer sacrifices for sins. . . . So also Christ did not glorify Himself to become High Priest, but it was He who said to Him: 'You are My Son, Today I have begotten You.' As He also says in another place: 'You are a priest forever according to the order of Melchizedek.'"
>
> – Hebrews 5:2–3, 5–6

In Hebrews 5, the writer compares and contrasts the priesthood of Aaron and the priesthood of Melchizedek. Aaron was the first in the line of high priests in the Old Testament which offered sacrifices to God for sin. These high priests were sinful themselves; therefore, when they offered sacrifices for the sins of the people, they offered sacrifices for themselves as well. What was significant of the Aaronic priesthood was God commanded sacrifices to be offered continually for sin, a reminder that their sacrifices never took sin away (Heb. 10:2–3).

In contrast, Jesus Christ, who is the Son of God, is now serving according to the order of the Melchizedek priesthood. In Acts 13:33 Paul quoted Psalm 2 by saying, *"You are My Son, today I have begotten You."* This was a declaration referring to the day of the resurrection of Jesus Christ, indicating the ministry of Melchizedek is in resurrection — Jesus entered that priesthood the day of His resurrection. When Jesus Christ died on the cross, He was the real sacrifice for sin, a sacrifice which permanently took away sins (John 1:29; Heb. 10:11–12). Instead of reminding people of their sins, through Jesus' redemptive death, God remembers sin no more. After accomplishing such an impactful death, and being perfected through

His resurrection, Jesus became the author of eternal salvation, which is the ministry of His eternal life. It was only after His resurrection wherein Jesus became qualified to be *the* High Priest according to the order of Melchizedek (Heb. 5:10). The death of the Lord Jesus was to take away sins, and His resurrection was for imparting life.

> "So he [Abraham] brought back all the goods, and also brought back his brother Lot and his goods, as well as the women and the people. And the king of Sodom went out to meet him at the Valley of Shaveh (that is, the King's Valley), after his return from the defeat of Chedorlaomer and the kings who were with him. Then Melchizedek king of Salem brought out bread and wine; he was the priest of God Most High. And he blessed him and said: 'Blessed be Abram of God Most High, Possessor of heaven and earth; And blessed be God Most High, Who has delivered your enemies into your hand.' And he gave him a tithe of all."
>
> – Genesis 14:16–20

> "For this Melchizedek, king of Salem, priest of the Most High God, who met Abraham returning from the slaughter of the kings and blessed him, to whom also Abraham gave a tenth part of all, first being translated 'king of righteousness,' and then also king of Salem, meaning 'king of peace,' without father, without mother, without genealogy, having neither beginning of days nor end of life, but made like the Son of God, remains a priest continually."
>
> – Hebrews 7:1–3

The first time Melchizedek appeared was in Genesis when he met Abraham after Abraham defeated five kings who had captured his brother (nephew), Lot. At that point Abraham was a victorious fighter, not a defeated sinner. As a sinner, he would have needed a sacrifice for sins on his behalf. However, Melchizedek blessed Abraham — the victorious fighter — and ministered to him bread and wine. Unlike the Aaronic priesthood, which reminded people of their sins, the Melchizedek priesthood ministered bread and wine to those in victory.

This is a picture of God's eternal salvation. Jesus Christ has already completed the sacrifice for sins on the cross — the pardon for sins penalty has been secured. Christ's current function is to be High Priest ministering bread and wine to believers; no longer will poor sinners in God's eyes be awaiting judgment for sin but are free through the victory won on the cross in Him. In Jesus Christ, believers are in victory and qualified to partake of Him.

Teaching and Dispensing Food

Sadly, believers often remain babes becoming dull of hearing concerning ministering Christ to others – they neither teach nor dispense Christ as food to the hungry.

> ". . . of whom we have much to say, and hard to explain, since you have become dull of hearing. For though by this time you ought to be teachers, you need someone to teach you again the first principles of the oracles of God; and you have come to need milk and not solid food."
>
> – Hebrews 5:11–12

There is much to say about Melchizedek because He is the archetype of Jesus Christ in resurrection, ascension, and outpouring of the Spirit. His ministry as *the* Great High Priest has been continuing for 2000 years. Jesus ministered for three-and-a-half years – beginning His earthly ministry at about 30 years of age (Luke 3:23), whereby he took away sins and accomplished forgiveness. But now some 2000 years later, Jesus is still ministering life. The priesthood of Melchizedek, which is the ministry of eternal life with all His riches which shall continue into eternity.

However, though Jesus is unsearchably rich, the hearing of most believers has become dull and sluggish. There is little interest in the riches of Christ in resurrection beyond forgiveness of sins. Many are bored hearing about Christ's ministry of Himself as bread and wine. Christians in the main remain within the basic principles of Christ. These basic principles include such things as the forgiveness of sins emphasized through the Aaronic priesthood, as well as foundational doctrines like baptism and eternal judgment (Heb. 6:1–3). Believers who continue to crave instruction in these elementary doctrines will remain babes. Solid food is for those who move beyond these "*basic principles*" (Heb. 5:12). Believers must advance to participate in the priesthood of Melchizedek by ministering bread and wine to others. Their teaching concerning Jesus Christ to others, with all the riches of His person and work, in turn becomes *their* solid food. For those listening to the minister's teaching, it is milk. But to the one teaching, it is solid food. Once believers begin to teach others to advance beyond the stage of being babes — where they repeatedly hear the same teaching on forgiveness of sin — their ears will be opened. They will be interested and excited to hear more concerning Christ as the High Priest in resurrection and ascension. Teaching others will strengthen believers by providing them with solid food to grow by His eternal-divine life they have received — into a deeper appreciation of Christ.

Just as newborns are immediately active and must use their muscles to grow, new believers should immediately teach others as well. Just as toddlers learning to talk cannot speak in full sentences, new Christians learning to speak Christ, though without all the scriptural citations, is music to their heavenly Father's ears. What has been learned of Jesus Christ, even though it may seem small, can be taught to those even less informed than they. No matter how little or much new believers learn or experience concerning Jesus Christ, it is good enough to pass on and teach others. Their teaching may be very elementary, even inaccurate, but it is the best way to start exercising! New believers will grow and learn more concerning Jesus Christ as they minister. Their teaching ability will improve over time.

The Ministry of the Spirit

The word "milk" is akin to listening and being taught the things concerning Christ. However, the "word of righteousness" refers to the believer's participation in Melchizedek, through ministering the bread and wine of the New Covenant to others — *the* ministry of the Spirit (2 Cor. 3:6). This is solid food, which is the ministry of righteousness.

> ". . . for everyone who lives on milk is unskilled in the word of righteousness, since he is a child."
>
> – Hebrews 5:13, ESV

> "... who has made us sufficient to be ministers of a new covenant, not of the letter but of the Spirit. For the letter kills, but the Spirit gives life. Now if the ministry of death, carved in letters on stone, came with such glory that the Israelites could not gaze at Moses' face because of its glory, which was being brought to an end, will not the ministry of the Spirit have even more glory? For if there was glory in the ministry of condemnation, the ministry of righteousness must far exceed it in glory."
>
> – 2 Corinthians 3:6–9, ESV

Those who depend on milk year after year are unskilled in the word of righteousness. The *word of righteousness*, in context, is the ministry of Melchizedek (or the ministry of bread and wine). Scripture reveals participating in this ministry *is* solid food for believers. In 2 Corinthians 3:6–9 Paul declared: God made believers sufficient ministers of the New Covenant. Paul made clear this is *not* the ministry of the letter of the law, which is a ministry of death. Believers are qualified to minister *the Spirit*. Speaking about the law as sufficient for righteousness will minister death to people. No one can fulfill the law; therefore, everyone who receives this ministry is condemned to death. But the ministry of the New Covenant is the ministry of the Spirit. It is also the ministry of righteousness. When people receive the ministry of the Spirit, the Spirit works within them to produce a life and character which is right with both God and man.

This is the true priesthood of Melchizedek: those who minister the bread and wine of the New Covenant — this is the ministry of the Spirit — the word of righteousness.

Exercise to Become Mature

Exercising to become mature means to practice teaching and ministering to others. Doing so will sharpen one's perception; while ministering to others, the believer will be able to discern what is useful or worthless to their listeners.

> "But solid food belongs to those who are of full age, *that is*, those who by reason of use have their senses [faculties for perception] exercised to discern both good [useful, precious] and evil [worthless]."
>
> – Hebrews 5:14

To better understand how teaching — ministering bread and wine according to Melchizedek — equates with exercising, think of physical exercise. Just as people need to physically exercise in order to grow, spiritual exercise is needed for a person to progress to maturity. This means being more than just a listener of the Word, but also a teacher. Every person needs to exercise, and every believer needs to be a teacher — a minister like Melchizedek. If believers do not exercise in such a way, they will stay as a babe and will become dull of hearing. The more believers exercise to teach others about Christ, the more their inward faculties for perceiving and discerning good and evil, will be enhanced.

The phrase "good and evil" may be misleading. Some might immediately associate it with being either morally upright or depraved. The actual meaning in Greek, and the better translation is, "to be able to discern what is useful or precious and that which is worthless." As believers exercise to teach and minister Christ to others, they will be able to discern through their ministering what is useful in their teaching and what is not necessary at that time. The more a person ministers Christ to others, the more their inner senses and perception will be sharpened.

First, they will be able to discern what is precious for food and what teachings are worthless. Not only that, they will be able know what they should teach, how to say certain things, and what to avoid at a given time. They will be more excellent in ministry and service to others through teaching just what is needed at the time when it is needed. The listener will then partake of bread and wine and be nourished with Christ. Teaching here does not necessarily mean teaching like a teacher in front of an audience in a big room! The best and most opportune time is when teaching happens in a group of two or three or in a home assembly. Only a few may have opportunity to teach in front of a larger audience, but everyone has opportunity to teach and minister to another person.

Leave the Elementary Principles of Christ

Contrary to Paul's request to not linger in elementary doctrines, it seems this is what most believers are continually taught year after year.

> "Therefore, leaving the discussion of the elementary principles of Christ, let us go on to perfection, not laying again the foundation of repentance from dead works and of faith toward God, of the doctrine of baptisms, of laying on of hands, of resurrection of the dead, and of eternal judgment."
>
> *– Hebrews 6:1–2*

The word "therefore" in Hebrews 6:1 is key to understanding this section. It reveals the writer's next words will be both a continuation of the last chapter, and a conclusion. Earlier in Hebrews 5:12, the writer of Hebrews spoke of the *first principles* akin to milk. Hebrews 6 lists these elementary principles: repentance, faith, baptism, the receiving of the Spirit (laying on of hands), and issues of eternal judgment.

This is basically what most believers are repeatedly taught. The problem is not with these teachings, but *lingering* as a student, always listening, instead of moving on to become a teacher. Leaving these elementary things does not mean they are never talked about; leaving refers to progressing on to be a teacher, a minister like Melchizedek. It means leaving the state of perpetually being taught to one teaching and ministering to others.

It is easy to be a passive listener, but it is an exercise to rise up to teach and minister.

> "For it is impossible for those who were once enlightened, and have tasted the heavenly gift, and have become partakers of the Holy Spirit, and have tasted the good word of God and the powers of the age to come, if they fall away, to renew them again to repentance, since they crucify again for themselves the Son of God, and put Him to an open shame."
>
> *– Hebrews 6:4–6*

Once believers have received all these wonderful gifts — once they have *"become partakers of the Holy Spirit, and have tasted the good word of God and the powers of the age to come"* (Heb. 6:4–5) from their faith in Christ — they need to move on. Even if they "fall away" and backslide, it is impossible to return to the beginning, repent, and start all over again as a new believer. Just about every believer has experienced a falling away from the Lord. Many think when this happens, they need to be re-taught the basics. They feel the need to hear the gospel and repent again, to participate in another "altar call."

This should not be! Christ's crucifixion is once for all. To repent again is like asking the Lord to die and shed His blood again. Accepting this deception is why many believers remain babes and continue to crave milk. Their experience is one of constantly being reminded of their sins, which is a function of the Aaronic priesthood.

Mature believers are not perfect. Indeed, they can fall into sin; likewise, they may experience times of falling away from pursuing Christ as well. However, they have enough trust in the work of Christ and their own solid foundation of faith to resume moving forward in Christ's victory. Thus, the mature believer continues his journey as a victorious fighter, a priest in the order of Melchizedek, who ministers bread and wine to others. This is spiritual exercise.

A mature believer is one like Abraham, who did not linger in his own condition but went out to rescue his brother and returned victorious. Mature believers don't linger in the apathy of being taught! Once the wonderful gifts have been tasted, they start teaching and ministering in the priesthood of Melchizedek, despite having repeatedly failed. Doing so results in seeing and enjoying more of the unsearchable riches of Christ.

Believers should learn higher points of truth beyond the teaching of the basics of Christ. They should be learning those things to "complete the word of God" for the building up the Body of Christ: God's economy for His eternal purpose; the ministry of the Spirit for renewing and transforming believers into His image; the New Covenant; and the New Commandment of loving one another. Nevertheless, even if they learn some of these things related to the ministry of Melchizedek, they will become dull from repeatedly hearing these things if they don't teach them. They will remain a babe if they do not exercise and begin ministering to others themselves. Maturity is not about knowing a lot of Bible knowledge or even having the highest revelations, but whether Christians are participating in the ministry of Melchizedek by serving bread and wine — the riches of Jesus Christ for others to partake and enjoy.

Cultivating Believers to Produce Food

God's purpose is to cultivate believers with His riches, so they produce food that satisfies others just as Melchizedek did with bread and wine.

> "For land that has drunk the rain that often falls on it, and produces a crop useful to those for whose sake it is cultivated, receives a blessing from God. But if it bears thorns and thistles, it is worthless and near to being cursed, and its end is to be burned."
>
> – Hebrews 6:7–8

The writer of Hebrews reveals God's purpose in providing a rich spiritual supply. This specifically refers to Hebrews 6:4-5 where one receives a share of the Spirit, and can taste the heavenly gifts, as well as the good Word. Each of these things is "rain" on believers (the land). God's expectation for providing rain is intended for producing food to those who need it. God is in the process of cultivating believers who will produce nourishing food.

There are many people around every believer whom God wants to feed with Christ as the nourishing bread and wine. They are hungry for spiritual food and drink; therefore, God wants every believer to participate in the priesthood of Melchizedek in order to feed the hungry. If after receiving God's gift of rain, Christians in turn produce something nourishing for others, they are blessed. If they do not minister Christ, they are a barren land with non-edible worthless thorns and thistles. Those are believers who only receive, but rarely give.

This is a serious warning to all believers. Those who embrace the idea that teaching, and ministering is only to be done by trained professionals such as pastors, ministers, or priests are making an essential mistake. *Every* believer is called to teach — to minister to others the riches of Christ as bread and wine — each needs to exercise toward this function (i.e., "the priesthood of all believers"). Otherwise, they will remain a babe and never mature. Sharing what a believer has learned should begin as soon as a person comes to know the Lord.

John 15 provides a similar warning. There the Lord Jesus warned the branches in the vine to bear fruit, to supply life to others for His multiplication; any branch without fruit is "cast into the fire." It is a kind of discipline from the Father.

Minister to Strengthen and Increase Godliness

It is important to spiritually exercise to be a good minister of the things of God's economy. This will strengthen and increase godliness. Godliness is the entire process of God becoming flesh to be dispensed into His household (the ekklesia), that it may grow unto glorification.

> "But if I am delayed, I write so that you may know how you ought to conduct yourself in the house of God, which is the church [ekklesia] of the living God, the pillar and ground of the truth. And without controversy great is the mystery of godliness: God was manifested in the flesh, justified in the Spirit, seen by angels, preached among the Gentiles, believed on in the world, received up in glory."
>
> – 1 Timothy 3:15–16

Paul's concern was Timothy's conduct in the household of God, the family of God, which is the ekklesia. This is composed of living members, because God is living and moves within His family members, the ekklesia.

In 1 Timothy 3:16 Paul continues and explains the mystery of godliness: God was manifested in the flesh (His incarnation and as the God–Man living on earth), justified in the Spirit (His resurrection after crucifixion), seen by angels (His ascension and enthronement), preached among the Gentiles (His outpouring of the Spirit to initiate the dispensing of Himself to humanity through the gospel), and believed on in the world (the multiplication of the members of His body). Finally, taken up in glory (the members of His body transformed and glorified). This description of the mystery of godliness is the truth. It is this truth which the ekklesia supports and uplifts as the pillar and ground of the truth.

The truth, this mystery of godliness, is not just the person of Jesus Christ, it also includes God's family, the ekklesia – His body. Godliness is comprised of God Himself processed through death and resurrection and dispensed into man, resulting in glorification – the manifestation of God and man joined and intermingled into one. God Himself is not separated from His household (ekklesia), but is intrinsically joined to her; therefore, it is impossible for Him to separate from His ekklesia. This is God's eternal purpose.

Proper Conduct in the Household of God

When one understands that God is intrinsically joined and integrated to His household, how then should believers respond? According to Paul, it should be by dispensing nourishment, or teaching the truth to others.

"Laying these things before the brethren, you will be a good minister of Christ Jesus, nourished with the words of the faith and of the good teaching which you have fully followed up. . . . Enjoin and teach these things. . . . Till I come, give yourself to [public] reading, to exhortation, to teaching. . . . Give heed to yourself and to the teaching. Continue in them; for doing this, you will save both yourself and those hearing you."

– 1 Timothy 4:6, 11, 13, 16, DBY

After exhorting his listeners regarding godliness, Paul charges Timothy to be a teacher, a minister of the truth, and a dispenser of life. This is how Timothy is to conduct himself in the household of God; thus, it is how every believer ought to behave. On the one hand, they are to be nourished up with the truth, and continue in it. On the other hand, they are to teach: to present the nourishing truth before their brothers and sisters, and to exhort fellow believers to imitate what they are doing by teaching and ministering.

Exercising Oneself toward Godliness

Believers who desire to be good ministers refuse that which is not truth and exercise themselves toward godliness

"If you instruct the brethren in these things, you will be a good minister of Jesus Christ, nourished in the words of faith and of the good doctrine which you have carefully followed. But reject profane and old wives' fables, and exercise yourself toward godliness."

– 1 Timothy 4:6–7

After believers eat and are nourished (1 Tim. 4:6), Paul writes "exercise" is needed next. In order for life to grow and mature, one must eat; however, exercise must not be neglected. This supports the underlying thought of this chapter, i.e., if life is to grow and mature, there is the need to eat; there is also the need to exercise. It cannot be overemphasized godliness here in context is not a matter of ethics or morality. Godliness was not defined as such in this chapter; rather, godliness is truth – the joining and union between God and humanity. Therefore, exercise toward godliness relates to the teaching of the nourishing truth in contrast to fables and other unhealthy teachings which corrupt.

Reject Fables, Endless Genealogies, and Law Teachers

> "Even as I begged you to remain in Ephesus, when I was
> going to Macedonia, that you might charge some not to teach
> other doctrines, nor to turn their minds to fables and endless
> genealogies, which bring questionings rather than further God's
> dispensation [*oikonomia*], which is in faith. But the end of what
> is charged is love out of a pure heart and a good conscience
> and unfeigned faith; which things some having missed, have
> turned aside to vain discourse, desiring to be law-teachers, not
> understanding either what they say or concerning what they so
> strenuously affirm."
>
> — 1 Timothy 1:3–7, DBY

Paul commanded to reject "profane and old wives' fables" (1 Tim. 4:7)
which is consistent with charging Timothy not to teach any doctrines with
characteristics of fables, endless genealogies, and teaching of the law (1 Tim.
1:3–7). Rather, believers are to continue with the teaching of truth which
furthers God's dispensation or economy.

A fable might be considered the adding of undue embellishments and
emphasis to someone's testimony or witness of a "miracle," making it into a
legend or myth. Endless genealogies may include elevating certain ministers
or preachers who have a proper theological lineage, listing the great things
they have done — their pedigrees. People consider these teachers as being
sound simply because of their genealogy, without questioning what they
are teaching and to examine if it is true or healthy. Conversely, instructions
from teachers without an acceptable genealogy are automatically rejected,
regardless of how healthy or true their teachings are.

Then there are the so-called "law teachers" who Paul says: *They want to
be teachers of the law, but they do not know what they are talking about or what
they so confidently affirm* (1 Tim. 1:7 — NIV). Their teachings are deceptive
because they teach principles and laws from the Bible, but they draw
believers back into the dictates of the *first covenant* (Heb. 9:1), establishing
their own righteousness under the law. They energize believers' fleshly
nature, teaching believers to use their best efforts to keep *the law of
commandments contained in ordinances* (Eph. 2:15), leading them away from
faith — from the Law of the Spirit of Life in Christ — *written on the fleshy*

tablets of the heart (2 Cor. 3:3). Paul's entire epistle to the Galatians was his effort to expose this evil and recover believers back to freedom in Christ. Any teaching or speaking that distracts believers from the nourishing truth in God's economy should be avoided, even rejected.

Stand Firm in Truth When Teaching Others

Exercising toward godliness requires remaining in the things of truth while teaching and ministering to others.

> "But reject profane and old wives' fables, and exercise yourself toward godliness."
>
> – 1 Timothy 4:7

In the context of 1 Timothy 4 godliness must refer to the proper teachings which encompass the items previously described as leading to godliness. Also, since Paul contrasted godliness with profane old wives' fables, godliness must be in the context of proper teachings. For divine life to mature in believers, exercise (teaching the proper nourishing truth to others) is imperative and necessary for the household (the ekklesia of God) to grow and be built up.

Not Taking Grace in Vain

Laboring is an exercise, and grace (food) given to believers is in vain if there is no laboring through testifying on behalf of Christ.

> "But by the grace of God I am what I am, and his grace toward me was not in vain. On the contrary, I worked harder than any of them, though it was not I, but the grace of God that is with me. Whether then it was I or they, so we preach and so you believed."
>
> – 1 Corinthians 15:10–11, ESV

Grace is the supply of the Lord Himself with all His riches for a believer's enjoyment. It is surprising to read God's grace towards Paul could be in vain or for nothing. Why was it not in vain to him?

Why? Because Paul worked in spreading the good news. Grace was like being food for Paul, giving him the inward energy to work. Only because of God's grace was Paul able to proclaim Christ and teach others. If Paul didn't do any of the Lord's work, then grace to him would have been in vain. *Work is exercise.*

This is true for all believers. The more grace believers receive, the more they need to exercise through teaching, ministering, and preaching to dispense Christ to others. The more they exercise, the hungrier they will become and subsequently, the more grace they will receive.

This is similar to physically eating food; if a person only ate, but never worked to produced anything useful for their family or society, their eating is kind of vain. However, the more people work, the more they need nourishing food. Therefore, for a believer to function normally, grow, and mature, he or she needs to eat (be nourished with Christ regularly), and to exercise (labor in preaching or teaching regularly).

Therefore, the typical clergy/laity system practiced among most churches is detrimental to believers. In this system only a professional class of people teaches and preaches, while most believers listen. This is not the scriptural way to build up the Body of Christ. Every member needs to rise up, take responsibility, and exercise what the Lord has given them: the grace to speak forth Christ.

A Good Conscience: Being Led by the Spirit

A person's conscience is like an inner guide which helps them to discern right from wrong; healthy or harmful. Spiritual exercise involves possessing a *good* conscience. This, to believers, is related to being led by the Spirit.

> "For when Gentiles, who do not have the law, by nature do what the law requires, they are a law to themselves, even though they do not have the law. They show that the work of the law is written on their hearts, while their conscience also bears witness, and their conflicting thoughts accuse or even excuse them."
> – Romans 2:14–15, ESV

Man's conscience (even the conscience of nonbelievers) accuses of guilt for certain actions or excuses from guilt when innocent. God's law matches the created human nature. God's law regarding human conduct in society is itemized in the Ten Commandments and encapsulated in this one commandment: *"love your neighbor as yourself"* (Matt. 22:39–40). This single commandment mirrors man's created *good* nature; a person's conscience will object and sense guilt when his action may be harmful to themselves or others. When this is about to happen, their conscience will sound an inner alarm to prevent them from going further. The conscience is the innate mechanism God created in human nature for preserving and multiplying life.

> "My little children, let us not love in word or in tongue, but in deed and in truth. And by this we know that we are of the truth, and shall assure our hearts before Him. For if our heart condemns us, God is greater than our heart, and knows all things. Beloved, if our heart does not condemn us, we have confidence toward God."
>
> ~ 1 John 3:18–21

Believers in Jesus Christ possess a conscience with feelings more intensified and sensitive. Since their redeemed human nature is lifted up and intertwined with God's divine nature, their new nature now matches the interior laws of the New Covenant such as those given by Jesus on the "sermon on the mount" found in Matthew 5-7. For example, the First Covenant law says, "do not murder," but the corresponding New Covenant law says do not get angry with others and verbally abuse them. The old condones hurting someone who has hurt others (an eye for an eye), but the new commands people to love their enemies.

Thus, if believers do not love others in deed as Christ has loved them, their hearts — which includes the conscience — will condemn them. If their conscience objects, surely God also objects since He is even greater than our hearts. To follow the Lord and live according to the new nature — Christ in the believer — those in Christ must follow the sense of their conscience. They must love others in deed, whether Christian or not. Loving others means much more than not harming others but doing something good for their benefit.

> "Now the Spirit expressly says that in latter times some will depart from the faith, giving heed to deceiving spirits and doctrines of demons, speaking lies in hypocrisy, having their own conscience seared with a hot iron."
>
> ~ 1 Timothy 4:1

The conscience leads a person away from that which is harmful, and toward what is beneficial.

Nerve endings in a person's fingers help prevent their fingers from getting seared; however, if those endings are damaged, and a person has no sensitivity to heat, their fingers could catch on fire without the person even being aware. In the same way, a person's conscience can be seared so it has no more sensitivity. When a person denies his conscience for too long, it can become seared. That person becomes susceptible to receiving and accepting all sorts of harmful and evil things. This is true for both believers and unbelievers. A seared conscience will open a person up to demonic spirits and activities; such a person can end up living a lie his entire life or even having an early and untimely death.

A Conscience without Offense

It is important for believers to exercise their conscience, so it is without offense toward God and men.

> ". . . having hope towards God, which they themselves also receive, that there is to be a resurrection both of just and unjust. For this cause I also exercise myself to have in everything a conscience without offence towards God and men."
>
> – Acts 24:15–16, DBY

Knowing that there is a resurrection of all men unto judgment, Paul exercised (or strove) to have a conscience without offense. This should be part of *every* believer's spiritual exercise. On one hand, believers should exercise to teach and minister to others; on the other hand, they should exercise to have a good conscience. Both need the nourishment of the grace of the Lord Jesus. Both are needed if believers are to grow and mature.

A Conscience without Offense toward God

> "Therefore, brothers and sisters, since we have confidence to enter the Most Holy Place by the blood of Jesus. . . . let us draw near to God with a sincere heart and with the full assurance that faith brings, having our hearts sprinkled to cleanse us from a guilty conscience and having our bodies washed with pure water."
>
> – Hebrews 10:19, 22, NIV

This is the most basic tenant of faith: by the blood of Jesus Christ believers have the confidence, the boldness to come into the Holiest Place, God's presence. They do not come to God because of merit, or because they never offend their conscience due to failures and sins, but because they have the redemptive blood of Jesus which fully forgave them of all their sins — past, present and future. Due to this wonderful fact, believers come forward to God continually without hesitation. Because of the blood of Jesus, believers do not have a guilty and accusing conscience before God.

> "If we confess our sins, He is faithful and just to forgive us our sins and to cleanse us from all unrighteousness."
>
> — 1 John 1:9

The word "confess" in 1 John 1:9 in the original Greek is the word *homologeō,* which literally means, "to speak the same thing," or "to assent, accord, agree with" (Vine's Expository Dictionary). With whom is Paul saying believers are to agree? They are to agree *with the Lord* speaking in their conscience. As they are living and walking in the Lord, the Lord in their conscience will point out things which are not according to partaking of the divine nature in them. Upon hearing this speaking from their conscience, they must agree and speak back to the Lord the sin exposed by His light. By confessing in this way, God is faithful and righteous to forgive believers of their sins and to cleanse them. This kind of confession is simply part of speaking to the Lord throughout the day (breathing prayer). While in conversation with the Lord throughout the day, a believer's conscience will speak here and there; the very moment they answer back to the Lord in agreement, they receive instant cleansing. For example, a husband might agree, "Lord, my attitude was not right with my wife just now," or "Lord Jesus, I am not loving this person as you." It is not because Christians need to confess their sins before they come back to enjoy the Lord; rather, they confess *while they are already in fellowship* with the Lord.

A Conscience without Offense toward Men

"Let all bitterness, wrath, anger, clamor, and evil speaking be put away from you, with all malice. And be kind to one another, tenderhearted, forgiving one another, even as God in Christ forgave you."

– Ephesians 4:31–32

"You have heard that it was said, 'You shall love your neighbor and hate your enemy.' But I say to you, love your enemies, bless those who curse you, do good to those who hate you, and pray for those who spitefully use you and persecute you, that you may be sons of your Father in heaven; for He makes His sun rise on the evil and on the good, and sends rain on the just and on the unjust."

– Matthew 5:43–45

The conscience of believers is more sensitive than the conscience of unbelievers, because as sons of their Father God, believers are born of Him with His eternal life and divine nature. An unbeliever's created human nature may agree with God's commandments such as, "honor your father and mother," "do not kill," "do not commit adultery," "do not steal," "do not bear false witness," and "do not covet your neighbor's things." But with an uplifted and divine nature, a believer's conscience will object to more than just the negative causing of harm to a person; it will feel guilty when the believer doesn't act on the positive. When believers exercise themselves to have a conscience without offense, they live according to the "New Creation" (Gal. 6:15) in Christ in a way which benefits those around them. In other words, their conscience will bother them, when they do not live out Christ.

"Therefore if you bring your gift to the altar, and there remember that your brother has something against you, leave your gift there before the altar, and go your way. First be reconciled to your brother, and then come and offer your gift."

– Matthew 5:23

When a believer's conscience alerts one to an offense, especially if it is causing a rift in a relationship, it is important to reconcile quickly with the offended person. The offending person may need to admit wrongdoing or apologize. Such a one may even need to offer some sort of financial restitution, if necessary. In any case, believers are charged to reconcile; not choosing to reconcile could become a hindrance in fellowship with the Lord. It is easier to possess a conscience without offense to God than to men. To appease men, material restitution might be necessary. Therefore, it is important for believers to follow their conscience in dealing with others. Paul teaches an important guideline for this in Romans 12:18: "*If it is possible, as much as depends on you, live peaceably with all men.*"

Those with a Good Conscience Are Led by the Spirit

"I tell the truth in Christ, I am not lying, my conscience also bearing me witness in the Holy Spirit."

– Romans 9:1

A believer's conscience relates to the Holy Spirit. It is because of the indwelling Holy Spirit they possess an uplifted conscience, able to sense whether they are living according to the Spirit and the divine nature within them. Whether acting positively (speaking truth in Christ) or negatively (lying), their conscience constantly reacts as the believer moves about their daily life; this reaction reflects the thoughts and feelings of the Holy Spirit.

"For as many as are led by the Spirit of God, these are sons of God."
– Romans 8:14

"But if you are led by the Spirit, you are not under the law."
– Galatians 5:18

When believers live and act according to their conscience, they are "led by the Spirit" (Gal. 5:18). The word "led" in Galatians 5:18 in the original Greek is the word *agō,* which communicates compulsion. Paul states there is no option for believers but to follow the Spirit's leading; they are being brought into or are compelled to go a certain direction. This is the believer's conscience: completely one with and led by the Holy Spirit. Of course, each follower of Jesus still must choose whether to follow the feelings of their conscience.

The more believers exercise to live according to their conscience, the more they will manifest their partaking of the divine nature (2 Peter 1:4) as sons of God. God's law as contained in the Ten Commandments demands men and women live in a way which corresponds to their created nature.

Believers led by the Spirit — those who live according to their conscience — will exceed the law given by God. Their life will be lived according to the superior law of God's divine life in them.

Most believers compare being led by the Spirit to that found in the Old Testament, where God told His people what to do or not to do. For example, a Christian might ask, "Shall I visit this place? Shall I buy this car? Shall I buy this house?" Though the Lord can absolutely answer this type of request, in the New Testament, such cases are rare. There were only a handful of records in the New Testament where God told believers or apostles directly to do or not to do something.

Under God's New Covenant, believers are endowed so that their minds are transformed; they have His mind. His law of life becomes a very part of their nature, their being. How they think and what they feel is one with the Lord. They live according to the divine nature. Believers become one with the Lord; He is in them, and they are in Him. This is why it is so important to know the truth in His Word, so the mind is transformed to His mind, and believers are filled in Spirit to walk according to their conscience.

Practice: Teaching a Verse or Two

Practice teaching others the "unsearchable riches" of Christ — His person and work. Each week explain a verse from a section of Scripture to another person. Teach and verify they understood your explanation. Find out which point of the truth impressed them in the Word. It is important people learn to read and understand the Bible for themselves.

Simply pass along the good news from the Word. Try not to argue to convince people in an attempt to "convert" them. Finally, avoid sounding "preachy."

There are many ways to teach the Scriptures, but here is a way you can practice. Let's use the second part of John 10:10 to demonstrate a teaching conversation with your friend, Bob:

You: Bob, let's turn to this wonderful verse in John 10:10. Here — why don't you read this portion out loud to me.

Bob: *I have come that they may have life, and that they may have it more abundantly.*

You: This is a wonderful verse speaking of the purpose for which Jesus came to earth. Do you know who the "I" is referring to?

Bob: Jesus?

You: Yes, you are absolutely correct. So according to this verse why did Jesus come?

Bob: To save me from sin?

You: That is true, but is that what the verse says? Here, read it again (pointing to the phrase).

Bob: *I have come that they may have life.*

You: So why did Jesus come?

Bob: That they may have life?

You: Yes, correct. Now who do you think "they" is referring to?

Bob: I don't know.

You: "They" there refers to people including you and me, all people including sinners. So now read again and replace "they" with "Bob," and say *Jesus* for the "*I*" in the beginning.

Bob: Jesus has come that Bob may have life.

You: Isn't that great! Jesus came to give you life, life abundantly. So, again why did Jesus come?

Bob: To give me life.

You: Amen! Isn't that something that the reason Jesus came is to give you life? Now what kind of life is that? Aren't you alive now? Why does He have to give us life if we are already alive?

Bob: I don't know.

You: Do you have God's eternal life?

Bob: No.

You: That is what Jesus wants to give you — God's eternal, divine life. He came to give you this wonderful life. Do you understand this verse now? Explain to me again.

Guiding people through the Word like this may seem slow at first, but after a short while they will start to understand more and more. There is a point in their reading where they will start understanding for themselves. It is in this understanding of the Word the Spirit works to either bring salvation to the unbeliever or nourishment for growth for a believer.

8

SLEEPING: RESTING IN THE DEATH OF CHRIST

As life grows and matures, life will spontaneously and innately become what is encoded in its DNA. Consider the life of an apple tree. Through growth, apples will be produced. If the life is a dog, the little tiny puppy at birth will grow into a chasing, barking and biting dog. If the life has human DNA, it would be impossible for that embryo to develop and grow into anything else but a human person. If the four ingredients necessary for life to exist and grow are present, there is absolutely no doubt life will mature, function, and express the DNA of that life.

The fourth essential for life is sleep or rest. Sleep deprivation is torture. In fact, a person can die from lack of sleep. When a person goes to sleep, they physically and psychologically experience rest; they receive a break from labor and a hiatus from anxiety. A person may have anxiety, anger, or disappointment, but when he or she sleeps, there is both physical and psychological rest. While a person is asleep, discontent, anger, and anxiety vanish.

If believers do not know and experience *spiritual* sleep, their spiritual life will not last. They will not be happy Christians. Enjoying sleep is key to a joyful, healthy, and productive spiritual life.

Biblically, Sleep Refers to Death

"'Our friend Lazarus sleeps, but I go that I may wake him up'. . . . However, Jesus spoke of his death."

– John 11:11, 13

"And they stoned Stephen as he was calling on [God] and saying, 'Lord Jesus, receive my spirit.' Then he knelt down and cried out with a loud voice, 'Lord, do not charge them with this sin.' And when he had said this, he fell asleep."

– Acts 7:59–60

"But I do not want you to be ignorant, brethren, concerning those who have fallen asleep. For if we believe that Jesus died and rose again, even so God will bring with Him those who sleep in Jesus."

– 1 Thessalonians 4:13a–14

In the Bible, "going to sleep," describes death. In John 11, Lazarus died, but Jesus said Lazarus had only gone to sleep, and He would go and wake him up. The story continues with Lazarus dying and Jesus resurrecting him from death. To Jesus, death means going to sleep and resurrection means waking up. While being stoned to death Stephen called on the Lord and prayed for his persecutors; then Scripture says he "fell asleep" (Acts 7:60). What a wonderful picture! Stephen's persecutors were stoning him to death, and he was terribly suffering since death by stoning is one of the worst ways to die. When Stephen "went to sleep," the suffering ended. His pain was over, and he rested. It is appropriate to say, "rest in peace" (RIP) for the dead in Christ, because when a person "sleeps," they experience true rest.

In Thessalonians 4:14-15 Paul referred to believers who died: there was no need to sorrow because they had only fallen asleep. One day, they will all wake up in resurrection. Death is the ultimate rest. There is no more suffering, pain, anxiety, unhappiness, sorrow, or labor. Everything negative ends and the person is simply resting in death. For believers death is, therefore, the *real* rest and sleep.

This does not mean believers should seek physical death. In fact, it is much better for believers to remain physically alive if possible until they have finished the course God has laid out for each one (2 Tim. 4:6–7). Believers should not have the thought to prematurely die, nor attempt to do so; it is important to stay physically alive as long as possible until they finish the course the Lord has laid out for each of them.

If that is the case, what is spiritual rest for believers *while they are still physically alive*?

Sleep and Rest: Experience Christ's Death

For believers, to "sleep" and rest is to experience the death of Christ.

> "Or do you not know that as many of us as were baptized into Christ Jesus were baptized into His death? Therefore we were buried with Him through baptism into death, that just as Christ was raised from the dead by the glory of the Father, even so we also should walk in newness of life."
>
> – Roman 6:3–4

Baptism is a symbol of being immersed into Christ's death. When a person believes into Christ, faith joins him *into* Christ which includes all He is and has accomplished. One of His accomplishments is death; therefore, the believers' faith joins them to His death – His wonderful and powerful death. Baptism is the symbol of that union – joining with Christ in His death.

Believers are even buried with Him – dead and buried. Their death with Christ is final, terminal, and eternal . . . just as Christ died once, never to die again. Through faith, believers are joined to Christ's death, spiritually dying to their old man once for all. This is wonderful news! Consider the peaceful rest believers have in the death of Christ, according to these verses:

> "Therefore put to death your members which are on the earth: fornication, uncleanness, passion, evil desire, and covetousness, which is idolatry. Because of these things the wrath of God is coming upon the sons of disobedience, in which you yourselves once walked when you lived in them. But now you yourselves are to put off all these: anger, wrath, malice, blasphemy, filthy language out of your mouth. Do not lie to one another, since you have put off the old man with his deeds."
>
> – Colossians 3:5–9

The "old man" is dead. The old man refers to the fallen man, the man without God. When Adam ate of the tree of knowledge of good and evil, he and all his offspring became the "old man." All of Adam's offspring are alienated from God. They possess their natural life from birth, but they do not yet possess God's divine, eternal life. Even a newborn baby is part of the "old man." Attached to the old man is sin and death, the very nature of the old man.

Greediness, pride, anxiety, lust, discontent, the desire for revenge, and all other negative attributes within a person are attached to this nature. All of man's problems stem from this old man. Thankfully, the old man is dead and buried through crucifixion providing rest from these problems. This is not so for unbelievers; when bothered and troubled by the old man, they have nowhere to go for relief. Many unbelievers try to fix their problems themselves. They may seek self-improvement regimens or religion to strengthen their moral character. They may degenerate themselves by abusing drugs or alcohol or drown themselves with material riches or achievements. These people have no rest, no sleep.

For believers, it is completely different. Believers can rest and sleep in the death of Christ; the old man is dead; all troubles related to their sin nature become distant history. They can rest in peace in the death of Christ, by putting off the old man.

Freedom from the Slavery of Sin

"For I know that in me (that is, in my flesh) nothing good dwells; for to will is present with me, but *how* to perform what is good I do not find. For the good that I will *to do*, I do not do; but the evil I will not *to do*, that I practice. Now if I do what I will not *to do*, it is no longer I who do it, but sin that dwells in me."
– Romans 7:18–20

A slave must do his master's bidding. Every human is born fallen — a slave to sin. How awful a life under slavery! People who are slaves of sin don't want to be angry, but they can't help it. They want to forgive, but they can't. They want to be content, but they are not. They don't want to hurt anyone, but they do. When these experiences are present, the person is a slave to sin.

Freedom from sin comes only through the death of Christ. What a rest in the death of Christ when man is no longer a slave to sin! Most people (including Christians) try their best to avoid sin. However, their focus tends to be on expending effort to *not* sin. This is a losing battle every time. Though a person may never commit more external and visible sins like murder, adultery or debauchery, they can never escape the more hidden sins of anger, greed or the desire for revenge. Therefore, instead of struggling through the effort of the old man to be a good person, the secret to freedom is focusing on Christ. Enjoying Christ, because only through the death of Christ can a person truly sleep and experience the joy of comfortable, peaceful rest.

Death Has No More Dominion

> "For the wages of sin *is* death, but the gift of God *is* eternal life in Christ Jesus our Lord."
>
> – Romans 6:23

> "O wretched man that I am! Who will deliver me from this body of death?"
>
> – Romans 7:24

> ". . . and release those who through fear of death were all their lifetime subject to bondage."
>
> – Hebrews 2:15

At the fall of man, sin entered mankind resulting in death; Scripture is clear the payment for sin is death. The more a person sins, the closer he is to death.

This death, however, is completely opposite to the death of Christ. The death of Christ brings freedom, while death from sin dominates – it will not release man (male and female) from its clutches. Eventually every person will succumb to physical death. However, before physical death, the power of death dominates, evidenced by sicknesses, weaknesses, aging, deterioration, depression, and hopelessness. Each is an indicator of death's control over man, its dominion starts at birth and continues until physical death. How pitiful are those dominated by death who have no way out!

Even when everything seems okay, bondage still exists in the form of *the fear of death*. Most everyone is afraid of death. Though this fear can be drowned out for a period, it often rears its head and grips its victim. This fear is real, and the bondage is powerful. There is no escape. What misery and torment to be in such a state through life!

Even when a man dies, he still cannot escape death because there is a death worse than physical death: the second death (Rev. 21:8; see also Rev. 2:11; 20:6, 14). The second death is the eternal lake of fire from which there is no escape. It will be like having a perpetual nightmare; never waking up since it is real. Truly, death is dreadful and horrible.

Believing into Jesus Christ and participating in His death and resurrection frees believers from this dominating, eternal death. Victory over death begins immediately and can be the believer's daily experience. This is the reality for all those who have believed into Christ and into His death and resurrection. It is in His rest believers are free from the dominion of death. Unfortunately, most Christians' concept of experiencing the death of Christ equates to a kind of suffering. Contrarily, those who truly experience the death of Christ do not suffer; the death of Christ *terminates* suffering.

Types of Sufferings Believers May Experience

For many people, when difficulties surface in life, they just want to go to sleep. At least when they fall asleep, they receive a temporary respite from the bad things weighing them down. Of course, when they wake up, whatever rough situations they wanted to escape are still there (in this life). Many times, suffering and hardships cause unbelievers and believers alike to turn to God for relief; true relief is to rest in the death of Christ.

There are two types of sufferings: involuntary and voluntary. Involuntary sufferings are those negative experiences a person doesn't seek out. Voluntary sufferings, on the other hand, are those believers sign up for by choice.

Involuntary Sufferings Result from Sinful Man and the Corruption of God's Creation

> "And since they did not see fit to acknowledge God, God gave them up to a debased mind to do what ought not to be done. They were filled with all manner of unrighteousness, evil, covetousness, malice. They are full of envy, murder, strife, deceit, maliciousness. They are gossips, slanderers, haters of God, insolent, haughty, boastful, inventors of evil, disobedient to parents, foolish, faithless, heartless, ruthless."
> – Romans 1:28–31, ESV

Many people ask as a challenge to God: If God is real and God is love, why is there so much suffering in the world? Why doesn't God stop the suffering?

The problem is this: Much of the suffering in the world is due to man himself and not God. Consider the following: War causes suffering to untold millions of people; theft causes suffering because of covetousness; and murder and maliciousness result from anger. How many children suffer at school because of a schoolmate's deceit or bullying? How many parents suffer because of disobedient children? How much suffering results from even two or three of the things listed above, regularly committed by virtually every human being?

It is highly unfair and illogical to blame God for all the suffering man causes, unless man also expects God to immediately judge and execute anyone who has ever caused someone to suffer or turn everyone into a robot. Every person alive has caused another person's suffering because of their sin nature. Likewise, they have suffered due to another person's sin nature.

> "For I consider that the sufferings of this present time are not worth comparing with the glory that is to be revealed to us. For the creation waits with eager longing for the revealing of the sons of God. For the creation was subjected to futility, not willingly, but because of him who subjected it, in hope that the creation itself will be set free from its bondage to corruption and obtain the freedom of the glory of the children of God. For we know that the whole creation has been groaning together in the pains of childbirth until now."
>
> – Romans 8:18–22, ESV

As a result of man's fall in Genesis, all of creation was cursed and is now in bondage to corruption. This includes animals, plants, the earth, the oceans, and the atmosphere; everything is subject to futility or vanity. Because harmony does not exist in creation today; therefore, earthquakes, hurricanes, diseases, drought, and pestilence result. Therefore, God's entire creation "groans," or suffers, but man especially experiences the weight of creation's corrupted state. Creation is groaning to be set free at the revealing of the sons of God when believers are matured and glorified.

Believers today have Christ in them as the hidden hope of glory. One day, this glory will break forth into a manifested glory at the second coming of Jesus Christ. At that time, the entire creation will be happy, as mountains "sing" and the trees "clap their hands" (Isa. 55:12). It can be said that believers seeking to grow and mature are the real environmentalists! Only through their glorification will the entire creation be healed. In the meantime, corruption continues to bring suffering to humankind.

Involuntary Sufferings Result from a Person's Own Destructive Choices

> "Let no one say when he is tempted, 'I am tempted by God'; for God cannot be tempted by evil, nor does He Himself tempt anyone. But each one is tempted when he is drawn away by his own desires and enticed. Then, when desire has conceived, it gives birth to sin; and sin, when it is full-grown, brings forth death."
>
> – James 1:13–15

> "But let none of you suffer as a murderer, a thief, an evildoer, or as a busybody in other people's matters."
>
> – 1 Peter 4:15

People bring on much of their own suffering. Rampant substance abuse is a huge source of suffering, often resulting in death. Uncontrolled lust destroys families and affects untold numbers of children. Poor personal diet impacts people's health.

God cannot be blamed for each person's personal actions; yet, these things have caused the most suffering on a personal level. It seems that what people want is freedom of choice to live how they want, without the consequences or the result.

Nevertheless, the consequences of these poor choices are still involuntary. Just because one may choose to drink and drive, for example, doesn't mean they volunteered to suffer the consequences of a crash.

Involuntary Consequences from Satan's Attacks Allowed by God

> "And the LORD said to Satan, 'Behold, he *is* in your hand, but spare his life.' So Satan went out from the presence of the LORD, and struck Job with painful boils from the sole of his foot to the crown of his head."
>
> – Job 2:6–7

"And lest I should be exalted above measure by the abundance of the revelations, a thorn in the flesh was given to me, a messenger of Satan to buffet me, lest I be exalted above measure."

– 2 Corinthians 12:7

The first two types of suffering due to the sinful nature of man and environmental corruption are indiscriminate and can happen to anyone on earth. Any citizen of this world – believer or not – can experience these sufferings. The third type of suffering, however, only seems to target God's people.

God allows Satan to do the "dirty work" to test His people. In Job's case, Satan can be seen marshalling his power over health, the weather, and ungodly people, to cause God's people to suffer. However, before Satan could do any of those terrible things, he needed God's permission. For example, God *allowed* Satan to test Job, because He knew Job would come out stronger and better off because of the testing. It is the same for all of God's people.

After Job's testing, Job saw and knew God differently. Job received back much more than he lost during the testing. Paul (who will be highlighted later in this chapter) also gained much through intense trials.

Even after Satan rebelled against God, he remained God's servant; when he tried to humiliate God, Satan was still serving Him. God ultimately remained in control of Satan's actions and used them for His purpose.

Voluntary Sufferings for the Ministry of the Word and the Building Up of the Ekklesia

Believers should participate in Christ's afflictions by being a minister of God's economy.

"Now, I rejoice in sufferings for you, and I fill up that which is behind of the tribulations of Christ in my flesh, for his body, which is the assembly; of which I became minister, according to the dispensation of God which [is] given me towards you to complete the word of God."

– Colossians 1:24–25, DBY

The apostle Paul didn't have to suffer. If he had refused God's call to carry out his mission, Paul likely would have become a respected lawyer in the upper class of society. But instead, he rejoiced in being able to suffer in order to minister to the Lord's ekklesia, to complete the Word of God to them. This is called "voluntary suffering."

Paul continued in the sufferings and tribulations of Christ in order to serve people for the assembly. He knew what he was getting into; he knew the sufferings he would experience; and, he knew why tribulations would come. Despite these things, Paul chose to accept and carry out his mission with joy.

Suffering and Enduring as a Soldier, Athlete and Farmer

Paul, writing to his young co-worker Timothy, encouraged him to be strengthened in serving the Lord due to these various difficulties. He knew a servant of the Lord would encounter suffering. He gave Timothy three analogies — serving the Lord as a soldier, an athlete, and a farmer — in order to inspire him to be a faithful servant.

> "You then, my child, be strengthened by the grace that is in Christ Jesus, and what you have heard from me in the presence of many witnesses entrust to faithful men who will be able to teach others also. Share in suffering as a good soldier of Christ Jesus. No soldier gets entangled in civilian pursuits, since his aim is to please the one who enlisted him. An athlete is not crowned unless he competes according to the rules. It is the hard-working farmer who ought to have the first share of the crops. . . . Remember Jesus Christ, risen from the dead, the offspring of David, as preached in my gospel, for which I am suffering, bound with chains as a criminal. But the word of God is not bound! Therefore, I endure everything for the sake of the elect, that they also may obtain the salvation that is in Christ Jesus with eternal glory."
>
> – 2 Timothy 2:1–7, 8–10, ESV

Making disciples for the building of God's ekklesia is no easy task. It is a lifelong mission that guarantees much opposition and disappointment; therefore, Paul charged those who follow in his footsteps to be strengthened by grace and be prepared to take part in suffering.

Again, this type of suffering is voluntary. Believers are not forced to serve as a soldier. Many believers are satisfied with simply knowing they are saved from eternal damnation. They have become complacent believers with little to no focus on the mission of the gospel or on the building up of the ekklesia. Therefore, they will bypass suffering reserved for the soldiers of Christ. Since few believers today are willing to suffer the challenges of being a minister of Christ; therefore, the Lord's move in the gospel and the building up of the ekklesia is inhibited.

Paul again reaffirmed he was suffering for the gospel. Although he was in prison for the gospel, the gospel was not hindered by his captivity. Instead, it spread and multiplied. Paul was truly transformed from being a persecutor of the saints to a passionate disciple with the heart of Jesus Christ, so much so that Paul would endure all sorts of sufferings in order that others might receive salvation. It takes this kind of willingness to suffer for salvation to spread and for the ekklesia to be built.

What were the sufferings for which Paul was preparing Timothy? Paul was not preparing Timothy to do something purposely to hurt himself in order to suffer; rather, as a soldier, Paul knew Timothy would not be entangled with the things of this world. As an athlete, Timothy would serve by the law of the Spirit of Life. And as a farmer, Timothy would be faithful and diligent in taking care of his crop in order to bear fruit. Believers who stand firm as soldiers in the warfare of the gospel will automatically forgo many worldly pleasures. One competing as an athlete cannot freely live according to their old fallen life but will have to be led by the Spirit's law of life. Finally, the farmer who makes disciples by bearing remaining fruit must be diligent and faithful to plant and water on schedule, without the freedom to serve only when he or she feels like it.

Suffering for the Word and His Testimony

Believers will naturally participate in tribulation, because of the Word and Christ's testimony.

> "John, your brother and partner in the tribulation and the kingdom and the patient endurance that are in Jesus, was on the island called Patmos on account of the word of God and the testimony of Jesus."
>
> – Revelation 1:9, ESV

The apostle John also voluntarily suffered on account of the Word of God and the testimony of Jesus Christ. John was not enjoying an island vacation while on Patmos; he was a prisoner, exiled by the Roman Empire because he would not stop preaching the gospel. John was a partner in the tribulation of Jesus Christ. According to the New Testament, all believers should be partners in the tribulation and kingdom with patient endurance for those who are in Jesus Christ.

Believers Voluntarily Bear the Cross of Christ

This voluntary suffering of the cross of Jesus Christ is what Jesus asks His disciples to bear. It is voluntary suffering for the sake of others — for their salvation, growth, and the building up of God's ekklesia. Jesus did *not* have to bear the cross for humanity; he willingly accepted this mission.

Many Christians mistakenly assume any kind of suffering is the cross for them. Even some unbelievers say, "That is my cross" when going through difficulties. Some may say, "My wife is mad at me; she is my cross I am bearing." No, she might be mad because her spouse is lazy and neglects caring for her, so that is not the cross. Others may say, "I am bearing the cross because the drought really hurt my business." No, that is not the cross either; that is making light of the cross and misapplying its meaning. Involuntary sufferings are not the cross, because the cross is only for believers who volunteer. More serious and "spiritual" Christians may think a form of asceticism (severe self-discipline) is the cross. That means a denial of any enjoyment for their physical and psychological self. They consider the cross to be denial of any pleasure. For example, if they like to look attractive, they should make themselves as plain as possible; if they like gourmet food and drink, they should avoid it at all cost. This kind of Christian will even feel guilty if they find themselves having fun in the world's amusement. Their view of the cross is to voluntarily place themselves in situations where they are devoid of any worldly pleasure. This is not the cross of Christ as described by the Lord in the Bible.

Any suffering that causes the believer to be downcast or to complain about suffering, even if it is for others, is also not the cross of Christ. Bearing the cross of Christ is a matter of joy, rejoicing and hope; it is in the power of the Lord's Spirit of glory for accomplishing the eternal mission of building up His eternal dwelling place.

In later chapters, there will be additional consideration on this important topic of bearing the cross of Christ.

Sufferings Often Causes Believers to Turn to God

Any trials and sufferings, whether involuntary or by choice, often cause believers to turn to God and away from sin and distractions.

> "Since therefore Christ suffered in the flesh, arm yourselves with the same way of thinking, for whoever has suffered in the flesh has ceased from sin, so as to live for the rest of the time in the flesh no longer for human passions but for the will of God."
>
> – 1 Peter 4:1–2, ESV

When unbelievers undergo any kind of suffering, there is no hope of any redeeming value. What will they gain from sickness? Or from being cheated of their wealth? Some philosophies may bring comfort in the immediate, such as, "This is an opportunity, think positively!" or "Look for the silver lining." But if sufferings pile up one after another, people can sooner or later become depressed.

For believers, however, it is different. Believers have a weapon: *the mind of Christ*. Believers can arm themselves and be prepared for all kinds of suffering. There is only one way to possess the mind of Jesus. It is when believers turn to Him and let Him live in them. Jesus Christ today is not just in the heavens – He is also in His followers. He is in every part of them, including their minds.

To prepare for future unexpected sufferings, believers need to abide in Christ and let Him abide in them. Then, when suffering comes, they will be able to turn to Jesus immediately in prayer, praise, song, and fellowship.

All sufferings – even involuntary ones – can work out positively to the believer's eternal benefit if they turn to the Lord through them. Even if Christians cause their own suffering, turning to the Lord will bring positive results. That is why many have found Christ in prison, though they have committed a crime to be there. Believers armed with the mind of Jesus will be sanctified through suffering. They will cease from sin and live for God. Something so negative will be turned into something positive – and the hinge for this is turning to Jesus Christ, to have *His* mind. While unbelievers dread the thought of calamities befalling them, while they fear evil people bringing pain to their families, while they are anxious about sickness or any kind of pain, believers are ready for calamities. They know suffering will help them cease sinning and live the rest of their lives for God. The suffering will turn them to Jesus Christ, to rest in Him. This is spiritual sleep; every believer needs to regularly experience it. Good sleep and rest in Christ places everything in the proper perspective — turning the negative into the positive.

Proving Faith Works

"In this you rejoice, though now for a little while, if necessary, you have been grieved by various trials, so that the tested genuineness [or proving] of your faith — more precious than gold that perishes though it is tested by fire — may be found to result in praise and glory and honor at the revelation of Jesus Christ. Though you have not seen him, you love him. Though you do not now see him, you believe in him and rejoice with joy that is inexpressible and filled with glory."

— 1 Peter 1:6–8, ESV

"Count it all joy, my brothers, when you meet trials of various kinds, for you know that the testing [proving] of your faith produces steadfastness."

— James 1:2–3, ESV

Faith is the ability to substantiate the unseen. Faith can be likened to a sixth sense with which believers can enjoy and realize all Jesus Christ is and has accomplished in the spiritual realm. In other words, believers are already sitting in the heavens with Christ, and Satan is already defeated; while the old creation is dead and buried. To a human being's five senses, this cannot be true; but when faith is activated, a person's presence in the heavens is truer than their presence on earth. That is reality. So, faith is the ability to see and realize the unseen realm of the Spirit.

This is the reason, while suffering, the revelation of Jesus Christ exists; and because of this, a believer's suffering fades. They rejoice in seeing the One they love. Though they cannot see Him with their eyes, Jesus is revealed to them through faith. They are filled with inexpressible joy and glory.

A believer's faith is really the faith of Jesus Christ. He originated this faith in His people — it is a gift of God. Faith is not something a person can muster up, nor generate on his or her own. Since faith is something of Christ from God, it does not need testing. It will pass any test all the time, any time. Yet, James writes, "*the testing* [proving] *of your faith produces steadfastness*" (James 1:3); and Peter writes about the "*tested genuineness* [or proving] *of your faith*" (1 Pet. 1:6).

What, then, does it mean to be tested?

The Greek word used in both "tested genuineness" and "testing" in these verses is the same word. It is better translated "proving." This means believers are to prove to themselves their faith works. They may not know how genuine and precious their faith is until they face trials and sufferings. Instead of being depressed and grumbling, they can persevere with joy. Their faith can be activated during difficulty – they see Jesus. They are substantiating reality in their environment; therefore, their trials become nothing to them. They received proof of their faith. They now know by experience the genuineness of their faith.

Of course, faith is precious, but to believers who are suffering, the "proving out" or the experience of this faith is more precious than gold. They actually experience being transferred from the worldly to the spiritual heavenly realm where they see Jesus, resulting in praise, glory and honor. They are no longer in the realm of suffering, but in the realm of glory where they respond with song and praise.

This is what happened with Paul and Silas when they were in prison. They were beaten and chained down in the dungeon of a prison; yet, they were singing and praising God (Acts 16:22–34); moreover, they were comforting and caring for a jailer who was about to kill himself. In the earthly realm, there appeared to be two men of God suffering in prison. However, in the realm of faith, Paul and Silas were in the heavens caring for those who were *really* suffering.

New believers may not have the experience of proving their faith; furthermore, they may encounter trepidation when facing any form of suffering. The more mature believer has proven the faith of Jesus more and more, having found joy in the face of suffering, because they know they can have a good rest and sleep through it all. Knowing how to experience Christ's death as spiritual sleep produces steadfastness in believers. No matter what is thrown at them, they will not tire nor be discouraged, because they are resting in Jesus. *Sleep, then, is being dead to the world and alive to Christ and experiencing the reality of the crucified and resurrected life of Jesus Christ.*

3 in 1 Experience: Death, Resurrection and Ascension

Many believers isolate the various stages of Christ as separate experiences. True, Jesus did die first before resurrecting, and then forty days later ascended. In His experience, these were separate, sequential events. But to believers today, they are now part of who Jesus is in His Spirit. Isolating and separating these experiences may cause some to say, "What I need now is Christ's resurrection because I am down." Others may say, "I am troubled by a hard situation; I need to experience Christ's death."

However, *all* aspects of Christ — his death, resurrection and ascension — are a part of Him; since believers have Christ, they simultaneously experience each stage. This simplifies the experiences for believers; moreover, it also puts the focus on Christ rather than an aspect of His work. These stages of Christ are for a believer's experience; they are distinct, but not separate.

Knowing Jesus Christ Experientially

". . . that I may know Him [Jesus Christ] and the power of His resurrection, and the fellowship of His sufferings, being conformed to His death."

– Philippians 3:10

Paul's aspiration was to know Jesus Christ in a way which was experiential to Him. This was not simply knowing facts about Him but *knowing* Him in the way of experience. For example, one may understand the ingredients that go into making a dish but knowing about the ingredients is much different from experiencing the food by tasting and being nourished by it. Paul aspired to know Jesus Christ by tasting all His goodness. Knowing Him means knowing the power of His resurrection. Paul didn't just know *about* the power of resurrection; he experienced it during tribulation. Since that was Paul's own experience, nothing could hold him down no matter the opposition. Paul also participated in Christ's suffering through his care for the ekklesia. He rejoiced in having the privilege of experiencing the same sufferings of Christ as He did for His Body. This is what it means to "take part" in His death, the spiritual "sleep" believers need.

Physically, people go to sleep when they are tired and wake up to start a new day refreshed. But in the spiritual realm, believers live in the state of being conformed to His death. In other words, believers are always resting.

They should never depart from resting in Christ. Whether working or going through trials, they are still resting.

Resting or living in the reality of the death of Christ should be the believer's daily, moment-by-moment experience. It is in this position of rest — death — that believers experientially know Jesus. It is in this state they know His resurrection power and participate in the suffering of Jesus for the sake of His body.

The Fruit of the Spirit in Resurrection through Death in Christ

"I have been crucified with Christ; it is no longer I who live, but Christ lives in me; and the [life] which I now live in the flesh I live by faith in the Son of God, who loved me and gave Himself for me."

– Galatians 2:20

"But the fruit of the Spirit is love, joy, peace, longsuffering, kindness, goodness, faithfulness, gentleness, self-control. Against such there is no law. And those [who are] Christ's have crucified the flesh with its passions and desires. If we live in the Spirit, let us also walk in the Spirit."

– Galatians 5:22–25

The "I" which was crucified with Christ Paul speaks of in Galatians is the "I" before the new birth in Christ. This is the old "I," the "I" without the life of Christ. Since the old "I" is dead, who is the "I" that is now living in the flesh?

This is the new "I" with Christ living in him. The new "I" is the believer living in faith, and Christ living in him. It is a mingled living or a living in union between the believer and Jesus Christ. Such a person expresses Christ's life through love for people around him, joy that's unquenchable, peace with God and man, and the ability to suffer through all sorts of difficulties. Those believers are kind in their actions toward all of creation. They do not have to *put forth effort* to act this way because that is their normal, divinely natural character. It is the fruit of the believer's new life in Christ, the fruit of the Spirit in them. They are not putting up a front; they are living out Christ because they are partaking in His fellowship.

A believer who does not "sleep" or live in Christ's death will always try to fulfill God's requirements in his own efforts. He or she will use the natural life of their old man to live out God's requirements. This believer will be exhausted, becoming a failure sooner or later. When a believer finds himself worn-out from being a Christian, depressed by his environment, irritated by people around him or wanting to give up, it is a sign affirming he is not sleeping. If he will just "sleep" in Christ, Christ will live in him and his experience will immediately return to the positive.

Experiencing the Killing of Jesus that Others May Receive Life

Paul described the death and life of Christ acting simultaneously.

> ". . . always carrying about in the body the dying of the Lord Jesus, that the life of Jesus also may be manifested in our body. For we who live are always delivered to death for Jesus' sake, that the life of Jesus also may be manifested in our mortal flesh. So then death is working in us, but life in you."
> – 2 Corinthians 4:10–12

Paul didn't bear the death of Christ for a certain period before he started to serve Christ to others; rather, while he was experiencing the death of Christ, others were experiencing the life of Christ through Paul. Paul ministered to them in ascension.

As ministers of Christ, Paul and his co-workers experienced tribulation and persecution, but those sufferings did not deactivate or destroy them; rather, they rested in the death of Christ. Concurrently, the life of Christ was manifested, giving life to those to whom they spoke. The "death" which was working in them was not the negative death of Satan, but the positive death of Christ. Satan's death is crippling, hopeless, crushing, destructive, and utterly despairing. On the other hand, the death of Christ is restful, comforting, hopeful, and life-giving. So, while Paul and his co-workers were "sleeping" in Christ's death, Christ's life was working in those to whom Paul was ministering. Although Jesus Christ died 2,000 years ago, His death is still active, effective and experiential today.

Being Comforted in Affliction to Comfort Others

"Blessed *be* the God and Father of our Lord Jesus Christ, the Father of mercies and God of all comfort, who comforts us in all our affliction, so that we may be able to comfort those who are in any affliction, with the comfort with which we ourselves are comforted by God. For as we share abundantly in Christ's sufferings, so through Christ we share abundantly in comfort too. If we are afflicted, it is for your comfort and salvation; and if we are comforted, it is for your comfort, which you experience when you patiently endure the same sufferings that we suffer."

– 2 Corinthians 1:3–6, ESV

Once again, Paul describes the death, resurrection and ascended life of Christ simultaneously working, so much so the word "comfort" can be substituted for both His death and the impartation of life. Comfort amid suffering is a much more experiential and identifiable word than even "death" or "life." Just as in the previous example in 2 Corinthians 4:10–12, here the experience of Christ's death and life when ministered brings comfort.

In these verses, the God of all comfort is active in a believer's affliction; moreover, it becomes a comfort for others as well. God's comfort is eternal; once given, His comfort continues to be passed on from person to person, and from generation to generation, to this very day. Believers are presently being comforted by the comfort which was given to Paul. Whatever comfort believers receive today is to be passed on to someone else tomorrow. These are the experiences of the crucified, resurrected, and ascended Christ lived out in Paul and all who would enjoy this comfort in their afflictions.

A Portrait of a Minister Who Knows How to "Sleep"

"But in everything commending ourselves as God's ministers, in much endurance, in afflictions, in necessities, in straits, in stripes, in prisons, in riots, in labours, in watchings, in fastings, in pureness, in knowledge, in longsuffering, in kindness, in [the] Holy Spirit, in love unfeigned, in [the] word of truth, in [the] power of God; through the arms of righteousness on the right hand and left, through glory and dishonor, through evil report

> and good report: as deceivers, and true; as unknown, and well
> known; as dying, and behold, we live; as disciplined, and not put
> to death; as grieved, but always rejoicing; as poor, but enriching
> many; as having nothing, and possessing all things. Our mouth
> is opened to you, Corinthians, our heart is expanded."
>   ~ 2 Corinthians 6:4–11, DBY

A person who knows how to spiritually sleep is a mysterious and wonderful person. He or she becomes like Jesus, a person hard to describe; one who cannot be put into a box. Although hard to understand and figure out, this person is an absolute delight to be around. There is something "attractive" about him or her.

In 2 Corinthians 6:4–11 Paul's description of God's ministers almost seems contradictory and impossible . . . even out of this world. This is because Paul was describing people living in another realm — the realm of the death, resurrection, and ascension of Christ. Such a person's heart is expanding and enlarging to include more and more people with their blessings. They pour out life and make those around them spiritually rich. All believers should be this kind of person. They can be this way by being with Jesus and experiencing His death, resurrection, and ascension.

Practice: "Voluntary suffering"

Consider someone whom you want to reach for the gospel or greet for fellowship. What might you need to do in order to speak the gospel of grace or the gospel of peace to them? Maybe it is as simple as taking some time out to spend with this person, or you need to get out of your own comfort zone because this person is very different than you, or you need to give this person something precious, or maybe to forgive this person of some offense. As you pray for this person, you will realize you will have to "deny yourself" in order to be effective in reaching this person for Christ. Take the resting and empowering Christ through prayer; take action to "voluntarily suffer" for the sake of Christ to reach this person.

Write down a person's name:

What is the Lord teaching you that you must deny in order to reach this person?

PART 2

GLORY FOR SERVICE

(Chapters 9–13)

I n this part of our text, the glory of Jesus enabling believers to work and to serve is the topic. For Christians to serve God and people in the same manner as Jesus Christ, something beyond their own human ability and strength are needed. Even when there is a desire to do good in human society and to serve God for His purpose, people are simply not able to endure prolonged hardship, humiliation, rejection, or even being faithful to do a service without a tangible reward. This is where the glory of Jesus is needed.

Miraculously normal service will certainly require the glory of the Lord as its unique source; nevertheless, the God-ordained way will also be needed to understand how to serve in the era of the New Covenant. It is one thing to have the energy to do a job, but it is another matter to do the correct job according to a plan. Certainly, carpenters need a source of energy every day in order to build a house, but if they do not build according to a blueprint, then the result of all their hard work is confusion and futility. Therefore, both a source of eternal energy and a clear blueprint for God's house, His ekklesia, is needed for all believers to do their part. When God's people are liberated for this service, God's eternal purpose will be fulfilled.

The Third Gift – Jesus' Glory

"And the glory which You gave Me I have given them, that they may be one just as We are one:"

—John 17:22

The Lord Jesus prayed the glory that was given to Him by the Father would be given to believers so that they may be one. *Glory* in the Greek means, "good opinion, praise, honor, an appearance commanding respect, magnificence, excellence, manifestation of glory" (Vine's Expository Dictionary). Human beings have their glory when they complete an excellent job, win a competition, or achieve outstanding goals. However, this human and worldly glory is fading and vain. The real, highest, and eternal glory is when God is expressed and manifested. When God is manifested, surely there will be praise, honor, magnificence, and excellence. This glory was given to Jesus whereupon He gave this glory to all His believers. This glory of Jesus, given to His followers, has everything to do with their ability to serve God and humanity.

In Jesus' opening prayer in John 17 He contemplated His hour had arrived for Him to be glorified. He was referring to His imminent crucifixion.

As the Son of God, the second of the Trinity, Jesus as God *already* possessed glory (John 1:14). In fact, it is the same glory as the Father (John 17:5). Since the glory of the Son in His divinity is the same glory as that of the Father, there was no need for the Father to give Him glory. The glory which was given to Jesus in the above-referenced verse was given to Him *after* His death and resurrection, affirming that the glory of the Father was given to Him *as a man*. Jesus in His humanity didn't possess the glory of God before His crucifixion, but after His death and resurrection, *still completely human*, He was glorified with the same divine glory as the Father and the Son. Jesus' humanity was brought into glory. It was through this process God was fully expressed in humanity and Jesus as a man was glorified.

It must be understood that the Son of God eternally existed with the Father before His incarnation (John 17:5 — "... *with the glory which I had with You before the world was*"); therefore, when Jesus prayed, "*And now, O Father, glorify Me together along side Yourself*" (John 17:5) He was praying for the glorification of His humanity — as a Man; for He was NOW to be both the glorified Son of God and Son of Man. Indeed, He was one with the Father as the Son of God, and was now to be one with the Father as the Son of Man.

The glory given to Jesus was through His death and resurrection, which was made clear in Luke 24:26. In John 12:23–24, Jesus said the hour had come for Him to be glorified; then He spoke of going to His death and resurrection in order to bear much fruit. He likened Himself to a seed of wheat which needed to die in order to bring forth many more grains in resurrection. His glory was displayed in resurrection.

Just as Jesus served God and man for His human glorification, even so, now His followers who have received His glory are on the same path. They are to serve God and man in humility, as a slave, to minister Christ to people on earth. Now, Jesus is interceding on the throne in heaven; moreover, His followers would continue the same service as the Christ on earth by preaching the gospel, teaching the truth, making disciples, and building up His ekklesia, His body. This is His unique purpose for all believers. They are one in this glory to fulfill God's purpose. While Jesus did this service before receiving glory, followers of Jesus are empowered by His glory to serve in miraculous normality.

Philippians 2 – A Description of How Jesus Obtained Glory

> "Make my joy full by being like-minded, having the same love, being of one accord, of one mind; doing nothing through rivalry or through conceit, but in humility, each counting others better than himself . . .."
>
> – Phil. 2:2-3 WEB

Philippians 2 describes the process from which Jesus received glory from the Father. The apostle Paul started by expressing the same aspiration as the Lord's prayer in John 17. Paul desired believers to become one: be in one mind, be of one accord, and have the same love for one another. However, he addressed a problem: "Vain glory" disrupted this oneness among His believers. Vain (or empty) glory is human glory which lifts oneself up and thinks of oneself as higher or better than others. This self-glory (or ego) caused strife and discord among those serving in Philippi.

The remedy for this discord, according to Paul, was believers were to have the mind of Christ.

> "Let this mind be in you, which was also in Christ Jesus: who, being in the form of God, thought it not robbery to be equal with God, but made Himself of no reputation, taking the form of a bondservant, and coming in the likeness of men. And being found in appearance as a man, He humbled Himself and became obedient to the point of death, even the death of the cross."
>
> – Philippians 2:5–8

These verses speak of Jesus' incarnation. The Son of God who was equal with God became a man. He left His glory and His reputation as God (Son of God) to become a lowly man, but not just *any* man; He became a humble bondservant who died performing His service. And it was after His death and resurrection whereupon Jesus, the man-slave, was glorified:

"Therefore God also highly exalted him, and gave to him the name which is above every name; that at the name of Jesus every knee should bow, of those in heaven, those on earth, and those under the earth, and that every tongue should confess that Jesus Christ is Lord, to the glory of God the Father."

– Philippians 2:9–11, WBT

As a man in resurrection and ascension, Jesus was glorified. His *humanity* received glory from the Father. Jesus was exalted with the highest name — Jesus Christ as both God and Man occupied the highest position in the seen and unseen universe. This humble Jesus, as a servant of God and man, received the highest glory, and in turn the Father was glorified. This is what Jesus meant when He prayed in John 17:1: "Glorify your Son, that your Son may glorify You."

This glory which was given to Jesus is the same glory given to believers. To have the same glory as Jesus, believers need to have the same mind as Jesus — a mind to become nothing but a servant to others. While ministers in Philippi were striving with each other in discord due to their vain glory (viz., Euodia and Syntyche — Phil. 4:2), they were forthwith charged to have the mind of Jesus. They could have this mind, this glory of Jesus, operating in them. It is either their vain glory motivating them as their source of service or the glory of Jesus as their energizing source.

Glory in the secular or religious world typically means a person is served and their directives are followed. The higher one is exalted; the more people will serve them and attend to their needs and wishes. This is the vain glory of man, the fleeting glory of this world today. But the glory of the Lord Jesus is not so. Jesus said:

"Yet it shall not be so among you; but whoever desires to become great among you, let him be your servant. And whoever desires to be first among you, let him be your slave — just as the Son of Man did not come to be served, but to serve, and to give His life a ransom for many."

– Matthew 20:26–28

Just as the glory given to Jesus was not of this world, the glory He gave to His followers is not of this world; it is the exact glory given to Him by the Father. It is the glory through His death and resurrection.

As in Philippi, where there was discord among believers, much of that same discord today leads to sectarianism due to egotistical personalities. Individuals who have allowed pride and arrogance to take over (which is the world's glory) have caused disunity in the Body resulting in sectarianism. Even among small groups of believers, pride and ego among various personalities is a sure way to cause division. This kind of splitting up is generally not between young or weak believers, but between those who are prominent; those who have been effective in service. It is ironic how many who desire to serve God end up not being able to be in unity with other believers because of ego and self-glory. The solution to this disunity is to understand, receive, and serve according to the glory of Jesus Christ.

The glory which was given by the Lord to His people is contrary to the typical hierarchy of leadership among believers. Those in leadership expect others to follow them, and those under their leadership will identify themselves with their leaders to the detriment of fellowshipping with other believers outside their immediate group. The problem is not with mature believers serving diligently who may have garnered a title such as "Pastor," "Minister," "Elder," or "Priest," who have stayed in the position as a servant. Trouble occurs when leaders expect others to follow their directions or remain in those groups they are leading. They are offended when their directions are not followed, or they become frustrated when they lose followers. When this happens, it is certain they are no longer participating in the glory of Jesus Christ. Instead, they are manifesting: "*Their end is destruction, their god is their belly, and their glory is in their shame*" (Phil. 3:19).

It is only by the glory of Jesus the services of each believer can lead to unity. The more each serves in glory, the more oneness is produced and manifested. This is the Lord's glory given to every believer that they may be ONE, which is the building up of His ekklesia.

The Cross of Christ and His Glory

"Then Jesus told his disciples, 'If anyone would come after me, let him deny himself and take up his cross and follow me.'"

– Matt. 16:24 ESV

For believers to receive this glory from the Lord Jesus Christ means He, as the first man to receive this glory, will lead His believers on the same pathway to glory. Since He has already pioneered the way, He comes into

His believers with this glory and leads them into glory (Heb. 2:9–10). When believers follow Him on the same pathway, the result is glory.

In Matthew 16, after Jesus said He would build His ekklesia, He spoke of going to His death and resurrection. Peter objected to Jesus' pathway to the cross; whereupon, Jesus turned and called Peter, *Satan*, His adversary. After this, Jesus said those who follow Him in the building of His ekklesia must pick up their own cross to follow Him (Matt. 16:24). To follow Jesus and share in His commission, believers must deny themselves, and take up the cross, and follow Him.

Certainly, the believer's cross is not to die for redemption. The Lord Jesus was the only One who was perfectly qualified to die for the redemption of all creation. He died once for all. The purpose of the cross afforded believers to follow Him in service to God and man — not for redemption, but for life impartation. Just as Jesus served God and man by the ministry of life for the building up of His ekklesia, believers are enabled to do the same. Christians need to follow Jesus to complete what Jesus was sent to do to fulfill God's eternal purpose — build His ekklesia.

Unlike Jesus who went through the entire process of the cross before receiving glory, believers already possess His glory when they have faith in the Son. It is by this glory believers are empowered to bear the cross and serve — to serve as a humble servant without vain glory. In other words, Jesus bore the cross suffered on His own and alone before receiving glory; whereas, believers first receive glory via faith, and then can bear their cross of suffering by the empowering Spirit in all their services. Whoever would bear the cross to be a servant can be one with all other believers — this is His ekklesia. If they will not bear the cross, it is inevitable, at a certain point, a minister cannot be one with other Christians; thus, the Lord's ekklesia will be impeded.

> "... that I may know Him and the power of His resurrection, and the fellowship of His sufferings, being conformed to His death....."
>
> – Phil. 3:10

Jesus suffered, died, and was resurrected. The sequence is reversed for Christians. Paul pursued to know Jesus Christ; consequently, the first item in this experience is the power of His resurrection. It is the power of His resurrection which enables ministers to participate in the sufferings of Jesus. While Jesus suffered as a man alone, believers participate in His suffering with the power of His resurrection. Without knowing Jesus and His resurrection, no one can suffer as He. It is in the fellowship of His sufferings that His followers are conformed to His death. All the items in this sequence are related to HIM. It is not the believer's own suffering and death but HIS. Only His sufferings include joy – His death is life-giving. Again, the glory of His resurrection empowers His people to serve through all sorts of afflictions for them to minister eternal life, giving spiritual nourishment to people.

"Bearing the cross" is not suffering just for suffering's sake. It is not asceticism. It is not silently accepting mistreatment. It is not denying the things of the world in order to be "holy." It is absolutely related to putting self aside in humble service to God and man. For this, the glory of the Lord is essential. The source of such humility is only accessible by those enjoying the glory of Jesus.

Consider the night Jesus prayed His last prayer in John 17 where this gift of glory was given, at the beginning of the evening when He washed His disciples' feet (including Judas' feet – the one who betrayed Him). Washing feet was a normal occurrence in those days. It was done by the lowliest of slaves. Jesus did this for His disciples. He asked them to do the same for one another (John 13:14).

Washing each other's feet, according to Jesus, was a symbol of love for one another – serving and caring for another shows the person's love. Jesus, knowing Judas would soon betray Him, still washed his feet. How hard it is for the person who was offended and disrespected to love the very person who made such an offense. How hard it is to serve that person. Certainly, Jesus denied Himself with all the glory of the Son of God in order to be in such lowliness. Naturally, it is impossible for Christians to fulfill such a command; therefore, the source for being so loving, humble and such a faithful servant can only find its source in the glory He gave His believers. It is this glory which strengthens and empowers believers to deny themselves, and to take up the cross to serve as He did.

Glory in Bearing Much Fruit

> "But Jesus answered them, saying, 'The hour has come that the Son of Man should be glorified. Most assuredly, I say to you, unless a grain of wheat falls into the ground and dies, it remains alone; but if it dies, it produces much grain. He who loves his life will lose it, and he who hates his life in this world will keep it for eternal life. If anyone serves Me, let him follow Me; and where I am, there My servant will be also. If anyone serves Me, him My Father will honor.'"
>
> – John 12:23–26

The best thing for a physical seed is burial — "death" by being covered in dirt. If a seed does not "die" then it remains alone. However, if it dies it will resurrect, not by itself, but with many other seeds just like it. The glory of the seed, then, is its fruit. All the beautiful and tasty fruit which appears is the duplication of the seed which was planted. Before a seed is planted, it typically does not appear beautiful. It is just a seed. But after its death and resurrection, the fullness of its beauty is manifested — a tree laden with fruit.

In the same way, the Lord's suffering and death was not just for redemption but for the impartation of life. His ultimate service was not simply dying for man's sins, but to give humanity His eternal life and glory. His purpose was to reproduce many sons just like Himself as brothers. Those produced through His death and resurrection would be His duplicates, bearing His image and likeness (Rom. 8:29). This is not only redemption for the forgiveness of sins but also regeneration for an assembly of believers as God's family, the Body of Christ. This is the building up of His ekklesia, which in the beginning was God's eternal purpose. This built-up ekklesia is to the praise of His glory (Eph. 1:12; 3:21).

The Lord's glory given to believers means they are to follow the Lord in the same path to glory. When believers are told to serve and follow the Lord in John 12:25–26, they must also not love this life of self and the glory of this world but be willing to serve as Jesus did and produce much fruit. In John 15, the Lord told His followers exactly this: He told them they are all branches in the vine, and each branch needs to produce and bear fruit. It is through this fruit the Father is glorified as the caretaker and source of the vine (John 15:8). The glory produced through bearing fruit results in fullness of joy (John 15:11); it results in the manifestation of love for one another (John 15:12).

Although believers cannot suffer for redemption; however, like Jesus, they can suffer with Him for the bearing of fruit that shall remain — this is for the building up of His ekklesia. The apostle Paul in Colossians 1:24 said he rejoiced in his suffering, for he was filling up that which was lacking in the afflictions of Christ for His Body, the ekklesia. From a human point of view, there is only one similar kind of affliction which involves rejoicing while in anguish: childbirth. Jesus used this exact metaphor for rejoicing in suffering in John 16:21–22. Women undergo much affliction and suffering to bring a child into the world, but it's all worth it once the baby is born. This is "rejoicing in suffering," the suffering of "death" in which believers should participate. Through this suffering of death, the believer shares in the same glory of producing much fruit.

Ministering Christ to others, so Jesus Christ might be reproduced, is the highest service to both God and man in growing God's ekklesia. This reproduction of remaining fruit results in the maturity of the ekklesia in Christ (Col. 1:28–29). This glorious service requires an attitude of a humble servant. It is not just a matter of preaching or motivating people for an "altar call" to come forward to receive Jesus Christ. It is a continuing service like that of a nursing mother, cherishing people in a very practical way, serving them for the sake of dispensing the grace of Jesus Christ to them. People who are practically served by those in this pathway to glory will become open to receive the gospel of Jesus Christ: both the gospel of grace and the gospel of peace thereby manifesting the Kingdom of God.

When this understanding and experience of glory takes hold of believers, they will treat everyone around them, whether believers or non-believers, in the way Jesus Christ would treat them: not as a lord or superior, but as a servant. This is the manifestation of loving and esteeming others better than yourself. It means being willing to be wronged by others; taking the status of a slave who has no ground to be offended. It involves feeding and caring for others. A person in this place of glory will not cause friction and division with other believers; rather, this person is one with all believers as a servant exemplifying the Lord's glory.

A Pattern of Ministry by the Lord's Glory

"Not that we are sufficient in ourselves to claim anything as coming from us, but our sufficiency is from God, who has made us sufficient to be ministers of a new covenant, not of the letter but of the Spirit. For the letter kills, but the Spirit gives life . . .. And we all, with unveiled face, beholding the glory of the Lord, are being transformed into the same image from one degree of glory to another. For this comes from the Lord who is the Spirit."

— 2 Cor. 3:5-6, 18 ESV

"But we have this treasure in jars of clay, to show that the surpassing power belongs to God and not to us. . . .. So death is at work in us, but life in you."

— 2 Cor. 4:7, 12 ESV

In 2 Corinthians chapters 3 and 4, the apostle Paul linked service (ministry), glory, and the cross (death) together — these three are interrelated. Paul and those with him were empowered by the Lord's glory in order to fulfill their ministry to serve eternal life to people wherever they went. That empowerment enabled them to experience the death (i.e., the cross of Christ). Therefore, in order to minister life, there is this bearing of the cross. In the death of Christ, there is the empowering of the Lord's glory. Without beholding the glory of the Lord, ministers will not be able to experience death or bear the cross. It is in the death of Christ; life is ministered to people around them.

Paul stated God is the source of His servants being sufficient to minister the Spirit to others as life. How did God make them sufficient ministers? According to 2 Corinthians 3:18, their sufficiency was secured by beholding the glory of the Lord: The incarnated Jesus, who laid aside His equality with God to suffer death as a human servant, Who then was resurrected and ascended to receive glory as a Man. Through beholding this glory, they are being transformed into the same image from one level of glory to a deeper and higher level of glory. They are beholding and are motivated by the incarnated, crucified, and glorified Jesus. As they are beholding, the Spirit is transforming them into the same glory. It is in this glory of Jesus they have become sufficient ministers of the life-giving Spirit.

In 2 Corinthians 4 Paul continues to unveil the source of this glory in them liking it to a treasure in jars of clay. The ministers were nearly worthless, earthen jars or vessels. As vessels, they were created to contain the treasure. Without this treasure, these vessels would be empty; simply put: jars of vanity. Jesus the Lord as the Spirit is the treasure in them. The treasure being in them was not to beautify the vessels; rather, it was the power within the vessels to endure sufferings for the sake of service. The ministers were able to persevere through all sorts of afflictions, which is the very bearing of the death of Christ. They were denying themselves taking up the cross. The issue of this death was producing life as they ministered to others. While death worked in them, people around them received life.

> "If you are insulted for the name of Christ, you are blessed, because the Spirit of glory and of God rests upon you."
>   – 1 Peter 4:14 ESV

Peter in his epistles directly called the Spirit, the Spirit of glory. When believers are despised and insulted for the name of Christ, the Spirit of glory is resting upon them. A servant of the Lord is willing to be despised. It takes genuine humility to be a servant of Christ and receive insults and abuses. In this position or state of service, the Spirit of glory is resting upon those ministering saints. *Resting* means ceasing from labor. The Spirit of glory is resting while the serving saints are also resting. They are resting or sleeping in the death of Christ. It is the Spirit of glory giving them rest while they are serving in the name of Christ. It seems contradictory: saints are serving for the name of Christ and yet they are resting in the Spirit of glory. This is miraculously normal service — the glory of Jesus empowering believers to rest in the death of Christ while they are suffering in the ministry of life to others.

The Need to Be Faithful

> "Let a man so consider us, as servants of Christ and stewards of the mysteries of God. Moreover, it is required in stewards that one be found faithful."
>   – 1 Corinthians 4:1–2

In this part of our text, the miraculously normal service will be explored. The most popular Greek word for "minister" is *diakonos,* which means, "a servant," or "one who executes the command of another." The other Greek word used is *hypēretēs,* which literally means, "the under-rower," or the subordinate who is doing the rowing of a boat. Thus, a minister works for both God and man in service. Just as Jesus was a servant to both God and man, so should all believers so serve.

Faithfulness is one of the basic requirements of a servant. The word "faithful" in 1 Corinthians 4:1–2 means to be reliable, dependable, or trustworthy. It is not the amount of service one has undertaken that counts. Notwithstanding how little one has undertaken in service, what counts is how faithfully it was performed. A person can be faithful in a few things and still receive a reward from the Lord (Matt. 25:21). In service and ministry, faithfulness needs to be kept in mind before the Lord. In just about all the service items described in which a believer can participate, they are not burdensome or hard to do. The requirement is whatever action one decides to take, he or she should faithfully practice; otherwise, the result will be minimal or disappointing.

For example, if one is to take up the service of prayer, then pray – if not every day – at least once a week. If not for an hour, then try to pray at least a few minutes per day. The same can be said concerning visitation. If one can't take time out to visit every week, then how about visiting once a month? The point of faithfulness here is consistency in service. Then the Lord will have a way to work and produce results within one's service.

Being a Minister in Four Stages

What does God want and how can He be served? God desires all men to be saved and come to the full knowledge of the truth (1 Tim. 2:4). The Lord Jesus desires the building up of His ekklesia. Ministers are the ones who serve Christ to humanity by preaching the completion gospel of Jesus Christ; i.e., the gospel of the grace of God for individual salvation and the gospel of peace for the building up of His ekklesia. Ultimately, God will have His eternal purpose fulfilled – He will be glorified by those participating in the anointing of Christ. The need of humanity mirrors God's needs. Yes, man (male and female) has various necessities relating to poverty, health, and relationships . . . but his ultimate essential is salvation in God's eternal purpose – becoming filled with God and built-up as a part of God's household. Therefore, serving God and man is really performing and working toward the same objective. When Christ is ministered for man's salvation, and the teaching of Jesus Christ is taught for growth with the purpose of building up the ekklesia, then both God and man are satisfied. The servants or ministers have completed their job.

When the Lord's glory has been received, believers will be energized to serve both God and humanity with unfailing power. Believers can be faithful ministers according to the way God has ordained according to Scriptures. There are four stages ordained by God for the building up of His One Body in expressing His glory:

The First Stage

The first stage is accomplished through a begetting father, as Paul said about himself in 1 Corinthians 4:15: ". . . *I have begotten you through the gospel.*" Through the gospel, Paul ministered God's eternal life to people; they became born anew. That was his service as a father: to beget life.

The Second Stage

The second stage was shown in 1 Thessalonians 2:8 where Paul said the ministers are as nursing mothers. The function of a nursing mother is to cherish and nourish new and young believers so they may grow. Paul didn't just bring forth new birth through his gospel; he wanted to help new and young believers grow. Ministers are to serve as nursing mothers caring for young believers until they are established in the faith.

The Third Stage

In the third stage, Paul functioned as a father again, exhorting and encouraging the maturing of believers. This is the stage of discipling believers toward serving and working as the apostles; learning to do what the apostles are doing. In this function, believers are being called and encouraged to work and serve alongside those who are cherishing and nourishing them. Ministers are equipping believers under their care to participate in ministry (Eph. 4:11-12).

The Final and Fourth Stage

The fourth stage is the work of building up for the manifestation of the Lord's ekklesia. The first three stages lead to this final stage, which is the building up of the one Body of Christ. Paul said in 1 Corinthians 3:10 he was the "master builder," building up the temple of God, which is the house of God — the Body of Christ, the ekklesia. As the master builder, he encouraged all believers to build up the local assembly with him. All believers should be co-workers and co-builders with Christ to build up His ekklesia according to the pattern given in 1 Corinthians 11:17 through to the end of 1 Corinthians 14.

Practice! Enjoying the Lord through Singing

In addition to considering, praying and praising of the Word, a simple and enjoyable way to enjoy the Lord is through singing. Sing hymns and songs from songbooks or from memory. Singing hymns and songs to the Lord will cause you to turn to the Lord and focus on Him. You will forget your anxieties and problems.

Better yet, make up your own songs by singing Scriptures using an existing tune or come up with your own tune. Get out of your comfort zone! It is not a matter of how good your voice is or how well your lyrics and rhyme is synced. What counts is making a joyful sound from a melody in your heart to the Lord.

Find a hymn online this week and spend 10 minutes to sing to the Lord. Then spend another 15 minutes to sing a song to the Lord using a verse from the Bible that inspires you. Use a tune you know or just make up your own tune. The key to this exercise is to forget about how well you can compose or how well you carry a tune, just focus on singing to the Lord and enjoying Him.

After you have enjoyed singing this new song to the Lord, then share it and sing it to someone else or sing it at the next fellowship gathering. The Lord will be fresh in your experience of Him through your singing.

9

SPEAKING TO
PROPAGATE CHRIST

Believers Have a Unique Service

Many people, including unbelievers and sinners, do a variety of good works for humanity. Believers should also remember to serve the poor and do what they can toward improving society; but the highest and best service believers can provide to humanity, which no one else can provide, not even the angels, is to minister Christ to people — that they may receive faith and have eternal life by being begotten of God. Believers are the only ones on earth today who have such a privilege and responsibility to minister Christ to all people around them. This is the propagation of Christ: believers begetting more believers to become sons of God.

Just as life is defined by the ability to reproduce itself, God, possessing eternal, divine life, and being the *real* life, also reproduces that life. It is God's desire and pleasure to have many children, many mature sons of God. It is through this proliferation of His life He is expressed, and His enemy is defeated — put to shame. God's salvation for men is much more than whether a person is going to heaven after they die. God's salvation is to give humanity heavenly, divine, eternal life — moment by moment — for them to live and enjoy Him as children of God on earth *today*.

It is an utterly amazing mystery the way the eternal life of God can be transferred to men through faith. People cannot work up this faith; this faith is a gift of God which is transmitted as people hear the wonderful things concerning Jesus Christ. The greatest gift in the entire universe is free — there is nothing anyone can "do" to deserve it. There is life-giving power in speaking forth Jesus Christ being both God and man, His crucifixion, and resurrection. This kind of speaking brings faith whereby salvation is granted to the hearer.

Every believer, the instant they receive Jesus Christ as their Savior, has the privilege and responsibility to spread the good news of Christ to others around them in order that they too may come to salvation. There is no training needed, no methods to learn; they only need to speak concerning the Christ they have heard, received, and experienced. The spreading of Christ to others is called "fruit bearing." Every believer is called to do this service.

As believers present the person and work of Christ to others, the God of glory will have a way to appear and call more people to Himself. The believer's job is not to have all the answers for skeptics or to convince people concerning the reality of Christ; they are simply there to present — then watch God's Spirit work in the hearers. Therefore, believers should always maintain a cordial relationship with friends and relatives, with the hope they will have opportunities to speak Christ to them again and again. This friendship is not superfluous or trite — it is genuine in that Jesus was the friend of sinners; even so, through His friendship in us, so are we.

The Propagation of the Life of Christ

God's purpose is the propagation of the life of Christ in order to beget many children. The definition and natural function of life is the cycle of metabolism and reproduction. Life is expressed and dominates through propagation.

> "Then God said, 'Let Us make man in Our image, according to Our likeness; let them have dominion over the fish of the sea, over the birds of the air, and over the cattle, over all the earth and over every creeping thing that creeps on the earth.' So God created man in His *own* image; in the image of God He created him; male and female He created them. Then God blessed them, and God said to them, 'Be fruitful and multiply; fill the earth and subdue it; have dominion over the fish of the sea, over the birds of the air, and over every living thing that moves on the earth.'"
> – Genesis 1:26–28

The first outstanding point revealed in Genesis 1:26–28 is man (male and female) was created in God's image and likeness. God wanted to be expressed and manifested through man. Since man is in God's image and likeness, when all creatures see man, they see God. That is the meaning of "expression." Man *expresses* God.

The second outstanding point is for man to have dominion and subdue the earth. There was something on the earth which needed subduing. Man was appointed to do this work and have dominion. Finally, God made clear how both intentions were to be carried out by man; man should be fruitful, multiply, and fill the earth. In God's purpose, being fruitful through the multiplication of human life was critical to fulfilling His desires.

God is rich in every facet of His character. If there were only one man on the earth bearing His image and likeness, how small and insignificant would His expression on the earth be! By being fruitful, man multiplied himself to millions and billions. How rich is the expression of God!

If the evil aspect of man (because of his fall into sin) did not occur, then the various characteristics of love, care, honor, creativity, faithfulness, diligence, righteousness, and goodness in man expressing the attributes of God could be seen. When this man is spread throughout the earth, due to generations upon generations of fruitfulness, God can then be expressed in every corner of the earth.

God's intention in creating man (male and female) was for man to have dominion ". . . *over all the earth*" (Gen. 1:26). This phrase should already include *everything* that is on the earth, but God added, "*and over every creeping thing*." These creeping things must be something special in addition to all creatures on earth — a special category of creatures called out by God.

In Genesis 3:14 God cursed the serpent to creep on his belly on the earth. Then in Revelation 12:9, John writes: the serpent is Satan — the devil — and he, along with his angels, would be cast to the earth. This indicates Satan (the snake) is the leader of all the creeping things, including demons and angels who follow him. God's intention is for man to be the one to defeat and have dominion over Satan, the "creeping things." God didn't want to deal with Satan directly — it would be beneath His divine dignity, if you would; that is the reason Satan is not afraid of God. This is revealed in Satan's freedom to approach God whereupon Satan challenged Him in the book of Job.

Man was appointed by God to subdue and defeat Satan. Dominion occurs through God's command to be "fruitful and multiply." As human beings, God's command for man to obtain dominion over all the earth is certainly fulfilled through the multiplication of human life on every continent on earth. Most importantly, God's desire is for man to ultimately defeat and subdue Satan through the multiplication of life.

"You did not choose Me, but I chose you and appointed you that you should go and bear fruit, and that your fruit should remain, that whatever you ask the Father in My name, He may give you."
— John 15:16

In Genesis, created man became the old creation as a result of man's disobedience and consequent fall into sin. Instead of expressing God, man expresses evil because of the fall. Rather than subduing and dominating Satan, man became allied with Satan, God's enemy, thereby becoming an enemy of God (Rom. 5:10). Therefore, the Lord Jesus terminated the old and brought in a New Creation in Himself (2 Cor. 5:17; Gal. 6:15). This New Creation started with the Lord Jesus Himself, then He multiplied Himself when He brought forth much fruit (John 12:24). Now, based on His resurrection life, God is charging His believers as branches of the vine to go and bear remaining fruit — extending the New Creation.

This echoes what was spoken of in Genesis when God told man to be fruitful and multiply. It is through fruit-bearing — the multiplication of the eternal life of Jesus Christ within humankind — whereby men are born anew: *a New Creation*. Thankfully, early believers took the Lord's charge and spread the Word, bearing fruit. Many generations and billions of believers on earth later, this New Creation continues to bear remaining fruit.

Through fruit bearing and the multiplication of the divine life in man, the New Creation (the ekkelsia — the New Man, the Body of Christ) is realized. This is what the first man in Genesis failed to do: express God and subdue Satan (God's original purpose). The corporate New Man with Jesus Christ as the Head, and all believers as His body, fulfills God's original intention with man. Through the Body of Christ, God is fully expressed (Eph. 1:22–23) and Satan is destroyed (Luke 10:19; Rom. 16:20).

"And they sang a new song, saying: 'You are worthy to take the scroll, and to open its seals; for You were slain, and have redeemed us to God by Your blood out of every tribe and tongue and people and nation, and have made us kings and priests to our God; and we shall reign on the earth.'"
— Revelation 5:9–10

This fruit — born from every tribe, tongue, people, and nation — becomes the kings and priests of God. This brings in God's kingdom which expresses His life through reigning on the earth for eternity. Here in Revelation, the conclusion of the Bible, God's eternal-divine life has spread and multiplied among people of every tribe, tongue, and nation. Fruit-bearing through believers has reached every part of the earth. All those reached who have received God's life are made kings and priests to God. This mirrors the idea of God's purpose: dominion and expression. The "kings" are for dominion over enemies while the "priests" express God. Satan is subdued, and God is expressed. No wonder there is fullness of praise to the Lord Jesus Christ who has accomplished this . . . is there any wonder then that we look forward to a "Renewed heaven and earth" (2 Peter 3:13)?

The God–Man Life of Christ Spread to All Men

> "For God so loved the world, that He gave His only begotten Son, that whosoever believes into Him may not perish, but have eternal life. For God has not sent His Son into the world that He may judge the world, but that the world may be saved through Him."
>
> — John 3:16–17

The common misconception about God is He is a judge coming to condemn man. That is the opposite from the truth. The truth is God loved man and sacrificed His most precious and dearest only begotten Son for humankind. He didn't come to condemn man; man was already lost and condemned. God came to save man through Jesus Christ who died for all of God's beloved mankind.

Due to sin, man was already judged and marked for death. Jesus Christ came and saved man first by dying for man to save man from the wrath of God, from the penalty of sin, death; and then to give man not only a pardon from sin's penalty but eternal-divine life through His resurrection. This is the propagation of life, the multiplication of life, from one man to billions of men.

> "I [Jesus] have come that they may have life, and that they may have it more abundantly."
>
> — John 10:10

Certainly, the life spoken of in John 10:10 cannot be physical life since humankind was physically well and alive without the coming of Jesus Christ. The life John spoke of must be very special — only Jesus Christ can give this life. Some have interpreted this to mean a life of material blessing — that Jesus Christ came to give mankind a bigger house, a better car, and more money to spend. The problem with this interpretation is this: Jesus Himself and all His disciples, as well as all the early apostles, did not gain material riches.

The abundant life Jesus came to give man is the eternal-divine life of God, which is incomparably better than any material riches. This is consistent with the rest of the New Testament. Jesus Christ came through incarnation, crucifixion, and resurrection so humanity may have God's eternal and divine life. His goal was not just to save man from sin's penalty, death, but also to provide man eternal life in abundance. This eternal life is not just in the future, something men need to wait for until after their death; this life is now. Jesus came so every believer could know, experience, grow, and reproduce fruit as a result of this life now.

> ". . . who [God] desires all men to be saved and to come to the knowledge of the truth."
>
> — 1 Timothy 2:4

Paul unveils God's heart for man in 1 Timothy 2:4 — His loving, caring, and merciful heart for every man (male and female). God does not have any ill will or hurtful thoughts toward man . . . any man. God desires all men to be saved and not to perish; therefore, He needs His believers to reach all men, so all men may know the truth and come to salvation. Based on this verse, believers do not need to decide to whom God has chosen to preach the gospel, or to whom to teach the truth, since God has no such preference. He desires for all men to be saved.

The Increase and Duplication of Christ

> "But as many as received him [Jesus Christ], to them gave he *the* right to be children of God, to those that believe into his name; who were born, not of blood, nor of the will of the flesh, nor of the will of man, but of God."
>
> — John 1:12–13, DBY

What does it mean to be saved, to have this eternal-divine life? It is to be born of God. How can man be born of God? Men are born of God by receiving Jesus Christ and believing into His name. This very act ignites the human spirit whereby man is "born of the Spirit is spirit" (John 3:6). To receive the Lord Jesus is to believe into His name. The immediate result is the person is born of God — that is, one receives God's life. Since believers have God's life, they have the birthright to be children of God. There is no other condition to be a child of God other than to receive Him — to believe into the name of Jesus. It is this simple faith in Jesus whereby He gives all His believers the new birth in Christ. Jesus Christ is the good news able to reach all men.

> "... having predestined us to adoption as sons by Jesus Christ to Himself, according to the good of His will."
>
> – Ephesians 1:5

"Adoption" does not accurately translate the Greek word *huiothesia* used by Paul in Ephesians 1:5. *Huiothesia* is a compound word made up of "son" — an offspring by birth — and "appoint" which means, "to set in place."

The normal understanding of "adoption" is merely a legal procedure without the birth of a genuine offspring, whereas this Greek word clearly defines believers as sons by birth with God's life. However, believers also have a place in maturity — a legal standing — to be God's appointed sons. This is the Father's will. How great and wonderful is Father God, who has begotten millions upon millions of sons, who have matured for the universe to glorify the Father in His many sons.

> "For whom He [God] foreknew, He also predestined to be conformed to the image of His Son, that He might be the firstborn among many brethren."
>
> – Romans 8:29

God's children are the many brothers of Jesus Christ. The destiny of all God's children is for them to be conformed to the exact image of God's firstborn son, Jesus Christ. Those who follow Jesus are His exact reproduction; they may not look like Him or act like Him now, but one day, all believers will bear the same image as Jesus Christ, their eldest Brother.

Jesus Christ as the "firstborn" refers to both His divinity and humanity. The "only begotten Son" refers to His divinity alone and His position within the Triune God. Men, upon receiving divine life, become brothers of the firstborn Son of God, by partaking in both His humanity and His divine life — "*sons of the Living God*" (Rom. 9:26).

The Faith to Receive Life Is Transfused through Speaking Forth Christ

> "But that no one is justified by the law in the sight of God is evident, for 'the just shall live [alive] by faith.'"
>
> ". . . that the blessing of Abraham might come upon the Gentiles in Christ Jesus, that we might receive the promise of the Spirit through faith."
>
> "For you are all sons of God through faith in Christ Jesus."
>
> – Galatians 3:11, 14, 26

Anyone would gladly pay any price to receive something so precious and unspeakably costly as the life of God whereby one becomes a "son of the Living God." If the price is not material riches, then at least man should pay by being a good person and obeying God's laws. While inconceivable to humanity, God's desire is to give His life to man at no charge and with no preconditions. In fact, it is His good pleasure to freely give His eternal life to man. The conduit and means of receiving His eternal divine life is *simply by faith*. This is mysterious, yet true! It is uniquely simple faith in Jesus Christ which makes a person righteous and alive through the Spirit; they are born anew as sons of God. There are no other conditions or requirements other than faith in Jesus Christ. Begetting this life can never happen by attempting to fulfill God's law. Even while sinners, living faith in Jesus Christ transfers believers from being condemned to being righteous as living sons of God.

Hearing the Word: Christ

Faith with regenerating power comes through hearing the Word, which is Jesus Christ.

"For by grace you have been saved through faith, and that not of yourselves; it is the gift of God."

— Ephesians 2:8

Faith is needed to believe into Jesus Christ; yet, it is not something a person can create. Faith is not initiated by man; rather, it is a gift of God. A person cannot take credit nor boast it was their own ability when they believed. Faith is a gift which comes to people from God. This is just amazing!

People may think, "Okay, I don't have to pay for God's life, but surely I need to pay for faith." Or, they may think, "Well, faith is the hard part because I just can't believe all this stuff about Jesus Christ and eternal life." There is more good news! There is no need to try to believe or work up faith on your own . . . you can just let it happen!

"So faith comes from hearing, and hearing through the word of Christ."

— Romans 10:17, ESV

This gift of faith is transmitted from God through hearing. It is the Word of Christ which people hear which gives them faith. As people hear the things of Christ, something in them stirs; they start to appreciate the Christ they are hearing. On the one hand, there may be protests within them: "This is a fairy tale — it cannot possibly be true." On the other hand, they are being drawn and attracted to Christ; it is the beginning of faith percolating in the deepest part of their being. At a certain point in their hearing, they will react by receiving and calling on the name of the Lord Jesus. Whether they respond at the first time or after many times of hearing, in any case, faith gets through. When faith takes root, believing is no longer an option.

For believers who are speaking the good news of Jesus Christ, there must be confidence God is working whenever Jesus Christ is preached: Who He is and what He has accomplished. If believers have this confidence, they don't need to be anxious about whether they are preaching properly or with the correct "technique." They can trust the working of the Spirit and the hearing of faith. They don't need to argue or try to convince people. Their responsibility is to present Jesus Christ as best they can and allow the hearing of faith to work in the listener.

182 | ONE Life & Glory

> "This only I want to learn from you: Did you receive the Spirit by the works of the law, or by the hearing of faith? Are you so foolish? Having begun in the Spirit, are you now being made perfect by the flesh?"
>
> "Therefore He who supplies the Spirit to you and works miracles among you, does He do it by the works of the law, or by the hearing of faith?"
>
> – Galatians 3:2–3, 5

These questions from Paul were rhetorical. The answer for whether the Galatians received the Spirit by the works of the law or by faith was obvious: it was by the hearing of faith. It is also the hearing of faith which supplied the Spirit to the Galatians.

Believers begin by the hearing of faith and continue the Christian journey by the hearing of faith. A person's own works or effort do not give them the new birth, nor does it provide the continuous supply of the Spirit. Many believers mistakenly think (tragically, under deception by so-called Bible teachers) after becoming a Christian, they then need to keep God's laws to merit God's favor. If they do not, God will withhold His blessings from them, and they will lose God's smile on their lives. This was the case with the Galatians. They drifted back into keeping the Law under the influence of some Jewish Christian teachers who taught them that their righteousness was predicated on keeping the Law. Paul was fighting for them to come back to faith — justification was by faith alone, not by the works of the Law. One is made righteous by faith and not by the works of the Law. Believers start their journey in faith and should continue in the same faith — to live the Christian life by "the faith in the Son of God" (Gal. 2:20).

At this juncture, it must be pointed out that speaking to infuse faith is not just to unbelievers, but also to other Christians. When the riches of the truth of Jesus Christ are spoken to Christian, they receive the supply of the Spirit; moreover, this is the gospel of peace. Many times, believers may avoid fellowshipping with other Christians not in their own church or those with a contrary doctrine as theirs. However, if one would start to speak the truth of Jesus Christ to the other, then not only will there be a supply of the Spirit to the hearer, but it will also break down any walls of separation. Fellowship would initiate and unity will be expressed.

Not only do unbelievers need faith, but Christians also can use more faith. In Romans 10:17 when Paul said *faith comes by hearing*, he was not referring to unbelievers, but believers who already have the Word, Jesus, in their hearts. Nevertheless, they were distracted by law-keeping for righteousness or holiness. They needed to hear the gospel of Jesus Christ again to obtain more faith to come back to Jesus. This was the preaching of the gospel of peace to believers. Therefore, one cannot go wrong speaking the riches of Jesus Christ to people, it will either be the gospel of grace to the unbelieving or the gospel of peace to believers. The "gospel of grace" brings peace with God for the individual (aka, salvation); however, the "gospel of peace" brings peace with and among previously divided brethren — the one, if you would, satisfies the individual; but the other satisfies God's purpose in bringing His people into oneness with each other to "crush Satan under" their feet (Romans 16:20).

> "Truly, truly, I say to you, whoever hears my word and believes him who sent me has eternal life. He does not come into judgment, but has passed from death to life. Truly, truly, I say to you, an hour is coming, and is now here, when the dead will hear the voice of the Son of God, and those who hear will live."
>
> – John 5:24–25, ESV

It is interesting to note that hearing takes the least effort, when compared to eating, drinking, or even breathing. There is not even a muscle relating to hearing. Even with breathing, a little effort is needed! But hearing is so easy and effortless whereby even "the dead" can hear His voice and live. This is the greatest miracle of the gospel: dead men receiving life and living thereby.

> "Most assuredly, I say to you, the hour is coming, and now is, when the dead will hear the voice of the Son of God; and those who hear will live."
>
> – John 5:25

> "…having been born again, not of corruptible seed but incorruptible, through the word of God which lives and abides forever."
>
> – 1 Peter 1:23

Even though fallen man was condemned to death, God did everything to save man. The only thing man needs to do is stop and hear the good news of God's salvation — Jesus Christ. They don't need to agree or try to believe. Even in their skepticism, they just need to hear, consider the Word, and let it sink in to do its work of generating faith in them. It is effortless and simply amazing!

Speaking about the person and work of Christ transmits faith and life into others. An example of Jesus speaking to unveil Himself may be found in John 8:28–30, where Jesus spoke of Himself as the "Son of Man" and the "I AM" — the name of God.

> "Jesus therefore said to them, 'When you shall have lifted up the Son of man, then you shall know that I AM, and that I do nothing of myself, but as the Father has taught me I speak these things. And he that has sent me is with me; he has not left me alone, because I do always the things that are pleasing to him.' As he spoke these things many believed on him."
>
> – John 8:28–30, DBY

In the Hebrew Scriptures, God's name was unveiled as "I Am" meaning "self-existing" or "ever-existing." Here in John 8:28–30 Jesus also spoke of His crucifixion. As He spoke these things concerning Himself, Who He is and what He is to do, faith was transmitted, and many believed.

The First Gospel Message

The first gospel message, declared by Peter, concerned Jesus Christ:

> "Men of Israel, hear these words: Jesus of Nazareth. . . ., — Him, being delivered by the determined purpose and foreknowledge of God, you have taken by lawless hands, have crucified, and put to death; whom God raised up, having loosed the pains of death, because it was not possible that He should be held by it."
>
> ". . . he, foreseeing this, spoke concerning the resurrection of the Christ, that His soul was not left in Hades, nor did His flesh see corruption. This Jesus God has raised up, of which we are all witnesses. Therefore being exalted to the right hand of God, and having received from the Father the promise of the Holy Spirit, He poured out this which you now see and hear."

"'Therefore let all the house of Israel know assuredly that God has made this Jesus, whom you crucified, both 'Lord and Christ.' Now when they heard this, they were cut to the heart, and said to Peter and the rest of the apostles, 'Men and brethren, what shall we do?' Then Peter said to them, 'Repent, and let every one of you be baptized in the name of Jesus Christ for the remission of sins; and you shall receive the gift of the Holy Spirit.'"

– Acts 2:22–24, 31–33, 36–38

This is the first gospel message after the Lord's death and resurrection. It is full of description concerning Jesus (both God and man), His work of crucifixion, resurrection, and ascension, and how as a man He is also made both Lord and Christ. The speaking of this complete gospel message caused men to believe, repent, and be immersed into Jesus Christ.

Those who asked Peter, "*What shall we do?*" must have already received faith as they were hearing the gospel of Jesus Christ. They started to see with the eyes of faith the One they had crucified as Lord and Christ in resurrection. Their question was initiated by the faith which was being infused into the deepest part of their being through hearing those things concerning Jesus Christ.

Answering, Peter said to them "repent." Repent or repentance means a change of mind or purpose (Vine's Expository Dictionary). At one time, those without faith were thinking Jesus was nothing. Their purposes were not of God – they were shutting out the Spirit. Now they needed to repent: to treasure Jesus Christ, to be for God's purpose, and to receive the Holy Spirit. Repentance is not merely to turn from evil to good, but to turn from idols to God, from death to life, and from sin to grace.

Although repentance is a gift from God (Acts 5:31; 11:18), it also needs cooperation from those receiving faith. Repentance includes making a reversal or change in the actions or directions in one's life based on a change in thinking. The first action they took was baptism, which was a distinct change in direction for them at that time. Each believer needs an initial repentance as in Acts 2; but repentance should continue throughout the Christian life whenever one is distracted away from God (Rev. 2:5). The stronger the repentance or the more drastic steps taken to change direction, the deeper the faith in experiencing more love, joy, peace, and power of the Holy Spirit. Additionally, a radical repentance in turning away from sinful practices and habits will bring in sanctification to keep a person on course in the Christian life. This will make it harder for a person's old lifestyle to impede his walking in the newness of God's divine life in him.

The Apostle Paul's Gospel

"For we do not preach ourselves, but Christ Jesus the Lord, and ourselves your bondservants for Jesus' sake. For it is the God who commanded light to shine out of darkness, who has shone in our hearts to give the light of the knowledge of the glory of God in the face of Jesus Christ."

– 2 Corinthians 4:5–6

"Moreover, brethren, I declare unto you the gospel which I preached unto you, which also ye have received, and wherein ye stand; By which also ye are saved, if ye keep in memory what I preached unto you, unless ye have believed in vain. For I delivered unto you first of all that which I also received, how that Christ died for our sins according to the scriptures; And that he was buried, and that he rose again the third day according to the scriptures."

– 1 Corinthians 15:1–4

Paul preached Christ Jesus the Lord. As Christ Jesus the Lord was presented, God did the work of shining in the darkened heart of the hearer. This light allowed us to see Jesus Christ in the gospel. As Paul preached the simplicity of His person, crucifixion and resurrection, the hearer received faith and was saved.

Speaking to Minister Christ

Every believer has the privilege and responsibility to bear fruit for God's purpose, through speaking, to minister Christ thereby continuing His ministry.

"Jesus said to them again, 'Peace be with you. As the Father has sent me, even so I am sending you.' And when he had said this, he breathed on them and said to them, 'Receive the Holy Spirit. If you forgive the sins of any, they are forgiven them; if you withhold forgiveness from any, it is withheld.'"

– John 20:21–23

This is a clear message in John 20:21–23 from Jesus Christ whereby believers are to continue His mission. Just as He was sent by the Father with the Spirit to accomplish God's eternal purpose, Jesus is sending those who believe *into* Him in the same way — with the Spirit. Not only do believers have the life of the Spirit, they likewise have the authority of Christ on His throne. He is sending believers with the life and power of the Holy Spirit; when they speak Christ as faith into people, then people believe and receive Jesus as the Savior — their sins are forgiven. Not bringing the good news of Jesus Christ to others, or if people do not receive the words of Christ, this will result in people remaining in their sins. What an awesome privilege and responsibility the Lord has given all His believers! This mission is not just for a few elite Christians or trained professionals; rather, everyone who has received the Spirit through faith has the God-given and innate capability to fulfill this directive from the Lord.

> ". . . because of the hope which is laid up for you in heaven, of which you heard before in the word of the truth of the gospel, which has come to you, as *it has* also in all the world, and is bringing forth fruit, as *it is* also among you since the day you heard and knew the grace of God in truth."
>
> — Colossians 1:5–6

Paul's use of the phrase, "*bringing forth fruit*" in Colossians 1:6 clearly refers to people who have heard "*the word of the truth of the gospel.*" When a person hears this word and receives faith, they know the grace of God in truth. Such a person is a fruit of the gospel. In every generation, and in every place, a harvest of such fruit is needed. Therefore, it is the believer's privilege and responsibility to spread and speak the word of the truth of the gospel.

> "And the things that thou hast heard of me among many witnesses, the same commit thou to faithful men, who shall be able to teach others also."
>
> — 2 Timothy 2:2

Five generations of passing on the Word of the truth can be seen in this verse. It was through this speaking by faithful men, people heard the truth and became believers. Now it is this generation's responsibility to find more faithful men to pass on what has been learned and enjoyed of Jesus Christ;

so, more faithful men will in turn teach others. Each one should have the clear realization no one should be the end or the terminal point; rather, believers are channels. If believers do not become a channel to pass on to others what they are hearing and learning of Christ, they will become a "dead sea," devoid of life. Therefore, Christians should continually seek to pass on the Word of Jesus Christ to others.

Each Believer Is a Branch in the Vine to Bear Fruit

> "I am the true vine, and My Father is the vinedresser. Every branch in Me that does not bear fruit He takes away; and every *branch* that bears fruit He prunes, that it may bear more fruit."
>
> "I am the vine, you *are* the branches. He who abides in Me, and I in him, bears much fruit; for without Me you can do nothing."
>
> – John 15:1–2, 5

A vine is basically all the branches combined. Without branches, the plant is just a stump and not a vine. Believers are "branches" making up the entire vine: Christ. Jesus Christ as the vine is being cultivated by the Father to bear much fruit for His glory. This is the Father's goal: to have a fruitful vine. The duty of each branch of this vine is to bear fruit. If a branch does not bear fruit, it is devoid of the supply and enjoyment of the vine. It is a blessing when a branch bears fruit and a loss when it does not. Believers have the responsibility and privilege to supply other people with Christ, so they too may bear fruit — His increase — for the Father's enjoyment and pleasure.

Fruit bearing brings joy to the Lord, resulting in the believer's fullness of joy:

> "These things I have spoken to you, that My joy may remain in you, and that your joy may be full."
>
> – John 15:11

Bearing fruit — bringing people to know and enjoy Jesus Christ — is the Lord's joy; likewise, it is the believer's *fullness* of joy. In Luke 15:7 it states there is more "joy in heaven" over one sinner coming to Christ than ninety-nine "righteous" persons. It is one of the greatest joys and causes for rejoicing that mere men and women could be instrumental in bringing someone to salvation and growth in the Lord. It is a real loss if a believer has not experienced this fullness of joy. Once a believer experiences the joy of ministering Christ to people, it can be "addicting." They will continually desire the fullness of joy resulting from the joy of the Lord in bringing men to salvation or to supply them for growth in the Body of Christ.

> "By this My Father is glorified, that you bear much fruit; so you will be My disciples."
>
> – John 15:8

The Father is glorified because of the expression of His rich life through reproduction.

As the cultivator and even the source of the entire vine, the Father is truly glorified as "much fruit" is borne. What a shame if a viticulturalist tended to a vine but there was no fruit! The Father is expressed and glorified through His many sons as the fruit. A disciple, as defined by the Lord, is one who bears much fruit. Christians shouldn't be just His believers, but even more, His disciples bearing much fruit that remains.

> ". . . and so also were James and John, sons of Zebedee, who were partners with Simon. Jesus said to Simon, 'Don't be afraid. From now on you will be catching people alive.' When they had brought their boats to land, they left everything, and followed him."
>
> – Luke 5:10–11, WBT

When the Lord called Simon (Peter) to follow Him, the mission He gave Simon was from then on, for the rest of his life on earth, he would be "catching people alive." Peter was to be like a fisherman for the Lord, catching men as fish. Unlike every fish (when caught fish die), people who are "caught" by the Lord come alive. They were dead *before* they were caught. No wonder Simon and the other fisherman with him left everything to follow the Lord. How much more glorious such a service and mission to catch men alive rather than dead fish! All believers are called with the same purpose.

Today with millions of believers, how many have followed the Lord's call to catch people alive? Most believers have been going to church for years; yet, they do not serve the Lord in the way of fruit bearing. They consider the task to be the clergy's job which is why they are paid. They are "professional shepherds." Believers need to wake up to hear the Lord's call to arise to serve the Lord Jesus and the people around them. They should act and go speak Christ to other people to fulfill their commission!

Go and Spread the Good News Now

> "'Go therefore and make disciples of all the nations, baptizing them in the name of the Father and of the Son and of the Holy Spirit, teaching them to observe all things that I have commanded you; and lo, I am with you always, [even] to the end of the age.' Amen."
> – Matthew 28:19–20

Immediately after the Lord promised He would always be with His followers; He charged them to go and make more disciples by baptizing and teaching them. No matter the obstacles in carrying out this charge, believers are assured the Lord is with them through it all. In fact, it is in carrying out this charge believers experience His prevailing presence.

The meaning of "go" does not indicate believers are to journey somewhere other than where they already are to fulfill this charge. In the original Greek, "go" is the word *poreuō*, which means, "to pursue the journey on which one has entered" or "to continue on one's journey" (Vine's). When Jesus told the disciples to "go," he meant discipling was to immediately commence as they went on their way. Thus, whether believers are "going" at work, at home, or through their daily living, they can fulfill this charge of making disciples. Disciples don't have to go to a foreign land to be a missionary; discipling starts now, regardless of location, concurrent with their daily life.

> "After these things the Lord appointed seventy others also, and sent them two by two before His face into every city and place where He Himself was about to go. Then He said to them, 'The harvest truly [is] great, but the laborers [are] few; therefore pray the Lord of the harvest to send out laborers into His harvest. Go your way; behold, I send you out as lambs among wolves.'"
> – Luke 10:1–3

> "Do you not say, 'There are still four months and then comes the harvest'? Behold, I say to you, lift up your eyes and look at the fields, for they are already white for harvest!"
> – John 4:35

The harvest refers to the gathering of fruit. All the people of this earth should be harvested for the Lord. God desires all men to be saved. How great is this harvest! As believers look at all the people around them, they should not assume certain people are not open or ready for receiving faith. With the Lord's eyes, it will be revealed they *are* ready to harvest. If a believer's goal is not to "convert" or convince but simply to speak Christ, and if they believe the Word of Christ heard will work in unbelievers, then they will indeed recognize people are ready to hear. It is important to pray for more laborers, because there are too few when compared to such a great harvest.

Friends and Relatives Are Chosen

It is important for Christians to start speaking to those closest to them both in relationship and in proximity.

> "And the following day they entered Caesarea. Now Cornelius was waiting for them, and had called together his relatives and close friends."
>
> "While Peter was still speaking these words, the Holy Spirit fell upon all those who heard the word."
>
> – Acts 10:24, 44

There is no need to wonder who is "chosen." Believers should consider at least all their relatives and close friends are chosen; therefore, speak Christ to them as if they are. Here, Cornelius invited all his relatives and close friends to hear the Word of Christ. As they were hearing, faith was activated — the Holy Spirit fell upon all of them who heard the Word. Christians' responsibility is to pray for and speak Christ to relatives and friends. There is no need to argue or try to convince them. Their job is to speak, and the Spirit's job is to work in the unbelieving — giving them faith to receive the Lord Jesus Christ and be saved.

Believers Should Start from Wherever They Are

> "But you shall receive power when the Holy Spirit has come upon you; and you shall be witnesses to Me in Jerusalem, and in all Judea and Samaria, and to the end of the earth."
>
> – Acts 1:8

The place and time to start speaking forth Christ is here and now. Where were the disciples in Acts 1:8? They were in Jerusalem; they started right where they were and then extended themselves to Judea, Samaria, and to the ends of the earth. Often believers grow discouraged from listening to Satan's lies, thinking they need to go somewhere else to preach the gospel as a missionary or to wait until they are trained to become qualified. It is truly commendable to travel to a foreign land to become a missionary. However, without going to a foreign territory, each believer has the awesome responsibility to speak about Christ in the place where they are and to speak to those closest to them.

Everyone is qualified, starting from the youngest to the newest in Christ. It is important for believers to guard themselves against letting past or present failures hinder them or worry about saying something wrong. Instead, they should be bold and say, "Come and see."

Nothing Can Disqualify a Believer from Speaking Forth Christ

"The woman then left her water pot, went her way into the city, and said to the men, 'Come, see a Man who told me all things that I ever did. Could this be the Christ?' Then they went out of the city and came to Him."

"And many more believed because of His own word."

– John 4:28–30, 41

The woman in John 4 had five husbands, but at this point she was simply living with another man; she would be considered a person living in sin. Despite her current sinful situation, after receiving faith, she went and told others in her town about Jesus. Through her speaking she influenced many to come to Jesus, and eventually many became believers. Believers who have not yet overcome all their sins are still qualified to tell others about Jesus. Many times, the liar — Satan — convinces believers because they are still struggling with sins and failures, they are not qualified to speak of Christ. They may think, "How can I speak about Jesus being my Savior if I am still a failure myself, struggling with sin?"

Accepting this lie, wherein a person needs to be a "good" Christian before they can preach the gospel, has kept many believers silent concerning Christ. That is a testimony — believers still struggling with sins can still have the joy of the Lord in speaking for the Lord! This does not mean believers should not grow and be transformed into His image; but how they grow and when they will be transformed is not in their own timing and by their work, but altogether the Lord's. A believer's service is to speak forth Christ right where they are, just the way they are. The Lord can prune and cut away the unwanted parts, as they bear fruit. According to John 15, the Father does His pruning work to shape His children as they are bearing remaining fruit — not when they are dormant, thinking they are unworthy to share the gospel of grace and peace.

It is important to note it was a woman, not a man, who was a sinner — hardly a pious person — who became the first account of a believer bringing the good news of Jesus Christ to people; this woman brought people to Jesus. This established the principle: *anyone* can bring people to the Lord no matter who they are or what their condition.

> "Immediately he [Saul] preached the Christ in the synagogues, that He is the Son of God. Then all who heard were amazed, and said, 'Is this not he who destroyed those who called on this name in Jerusalem, and has come here for that purpose, so that he might bring them bound to the chief priests?'"
>
> – Acts 9:20–21

Saul, who was also called Paul (Acts 13:9), started preaching Christ's person immediately after receiving faith. That was the reason the people were amazed; just a couple of days prior to this, he was persecuting Jesus, and now he was preaching Jesus. Saul was the one dragging Christians to prison and consented to the stoning of another believer. However, no matter how negative a person's past, as soon as they believe, they are qualified to start speaking forth Christ. This is miraculously normal!

God Can Still Use Inaccurate Preaching of the Gospel

> "Philip found Nathanael and said to him, 'We have found Him of whom Moses in the law, and also the prophets, wrote — Jesus of Nazareth, the son of Joseph.' And Nathanael said to him, 'Can anything good come out of Nazareth?' Philip said to him, 'Come and see.'"
>
> – John 1:45–46

The information Philip told Nathanael concerning Christ was not correct. Jesus was of Bethlehem, not Nazareth. Strictly speaking, Jesus was not the son of Joseph. He was the Son of God of Mary. Nevertheless, Nathanael came to Jesus and became a believer. Therefore, do not be concerned with the accuracy of your speaking. Many believers are silent concerning Christ, worried they may not know enough, or they will say the wrong thing about Christ. The Lord can use any believer's speaking, even in its infancy and inaccuracy. What can be said, most certainly, with one hundred percent accuracy is, "*I have found Him*" and "*come and see.*" Every believer can say this with confidence.

Be Patient . . . It Is God's Timing

God called Abraham by appearing to him multiple times, but it took years before Abraham responded to God's calling. Thus, Christians should not expect quick results either.

> "And he said, 'Brethren and fathers, listen: The God of glory appeared to our father Abraham when he was in Mesopotamia, before he dwelt in Haran,'"
>
> *– Acts 7:2*

> "The people who sat in darkness have seen a great light, and upon those who sat in the region and shadow of death Light has dawned."
>
> *– Matthew 4:16*

The first record concerning the God of glory appearing to Abraham was in Mesopotamia. Abraham did not obey nor follow God's calling there (Acts 7:2-7). It seems it was Abraham's father, Terah, not Abraham himself who took the first step to leave Mesopotamia and go to Haran. God then came and appeared to Abraham again to call him in Haran (Gen. 11:31 – 12:4). It was at this point after many years since God's first appearance to Abraham, that he followed God's calling. This shows us even Abraham, the "father of faith," did not follow God the first time he was called.

This can be the case with many unbelieving friends and relatives. It may take many years and multiple times for the God of glory appearing to them through speaking about Christ before faith is received – then they become a believer. Jesus Christ is the great light attracting people in darkness. A believer's job is to shine forth Christ in their living and in their speaking of Christ. It is up to the Lord's timing when and where those who are being prayed for and hearing Jesus will be attracted and come to Him. Therefore, be patient and be bold, but don't be "preachy," and don't argue to offend. If people are willing to hear concerning Christ, they then have a chance to receive faith and become a believer in Jesus Christ.

Practice: Speaking Forth Christ to Others

Every day this week decide to speak to someone – anyone – about Jesus Christ. Speak about anything concerning Who He is and what He has done, even if it is for one or two minutes. You are not preaching, and you are not trying to convert, you just want to open your month to start saying something about how good Jesus is. Speak to your pet if there is absolutely no one available to speak to, because this practice is just to get your tongue loose in order to say something about Jesus.

You can even say something like this: "Hi _(John)__! I told God this week that I will do my best to say something about Jesus to one person. I just need a minute of your time (then proceed to say whatever is in your heart about Jesus).

You don't need a formulated message. You are simply letting the Spirit have a way to flow out of you. The Spirit can flow even if you are saying things that are not exactly correct. You can always give your testimony of how you came to know Jesus. Certainly no one can argue with your testimony!

10

CHERISHING: AN
OPENING FOR THE WORD

Bearing Remaining Fruit

Every believer has been called not simply to bear fruit, but to bear remaining fruit, which will in turn bear the next generation of fruit. To bear such remaining fruit means after a person is born anew three matters are needed: Cherishing, nourishing, and exhorting or discipling.

> "You did not choose Me, but I chose you and appointed you that you should go and bear fruit, and that your fruit should remain, that whatever you ask the Father in My name, He may give you."
> – John 15:8, 16

What a privilege for believers to be chosen — appointed to go and do His will regarding bearing remaining fruit. The word for "remain" in John 15:16, *menō*, is the same Greek word for "abide"; therefore, the fruit borne by the branches should be just like another branch which abides and bears fruit. This echoes 2 Timothy 2:2, where Paul instructs believers to pass on the truth to faithful men who would be able to teach others also. Thus, when believers ask the Father for "whatever" in relation to doing the Lord's will of bearing remaining fruit, He may give it to them.

Every believer's responsibility is not just to lead others to the Lord for regeneration, but those "born again" would continue for the rest of their lives in the Lord in bearing remaining fruit. *This is life.* Life begets generation after generation; this is how life multiplies.

It is good for a preacher who may be speaking the gospel to hundreds or even thousands of people at a time, but this is not what is emphasized here. Fruit-bearing is related to a personal and relational caring and feeding of another until that person is established in the faith; can spiritually fend for themselves, and are able to do the service of fruit-bearing as well. Even those who have come to know the Lord through a preacher at an event or on TV needs spiritual parenting from one or more believers until they reach maturity. Just like physical families, a set of parents gives birth and cares for a few children for many years until those children reach adulthood and have their own families. It is a tremendous matter for each believer to have a view of fruit bearing in order to bring up spiritual children. The Lord preached to thousands, but He personally took care of twelve disciples including a few women for a period of three-and-a-half years. Just as humanity has populated the entire earth through the multiplication of families; likewise, every believer simply must grow their own spiritual family for Christ, then there will be millions and millions of living and active believers on the earth.

If believers would be observant, they would notice that in every Christian gathering there are individuals who could benefit from personal care and shepherding. There are individuals at various times who could use personal fellowship and prayer; however, simply being in a group does not automatically provide such care. A person can be in a group, go through the "service" and the motions; yet, feel isolated, while lacking much needed personal care. If those with a serving heart take notice, the Lord will lead them to such individuals to provide cherishing and nourishing care. The opportunity to serve is everywhere if the heart is seeking and there is a willingness to act.

> "And the things that you have heard from me among [through] many witnesses, commit these to faithful men who will be able to teach others also."
>
> – 2 Timothy 2:2

In 2 Timothy 2:2, Paul describes multiple generations of fruit bearing which should occur from one generation to the next. Every believer who has heard the truth and received eternal life has a duty: to commit what he or she has received to faithful men, who will in turn teach others also. Christians up to this very day have been beneficiaries of multiple generations of believers passing on what they have heard and experienced of the Lord. Now, the followers of Jesus have the same responsibility to find more faithful disciples to pass on what has been received. When believers are not dormant, but are activated in this way to spread the gospel and engender the growth of believers which in turn will increase at an exponential rate — this is the pattern for all life forms.

The Way to Bear Remaining Fruit

In order to properly raise up a family, there should be three attributes performed by every parent over the course of their child's growth to maturity. Bearing remaining fruit would be applied here as people being brought from unregenerate sinners to becoming maturely established and active in the faith. Here is an overview of these three items in light of Scripture.

Cherishing: Tender Love and Care with the Intention to Nourish

The glory of Jesus to serve in His humble humanity is essential for service in caring for people. All individuals whether believers or unbelievers respond to love and care. The parental love and care provided to a human can only come from another human. Even though God is love, He Himself didn't display His love directly; rather, He sent His Son to take on humanity. It was Jesus' humanity Who truly transmitted love and care to the pinnacle of His creation, man. Therefore, in order to cherish others, the humanity of Jesus in His glory is needed. Believers need to live by and express the gift of His glory in order to cherish all kinds of people no matter how different they are.

To cherish is to "warm up" others in the humanity of Christ with tender love and care with the intent to nourish. A cherished person is comfortable, peaceful, happy and open; a person who is "warmed up" is ready to hear the truth of the gospel.

> "But we were gentle among you, just as a nursing mother cherishes her own children. So, affectionately longing for you, we were well pleased to impart to you not only the gospel of God, but also our own lives [souls], because you had become dear to us."
>
> – 1 Thessalonians 2:7–8

Although a nursing mother's goal is to feed her baby for life and growth, most of her time, energy, and attention are in fact focused on cherishing the baby. Paul and his co-workers were like such a mother, cherishing both the unbelieving and those new in the faith in order to nurse or nourish these babes. Every Christian needs to learn to cherish others as soon as they recognize they have been called to bear fruit as nursing mothers. Cherishing means fostering with tender care. Those being cherished are happy, comfortable, and open to receiving nourishment. I remember when my kids were babies, many times I had to act as if the food in the spoon was an airplane ready to fly into their mouth just to get them to eat. This "play" was my way of cherishing them to open their mouths to receive nourishment.

Being gentle means being mild and loving, even towards people who are difficult, stubborn, and hard to deal with. Many unbelievers are obstinate and argumentative when it comes to the gospel. Even in helping new believers to grow in the Lord, it is often difficult to feed them spiritually until they grow to the point where they can eat and drink the Lord on their own. Just as a good mother would never get angry and reject her child for becoming dirty or making mistakes, disciples who are nursing mothers (for the sake of fruit-bearing) also should forgive and love the spiritual babes when their words and actions are offensive or disappointing. If believers are to bear fruit, they need the gentleness of the Lord's humanity to continue cherishing those around them. The day will come when those being cherished will open their hearts to the gospel. Even Christians who already have faith need cherishing. If they are not yet mature spiritually, then they need nourishment to grow. However, at times, believers may harden themselves toward feeding on Christ; therefore, they need a servant to cherish them. It is when they are made happy and opened, they will receive nourishment and grow. If believers want to minister Christ to bear remaining fruit, cherishing will continue. Since the matter of cherishing is so essential for fruit bearing, it becomes the dominant theme of this chapter.

Nourishing: Feeding Others Christ through the Spirit and the Word

In addition to cherishing others, believers need to feed people Christ through the Spirit and the Word for them to partake of God's life and nature.

> "Husbands, love your own wives, even as the Christ also loved the assembly [ekklesia], and has delivered himself up for it . . . . . For no one has ever hated his own flesh, but nourishes and cherishes it, even as also the Christ the assembly."
> – Ephesians 5:25, 29

The Lord is nourishing and cherishing His ekklesia — His people — like a man takes care of his own body or as a husband lovingly cares for his wife. The Lord's "cherishing" is His loving care even to the point of sacrificing Himself for His wife, and His "nourishing" is His sanctifying work by the washing of water in the Word. As presented in previous chapters, this water represents the Spirit. As believers are filled with the Spirit, they are washed from within. A person's physical appearance reflects healthy nourishment (or the lack of it). To spiritually nourish someone is to supply the Spirit in the Word. If an unbeliever takes in such a nourishing Spirit, that person is born anew with the Spirit. If believers receive the ministry of such nourishment in the Spirit, they will grow and become transformed into His glorious bride.

> "So when they had eaten breakfast, Jesus said to Simon Peter, 'Simon, son of Jonah, do you love Me more than these?' He said to Him, 'Yes, Lord; You know that I love You.' He said to him, 'Feed My lambs.' He said to him again a second time, 'Simon, son of Jonah, do you love Me?' He said to Him, 'Yes, Lord; You know that I love You.' He said to him, 'Tend My sheep.' He said to him the third time, 'Simon, son of Jonah, do you love Me?' Peter was grieved because He said to him the third time, 'Do you love Me?' And he said to Him, 'Lord, You know all things; You know that I love You.' Jesus said to him, 'Feed My sheep.'"
>
> ~ John 21:15-17

When Jesus first encountered Simon Peter, He called Simon Peter to catch people alive. Now in His last physical encounter with Simon Peter, Jesus asked him to feed and care for His sheep — the people who were brought to the Lord and reborn in His divine life. First Simon Peter was to "catch" and bring people to the Lord; then, he was to feed them for growth. The way to love the Lord is to nourish and feed the Lord's people. Every believer who loves the Lord receives the same request from the Lord: to bear remaining fruit by shepherding and feeding — cherishing, nourishing, and exhorting.

Lambs may be considered new and young believers. Sheep are older (more mature) believers. Both the young and the more mature believer need nourishment; everyone who loves the Lord, even a newer believer, is qualified to nourish both the young and the mature.

Exhorting: A Father's Right and Responsibility

As a father that begets, there is the right and responsibility to exhort — to strongly encourage and admonish.

> "I do not write these things to shame you, but as my beloved children I warn [you]. For though you might have ten thousand instructors in Christ, yet [you do] not [have] many fathers; for in Christ Jesus I have begotten you through the gospel. Therefore I urge you, imitate me."
>
> – 1 Corinthians 4:14–16

A father is the one who begets or gives birth. Spiritually, a father gives life to another through the gospel of Jesus Christ. Paul was not only a begetting father — he was also the nursing mother. He cherished believers whom he had begotten. Since he gave birth, nursed, and cherished believers with gentleness, he was qualified to admonish, warn, and ask believers to imitate him. Today, as during Paul's time, there are many instructors who can pass on Scripture or spiritual knowledge while telling people what to do; however, what is needed are more begetting fathers able to bring forth children of God through the gospel — caring for them until maturity.

> "For you remember, brethren, our labor and toil; for laboring night and day, that we might not be a burden to any of you, we preached to you the gospel of God. You *are* witnesses, and God *also*, how devoutly and justly and blamelessly we behaved ourselves among you who believe; as you know how we exhorted, and comforted, and charged every one of you, as a father *does* his own children."
>
> – 1 Thessalonians 2:9–11

Paul didn't receive an appointment from an organization; he wasn't given a title as a "minister," "pastor," or "elder." It was completely out of love and life he cared for new believers in Christ. He didn't receive a salary to do this as a job. He worked night and day to support himself, in order to preach the gospel; to shepherd believers without being a burden to them. Just as parents who have children, their lifestyle and behavior changes for the sake of the child; likewise, when one takes up a burden to care for others in Christ, it affects their behavior, as it did Paul's. Being such a father, Paul exhorted and comforted the new and young believers as his own children.

To exhort someone does not mean telling a person to do something the father himself is not doing; rather, to exhort is to ask someone being shepherded to do what the one shepherding him is doing. In the Greek the word "exhort" is the word *parakaleō* which means, "To call to one's side" (Vine's) or to call alongside to participate in the same work or journey. A father's job in this sense is to encourage and ask those he is cherishing and nourishing to come alongside him to do the same work of begetting, and shepherding others in Christ for the building up of His body — this is the meaning of the word *exhort*.

Six Practical Cherishing Done by Jesus

Cherishing is the first essential and continuing attribute to bear remaining fruit. To "bear remaining fruit" is not simply bringing someone to faith, but to bear them, care, and feed them, until maturity in Christ. Christ cherished mankind by coming down from His glory to serve man for whom He ultimately died.

> "But Jesus called them to Himself and said, 'You know that the rulers of the Gentiles lord it over them, and those who are great exercise authority over them. Yet it shall not be so among you; but whoever desires to become great among you, let him be your servant. And whoever desires to be first among you, let him be your slave — just as the Son of Man did not come to be served, but to serve, and to give His life a ransom for many.'"
> – Matthew 20:25-28

A person who is cherishing is serving, while the one being cherished is being served. Think of a mother cherishing her baby: Her life centers on serving the baby. She will do whatever her child beckons. The rulers of the world expect others to serve them. Such rulers will never cherish their subjects. In the Body of Christ, the more believers can serve others, the greater and more mature they are. This is completely opposite to both the secular and the religious world. If people desire to bear remaining fruit as the Lord desires, then they need such a serving heart for the Lord. This, of course, is the essence of the glory given by Jesus Christ.

> "Blessed are those servants whom the master, when he comes, will find watching. Assuredly, I say to you that he will gird himself and have them sit down to eat, and will come and serve them."
>
> – Luke 12:37

Isn't it amazing to know the Lord Jesus in the coming kingdom will continue to serve His followers who are servants? He came as a man to serve men through His death on the cross, to rid humanity of sin. He continues to serve His people by supplying them with all His riches in their spirit — this will continue into His eternal kingdom.

Physically, a mother will continue to cherish her children and care for them with a serving heart even when her children are full grown and mature. So, too, in the future, will Jesus continue to serve faithful believers at His table for them to enjoy Him in His coming kingdom. What a cherishing Lord! The point here is for believers to have such a serving heart as the Lord; one which never stops and never rests but continues into the kingdom.

> "Who, being in the form of God, did not consider it robbery to be equal with God, but made Himself of no reputation, taking the form of a bondservant, *and* coming in the likeness of men. And being found in appearance as a man, He humbled Himself and became obedient to *the point of* death, even the death of the cross."
>
> – Philippians 2:6–8

In Philippians 2:6–8 Paul reveals the principle of cherishing: laying aside one's glory and honor and becoming a humble servant for the sake of caring for the needs of others. The Lord went from the highest position to the lowest so He might cherish and serve others, even those of the lowest status among humanity. How much have all His believers been cherished by the Lord! They were truly warmed up when they recognized His death on the cross which has solved all their problems of sin, death, Satan, and even self. Through this cherishing, they opened to receive His nourishing.

Below are examples of how the Lord Jesus cherished people in His humanity. His followers can imitate Him because they share in the glory of His humanity. This is miraculously normal to cherish both unbelievers and believers in such a way.

Eating and Drinking with Sinners

The Lord practically cherished, and warmed up people around Him, especially sinners, by fellowshipping with them over a meal.

> "The Son of Man has come eating and drinking, and you say, 'Look, a glutton and a winebibber, a friend of tax collectors and sinners!'"
>
> – Luke 7:34

> "And the Pharisees and scribes complained, saying, 'This Man receives sinners and eats with them.'"
>
> – Luke 15:2

> "But when they saw it, they all complained, saying, 'He [Jesus] has gone to be a guest with a man who is a sinner.'"
>
> – Luke 19:7

The Lord used the best way to a man's heart: through their stomach. A good meal with people is the easiest and quickest way to make them happy. They feel cared for, appreciated, and accepted. A good meal can also erase a lot of suspicion and bad feelings. Believers should learn from the Lord: Cherishing others for fruit bearing requires making opportunities to have meals with them. Note also it was religious people who condemned the Lord for having such meals with sinners. Religion is cold, strict, and impersonal, in contrast to the Lord who is warm, approachable, relaxed, personable, non-judgmental, and accepting.

Did Not Judge or Condemn Sinners

> "Jesus said to her, 'Go, call your husband, and come here.' The woman answered and said, 'I have no husband.' Jesus said to her, 'You have well said, 'I have no husband,' 'for you have had five husbands, and the one whom you now have is not your husband; in that you spoke truly.'"
>
> – John 4:16–18

In this conversation, Jesus was full of gentleness and love for an adulterous woman. He could have called her a liar for saying she did not have a husband, but he didn't. Even when he exposed her real shameful situation, there was not a tone or hint of condemnation. He accepted her though she was immoral and lived a loose lifestyle for years. What cherishing! What is the rest of this story? After their conversation, the woman received the Lord Jesus as the Living Water — she was satisfied. He didn't ask her to leave her shameful relationship of living with a man outside of matrimony or to patch up her failed relationships. He just gave her "Living Water" to drink without any condition. This was the Lord's cherishing so she could receive nourishment. Afterward, she told everyone in town to come and meet Jesus.

> "Then the scribes and Pharisees brought to Him a woman caught in adultery. And when they had set her in the midst, they said to Him, 'Teacher, this woman was caught in adultery, in the very act. Now Moses, in the law, commanded us that such should be stoned. But what do You say?' This they said, testing Him, that they might have *something* of which to accuse Him. But Jesus stooped down and wrote on the ground with *His* finger, as though He did not hear. So when they continued asking Him, He raised Himself up and said to them, 'He who is without sin among you, let him throw a stone at her first.' And again He stooped down and wrote on the ground. Then those who heard *it*, being convicted by *their* conscience, went out one by one, beginning with the oldest *even* to the last. And Jesus was left alone, and the woman standing in the midst. When Jesus had raised Himself up and saw no one but the woman, He said to her, 'Woman, where are those accusers of yours? Has no one condemned you?' She said, 'No one, Lord.' And Jesus said to her, 'Neither do I condemn you; go and sin no more.'"
>
> – John 8:3–11

Religious people use fear and condemnation to manipulate those who are afraid of God's judgment. This is pretty much a universal tactic of all religions. The religious have successfully spread the fear of God's judgment abroad to control people for centuries. However, this is not the Lord Jesus' way. His way is to forgive and save sinful people from certain death. How cherishing! If believers are to spread the Lord Jesus to friends, relatives, and others, then they need to both enjoy and express the Lord's forgiveness to others. To bear remaining fruit, believers should care for people without condemnation or judgment. People should feel comfortable and accepted when in a believer's presence. If so, they will have a way to present Christ as nourishment fostering regeneration and growth.

Forgave All Sin and Debts

"Then Peter came to Him and said, 'Lord, how often shall my brother sin against me, and I forgive him? Up to seven times?' Jesus said to him, 'I do not say to you, up to seven times, but up to seventy times seven. Therefore the kingdom of heaven is like a certain king who wanted to settle accounts with his servants. And when he had begun to settle accounts, one was brought to him who owed him ten thousand talents. But as he was not able to pay, his master commanded that he be sold, with his wife and children and all that he had, and that payment be made. The servant therefore fell down before him, saying, 'Master, have patience with me, and I will pay you all.' Then the master of that servant was moved with compassion, released him, and forgave him the debt. But that servant went out and found one of his fellow servants who owed him a hundred denarii; and he laid hands on him and took *him* by the throat, saying, 'Pay me what you owe!' So his fellow servant fell down at his feet and begged him, saying, 'Have patience with me, and I will pay you all.' And he would not, but went and threw him into prison till he should pay the debt. So when his fellow servants saw what had been done, they were very grieved, and came and told their master all that had been done. Then his master, after he had called him, said to him, 'You wicked servant! I forgave you all that debt because you begged me. Should you not also have had compassion on your fellow servant, just as I had pity on you?' And his master was angry, and delivered him to the torturers until he should pay all that was due to him. So My heavenly Father also will do to you if each of you, from his heart, does not forgive his brother his trespasses.'"

– Matthew 18:21–35

Sometimes it is easier for Christians to forgive unbelievers than to forgive fellow believers. The case above is a story about forgiving a fellow believer.

Christians can be much more demanding and unforgiving toward their own brothers and sisters in Christ, because they think they should know better. However, those who care for fellow believers — desiring to help them to grow in the faith — must take this story to heart having compassion to forgive. The ones having difficulties forgiving others seem to be those who have ignored or minimized their own sins and debt. In caring for younger believers over a prolonged period, it is inevitable those less mature believers will do or say something which will offend the one doing the shepherding. At such a time, the shepherding one may want to give up on caring for them. However, if the goal is to bear remaining fruit, the shepherding one cannot give up. Therefore, it is important to take the Lord at His Word and forgive 490 times. It is certain cherishing occurs when forgiving a person that many times; the forgiving disciple will be able to nourish the other person and help him to grow to maturity.

Received and Blessed Little Children

> "Then they brought little children to Him, that He might touch them; but the disciples rebuked those who brought *them*. But when Jesus saw *it*, He was greatly displeased and said to them, 'Let the little children come to Me, and do not forbid them; for of such is the kingdom of God. Assuredly, I say to you, whoever does not receive the kingdom of God as a little child will by no means enter it.' And He took them up in His arms, laid *His* hands on them, and blessed them."
>
> – Mark 10:13–16

Jesus specifically cherished children. Who brought the little children? It must have been their parents who wanted Jesus to touch their sons or daughters. Because Jesus cared for and cherished the little children, He cherished the entire family — including the parents. As shown in previous chapters, God's salvation is for the entire family. He wants to see family-by-family come to salvation. Therefore, if believers are to cherish and lead a family to the Lord thereafter to grow in the Lord, it is vital they also cherish the *children* of the family just as the Lord did. Sometime believers erroneously consider children as a distraction when they try to preach the gospel or teach the truth. On the contrary, Jesus cherished them and in turn cherished the entire family.

A Good Listener to the Ignorant

"Now behold, two of them were traveling that same day to a village called Emmaus, which was seven miles from Jerusalem. And they talked together of all these things which had happened. So it was, while they conversed and reasoned, that Jesus Himself drew near and went with them. But their eyes were restrained, so that they did not know Him. And He said to them, 'What kind of conversation is this that you have with one another as you walk and are sad?' Then the one whose name was Cleopas answered and said to Him, 'Are You the only stranger in Jerusalem, and have You not known the things which happened there in these days?' And He said to them, 'What things?' So they said to Him, 'The things concerning Jesus of Nazareth, who was a Prophet mighty in deed and word before God and all the people, and how the chief priests and our rulers delivered Him to be condemned to death, and crucified Him. But we were hoping that it was He who was going to redeem Israel. Indeed, besides all this, today is the third day since these things happened. Yes, and certain women of our company, who arrived at the tomb early, astonished us. When they did not find His body, they came saying that they had also seen a vision of angels who said He was alive. And certain of those who were with us went to the tomb and found it just as the women had said; but Him they did not see.' Then He said to them, 'O foolish ones, and slow of heart to believe in all that the prophets have spoken! Ought not the Christ to have suffered these things and to enter into His glory?' And beginning at Moses and all the Prophets, He expounded to them in all the Scriptures the things concerning Himself. Then they drew near to the village where they were going, and He indicated that He would have gone farther. But they constrained Him, saying, 'Abide with us, for it is toward evening, and the day is far spent.' And He went in to stay with them. Now it came to pass, as He sat at the table with them, that He took bread, blessed and broke it, and gave it to them. Then their eyes were opened and they knew Him; and He vanished from their sight. And they said to one another, 'Did not our heart burn within us while He talked with us on the road, and while He opened the Scriptures to us?'"

– Luke 24:13–32

Two disciples in Luke 24 heard about Jesus' resurrection and didn't believe; dejected, sad, and disappointed, they left Jerusalem where Jesus was crucified. On their way to Emmaus, Jesus, in resurrection, came alongside them, and started a conversation — but they did not recognize with whom they were speaking, for "*their eyes were restrained.*" Jesus asked questions; moreover, He let them speak out what was troubling them. It is almost comical how they were telling Jesus about Himself — and even got it wrong (Jesus was not only a prophet but the Son of God)! Yet, Jesus didn't rebuke, belittle, or judge them.

After Jesus patiently listened to these two men for a long while, He began to speak from the Scriptures concerning Himself. Eventually, when they broke bread together for a meal, they recognized it was Jesus, and they believed.

What the Lord did here is a great example of cherishing for nourishing. It is very cherishing for troubled people to be able to speak and pour out what is bothering them to someone willing to listen without passing judgment. To warm up and open the hearts of others. Indeed, believers need to learn to listen more and speak less (note: in the above portion of Scriptures, seven verses were of the Lord listening, but only three were of the Lord speaking). People's hearts are often opened when they can freely speak. If believers ask the right questions and listen to others without correcting or judging them, they are qualified — able to nourish them by unveiling Christ in the Scriptures, leading them to partake of Jesus Christ as food.

Condemning the Hypocrisy of the Religious

Jesus exposed and condemned the hypocrisy of the religious but cared for those beaten up by religion.

> "Then Jesus spoke to the multitudes and to His disciples, saying: 'The scribes and the Pharisees sit in Moses' seat. For they bind heavy burdens, hard to bear, and lay *them* on men's shoulders; but they *themselves* will not move them with one of their fingers. But all their works they do to be seen by men. . . . But woe to you, scribes and Pharisees, hypocrites! For you shut up the kingdom of heaven against men; for you neither go in yourselves, nor do you allow those who are entering to go in. Woe to you, scribes and Pharisees, hypocrites! For you cleanse the outside of the

cup and dish, but inside they are full of extortion and self-indulgence. Blind Pharisee, first cleanse the inside of the cup and dish, that the outside of them may be clean also. Woe to you, scribes and Pharisees, hypocrites! For you are like whitewashed tombs which indeed appear beautiful outwardly, but inside are full of dead men's bones and all uncleanness. Even so you also outwardly appear righteous to men, but inside you are full of hypocrisy and lawlessness."

– Matthew 23:1–2, 4–28

The Lord was harsh, exposing and condemning the leaders of religion — and this religion was even Scripturally-based. Religions, which are based on fear, teach people how to behave and live in a way that would please God. The religious practitioners are devoid of the presence and enjoyment of God. In fact, they become an impediment, a roadblock to God. It is very deceptive, because on the one hand they talk about God, and try to keep God's laws to please God, but on the other hand they drive people away from God through their demands and hypocrisies. In order to expose this deception, making a clear distinction between Himself and the religious, Jesus condemned and openly denounced them. He wanted to make the hypocrisy of religion clear — it is just for outward show, full of death — He had nothing to do with it.

This condemnation of the religious is a cherishing to those who are turned off, disappointed, and repulsed by them. Many who have been damaged and hurt by religion will recognize through the Lord's condemnation Jesus is *different*. Not only is He not part of a religion, but He is in opposition to religious leaders. This is a cherishing to many who have been afflicted under the hypocritical judging of the religious. The Lord Jesus liberated them from religion in order to attract them to Himself.

"Then Jesus answered and said: 'A certain *man* went down from Jerusalem to Jericho, and fell among thieves, who stripped him of his clothing, wounded *him*, and departed, leaving *him* half dead. Now by chance a certain priest came down that road. And when he saw him, he passed by on the other side. Likewise a Levite, when he arrived at the place, came and looked, and passed by on the other side. But a certain Samaritan, as he journeyed, came where he was. And when he saw him, he had compassion. So he went to *him* and bandaged his wounds, pouring on oil and wine; and he set him on his own animal, brought him to an inn, and took care of him.'"

– Luke 10:30–34

In response to a challenge by a religious law keeper, Jesus told this story of a man beaten up by thieves. The "thieves" refer to the religious law keepers who regularly expose, condemn, beat up, and leave half dead those who cannot keep their religious laws. This is why the priest and Levite (both referring to prominent religious personalities) did not stop to help him. The Samaritan, however, belonging to a people *despised* by the religion of the time, refers to Jesus who was despised and rejected by religion. He was the one Who came to take care of this wounded half-dead man. The man who was beaten up by religion received care from and was saved by Jesus.

Thus, believers need to cherish those who are dejected and wounded by religion so they will become cherished and thus receive the Lord Jesus — or turn back to Jesus — who is life and diametrically the opposite of religion.

The Practical Experience of the Crucified and Resurrected Christ

Cherishing and nourishing others is the real and practical experience of the crucified and resurrected Christ. This is the functional application of the glory of Jesus given and received, which has everything to do with fruit-bearing. Life through death is truly miraculously normal service every believer should normally experience in their daily living.

"But Jesus answered them saying, 'The hour is come that the Son of man should be glorified. Verily, verily, I say unto you, Except the grain of wheat falling into the ground dies, it abides alone; but if it dies, it bears much fruit. He that loves his [soul] life shall lose it, and he that hates his life in this world shall keep it to life eternal.'"

– John 12:23–25, DBY

Most serious Christians are familiar with the teachings of self-denial and hating the self-life of this world in order to be holy, thereby pleasing to God. Many then interpret this to mean they should not derive any pleasure from worldly things or things which bring worldly enjoyment. This becomes a big religious requirement which they put on themselves and fellow believers. Many believers, not able to keep this requirement, become discouraged; thus, spiritually deadened. However, this is not what the context of these verses is saying.

In John 12:23–25 and in later verses, Scriptures teach death produces much fruit — *life*. The purpose and outcome of Jesus' death is life for many others — *fruit*. Jesus was not denying Himself just so He wouldn't indulge in the things of this world; rather, His full attention was focused on the resulting "fruit," and it was for "fruit bearing" He died.

Likewise, when believers act for the sake of caring and bearing others, they are denying themselves. A mother does not go through changes in lifestyle and much suffering just because she must suffer with no outcome. No, she automatically does so for a new birth — for the joy and rejoicing of a new life — the fruit of her womb.

Sent to Speak the Word and Follow Christ for the Increase

The Word concerning "bearing the cross" and "denying the soul-life" is related to being sent to speak the Word and to follow Christ for the increase (building up) of the ekklesia.

> "And as you go, preach, saying, 'The kingdom of heaven is at hand.'"
>
> "And he who does not take his cross and follow after Me is not worthy of Me. He who finds his [soul] life will lose it, and he who loses his [soul] life for My sake will find it."
>
> – Matthew 10:7, 38–39

In the context of charging His disciples to go preach the gospel, Jesus spoke of taking the cross in following Him. For believers to follow Him by losing their soul-life and taking up the cross, does not mean suffering for suffering's sake; it is heeding the call of Jesus to go and share the good news and enjoyment of Jesus Christ to others around them. When believers experience the joy and rejoicing which comes with bringing people to salvation, they gladly consider whatever time, energy, and missed pleasure of the world, well worth the sacrifice. It is a privilege to witness a person coming to salvation or growing in Christ.

Contrary to Jesus' *physical* death, the Lord is not asking believers to lose their *physical* life since "life" in this verse does not refer to physical life. It refers to a believer's soul, or *psychological* life. To be worthy of the Lord is to go and bear fruit, even at the cost of losing the temporary pleasures of the soul life.

> "And I also, I say unto thee that you are Peter, and on this rock I will build my assembly, and hades' gates shall not prevail against it."
>
> "From that time Jesus began to show to his disciples that he must go away to Jerusalem, and suffer many things from the elders and chief priests and scribes, and be killed, and the third day be raised."
>
> "Then Jesus said to his disciples, 'If any one desires to come after me, let him deny himself and take up his cross and follow me. For whosoever shall desire to save his [soul] life shall lose it; but whosoever shall lose his [soul] life for my sake shall find it.'"
>
> – Matthew 16:18, 21, 24–25, DBY

Jesus unveiled His purpose in these verses in Matthew 16 concerning the building of His ekklesia — His kingdom. The way He would do it: by going to His death followed by His resurrection. After this, He told those who followed Him to build His ekklesia as He — by taking up the cross, denying one's self, and losing their soul-life. Again, this is not the same as the philosophy of asceticism — treating oneself harshly in order to control baser desires. It is also not the same as some erroneously think that in denying oneself a person should not do certain things they wish to do as an end in themselves. Many Christian leaders use verses like these to teach those under their leadership to deny themselves by not objecting, criticizing, while just continuing to support their leaders when those leading do things which are wrong. This type of "denying" is characteristic of a cult following; it is not in the nature and practice of the Lord's ekklesia. The next set of verses will practically discuss what is means to "deny yourself."

> "He said to him the third time, 'Simon, son of Jonah, do you love Me?' Peter was grieved because He said to him the third time, 'Do you love Me?' And he said to Him, 'Lord, You know all things; You know that I love You.' Jesus said to him, 'Feed My sheep. Most assuredly, I say to you, when you were younger, you

girded yourself and walked where you wished; but when you are old, you will stretch out your hands, and another will gird you and carry *you* where you do not wish.' This He spoke, signifying by what death he would glorify God. And when He had spoken this, He said to him, 'Follow Me.'"

~ John 21:17–19

The Lord asked Peter three times whether Peter loved Him. Each time after Peter answered in the affirmative, the Lord responded by commanding him to feed and care for His sheep and lambs. These lambs and sheep referred to the Lord's people from young to old. For Peter to *show* his love for the Lord, he was charged with feeding and shepherding God's people.

The Lord explained this feeding and shepherding of His people meant others would lead Peter to do things he would not want to do. Caring for others by feeding and shepherding often requires believers to go somewhere or do something which may not be convenient. It would not be the wish of the shepherding one, but for the sake of those being shepherded, he or she will do what is required. Maturity is manifested when a believer is led by the needs of those they are feeding and shepherding. This is the practical denial of oneself in order to care and feed the Lord's people; to follow Jesus to build up His assembly, His body. This is the kind of "death" which glorifies God because it issues in much fruit.

Again, consider a new mother. Before she has her baby, she can stay out late and party if she wants. Once she conceives, however, she is controlled by the life and need of her child. In that sense, concern for the child's well-being will lead her, even when it goes against her wishes. Likewise, when believers take up the care for the spiritual well-being of others, the need to feed and shepherd them will direct how those caring for them live.

Bearing the Cross for the Ministry of Life

The apostle Paul experienced the crucified Christ in caring for those he was bearing.

"For we who live are always delivered to death for Jesus' sake, that the life of Jesus also may be manifested in our mortal flesh. So then death is working in us, but life in you. And since we have

the same spirit of faith, according to what is written, 'I believed and therefore I spoke,' we also believe and therefore speak."
— 2 Corinthians 4:11–13

In the apostle Paul's case, it was his activities of spreading the gospel and ministering Christ to people which resulted in much persecution and suffering. This was his life-style — denying himself and taking up his cross — "*delivered to death for Jesus' sake*." However, the suffering spoken of in these verses was not an end in and of itself; there was a positive outcome. The result was the resurrection life of Jesus worked into those to whom he ministered. While he went through "death," those watching and listening to him were receiving life. Though he was suffering, his spirit of faith was active and strong. Continuing to speak and minister Christ was Paul's demonstration of inwardly seeing the glory of Jesus while in death experiences. He was not murmuring and complaining about his suffering; rather, in his speaking out the glorified Jesus by the spirit of faith, life was imparted.

"Now, I rejoice in sufferings for you, and I fill up that which is behind of the tribulations of Christ in my flesh, for his body, which is the assembly [ekklesia]; . . . Christ in you the hope of glory: whom we announce, admonishing every man, and teaching every man, in all wisdom, to the end that we may present every man perfect [mature] in Christ. Whereunto also I toil, combating according to his working, which works in me in power."
— Colossians 1:24, 27b–29, DBY

How could Paul rejoice in his sufferings unless he was looking at the outcome of his labor, and not at the sufferings? Paul had the same heart and motivation as Jesus to build His ekklesia — His Body. Just as Jesus suffered and went to the cross for building up His ekklesia, Paul did the same. Paul participated in the Lord's tribulation for dispensing the riches of Christ through ministering the Word for believers to see and live according to the reality of Christ in them, the hope of glory.

This is both for cherishing and nourishing believers under his care — they would grow to maturity and be perfected in Christ. Today, believers also can partake of the afflictions of Christ for the sake of cherishing and nourishing others for the building up of the Body. The correct understanding of suffering for believers, therefore, is related to the labor of building up His Body.

Denying Self in Order to Save Some

Paul cherished others by being flexible for diversity among people making them comfortable with him so that they might receive the Christ he was ministering. It is also by this flexibility he earned the title of an approved one, a peace maker in unifying the Lord's ekklesia with a multitude of different kinds of individuals.

> ". . . and to the Jews I became as a Jew, that I might win Jews; to those *who are* under the law, as under the law, that I might win those who are under the law; to those *who are* without law, as without law (not being without law toward God, but under law toward Christ), that I might win those *who are* without law; to the weak I became as weak, that I might win the weak. I have become all things to all *men*, that I might by all means save some. Now this I do for the gospel's sake, that I may be partaker of it with *you*."
> – 1 Corinthians 9:20–23

Paul was a Jew who grew up under strict Jewish customs. Yet, he denied himself and left His comfort zone, culture, natural inclinations, and biases in order to fit in with different kinds of people around him for whom he was burdened to gain for Christ. If a minister expects others to be like him and be compatible with him before serving them, it would be nearly impossible for such a minister to bring people to Christ and to nurture them for Christ. Consider Jesus Christ: He left His "comfort zone" of being God and came to fit into every person's environment and culture around the world. No matter a person's ethnicity or socioeconomic situation, nobody must first change before receiving and believing into Christ. Jesus stepped out of His heavenly environment to fit into man's lowly and earthly surroundings in order to gain every person.

The more believers are willing to deny themselves, leaving their own comfort zones while being genuinely comfortable with people from diverse backgrounds, the more the Lord can use them to minister to others while participating in the ekklesia. This teaching of "denying yourself" according to Scripture can be practiced only in the context of doing a ministry to serve others for the building up of the Lord's ekklesia.

When the Lord's ekklesia gathers as described in 1 Corinthians chapters 11-14, believers from contrary factions are included. In such as an environment the "approved" or "genuine" ones are manifested (1 Cor. 11:19). Those so approved are experiencing flexibility by denying themselves in order to be open for fellowship with every believer. Moreover, they bring peace and fellowship between those who normally do not communicate. They have become "*all things to all men*" in order to gain some for Christ and His ekklesia.

A Portrait of a Cherishing Person

What is it like to live in the humanity of Christ and express His divine attributes?

> "Love is patient, love is kind. Love does not envy, is not boastful, is not conceited, does not act improperly, is not selfish, is not provoked, and does not keep a record of wrongs. Love finds no joy in unrighteousness but rejoices in the truth. It bears all things, believes all things, hopes all things, endures all things."
> – 1 Corinthians 13:4-7, HCSB

This chapter on love is embedded in the chapters relating to the building up of the Lord's ekklesia (starting from 1 Cor. 11:17 through to the end of 1 Cor. 14). It is in this context love is defined, because it is only in this real love believers can minister Christ and build up others. Without experiencing Christ and having this love expressed through His children, it is impossible to care for others for the building up of His body.

The closest example of this kind of love is, again, between a mother and child. That is why if believers are to serve the Lord and be fruit bearers, then everyone needs to be such spiritual mothers and fathers caring for both non-believers — that they will come to Christ — and for the newer, younger, or weaker believers — that they may grow and become such ministers themselves. This is what it means to, "*love one another just as I* [Jesus] *have loved you*" (John 13:34). Unlike today's popular usage of the word "love," the biblical usage is much deeper with the implication of sacrificing something for the person being loved.

Therefore, loving "sinners" by caring for their salvation, and loving other believers by caring for their growth, touches the core of one's character and motivation. This kind of love, truly, means death to the self, requiring the denial of natural, selfish inclinations. Every believer should express this kind of love, not just a few select clergymen.

Practice: Cherishing!

Spend time cherishing others for the sake of nourishing them with Christ.

Try going out of your comfort zone; out of your way to do something for someone else. Reach out to cherish someone close to you (or around you) by considering one or two of the examples of Christ and how you can follow His pattern to do the same to cherish another person.

List a few names of people close to you who need cherishing:

After each name, write down what you may want to do to cherish that person in the coming days or weeks:

Person #1:_____

Prayer: _____

What can I do: _____

Person #2:_____

Prayer: _____

What can I do: _____

11

NOURISHING AND MAKING DISCIPLES IN HOMES

Before starting this chapter, there needs to be a clear understanding a minister, servant, or worker of the Lord Jesus is not a "special" believer belonging to a "special group" or "class." According to the New Testament revelation, *every* believer should be a minister, servant, or worker. Every believer should serve the Lord according to their God-given capabilities. Since the time of Martin Luther, the "priesthood of all believers" has been a cardinal doctrine recovered for His people. Some ministers may be much more capable than others or may have a much larger impact on people. However, every believer needs to understand he or she is a minister, even if they can only impact one person.

As pointed out earlier, human civilization is not built by a few but by every working human being. It is built by each family — children from generation to generation. This is the same for God's ekklesia — the divine kingdom is spiritually built family by family. The goal of these chapters is not to motivate the few to become big ministers (in the sense of having an impact on thousands of people). Rather, it is to inspire every believer to do their little part according to their capacity. What is presented in these chapters is something every believer can do. It does not require any special gift or talent, only faith wherein God is co-working with us coupled with our diligence to start caring for just one other person's spiritual well-being — at a minimum.

Nourish: To Unveil the Person and Work of Jesus Christ

> "I planted, Apollos watered, but God gave the increase. So then neither he who plants is anything, nor he who waters, but God who gives the increase."

> "For we are God's fellow workers; you are God's field, *you* are
> God's building. According to the grace of God which was given
> to me, as a wise master builder I have laid the foundation, and
> another builds on it. But let each one take heed how he builds
> on it. For no other foundation can anyone lay than that which is
> laid, which is Jesus Christ."
>
> ~ 1 Corinthians 3:6–7, 9–11

Paul and Apollos are good examples of effective servants — ministers of the Lord. They planted and watered. Paul first went to Corinth to plant the seed of life. Apollos followed and watered the saints. Paul then wrote letters to the distracted Corinthians to water them more by pointing them back to Jesus Christ during the various problems the Corinthians were facing. No matter the difficulties the Corinthian believers were facing, Paul unveiled and applied Jesus Christ for their focus and experience. It is the Word conveying Jesus Christ Who is the seed of life. It is the Spirit of Jesus Christ Who is the water of life. Scripture by itself is not the seed of life — if Jesus Christ is not the focus of the message. If the Spirit of Jesus Christ is not ministered in our teachings, then the listener is not being watered. It is the planting and watering from ministers which allows God to grow in believers.

As shown in earlier chapters, receiving Christ as the Word comes through logical understanding, and receiving the Spirit as water comes through faith. This is what it means to "nourish" wherein they appreciate the knowledge of Jesus Christ and receive by faith their understanding of Christ. The cherishing of people as discussed in the previous chapter is for this type of nourishing. Without nourishing, the best a minister can be is a good humanitarian worker or a good friend to provide sympathy. However, caring for people's physical and psychological needs (cherishing) should lead to satisfying people's deepest and eternal needs, which is Jesus Christ — their true requirement. Therefore, cherishing is for nourishing. Cherishing is loving with His love; but this cherishing must be accompanied with nourishing — supplying that same person(s) with the nourishment of Christ to produce the growth in life.

Ultimately, nourishing is for God's building. The Corinthians weren't just a "field" — a farm — for growing. "Growing" is God's act of "building." God is building His ekklesia through the growing of believers. God's building (the ekklesia) is not physical. The ekklesia is a spiritual building made up of Christ growing in men. The more Christ grows in many diverse men (male and female), the more God's spiritual house is built, His building. All ministers — servants and workers of the Lord — are for this one building. All their work of service is for God's eternal purpose of having this building, God's ekklesia which is the Bride of Christ and the Body of Christ. There should be as many ministers as there are believers who work together with the same goal: fulfilling God's eternal purpose of having His ekklesia.

Since the foundation laid by Paul is Jesus Christ, all those coming after him involved in the building need to take heed to construct with precious materials which are produced by the Seed of Life and the water of the Spirit. Understanding the truth will help believers know teachings which are healthy to use for planting and watering. The subject of truth will not be discussed in these chapters since it is the focus of the first two books by the same author: *One Ekklesia* and *One Truth*. If there is an understanding of what is nourishing — the unveiling of the person and work of Jesus Christ — then it can be passed on in service to others whereupon nourishing will happen. Those being supplied will grow, and the Lord's ekklesia will be built up.

Leading and Discipling Believers towards Growth and Maturity

Every follower of Jesus should participate as begetting fathers by feeding others and raising them as their own "children" so they may walk worthily of God. One who feeds also has the authority to lead and disciple others.

> ". . . but have been gentle in the midst of you, as a nurse [nursing mother] would cherish her own children. Thus, yearning over you, we had found our delight in having imparted to you not only the glad tidings of God, but our own lives also, because you had become beloved of us. For you remember, brethren, our labour and toil: working night and day, not to be chargeable to any one of you, we have preached to you the glad tidings of God. You are witnesses, and God, how piously and righteously and blamelessly we have conducted ourselves with you that believe: as you know how, as a father his own children, we used to exhort each one of you, and comfort and testify, that you should walk worthy of God, who calls you to his own kingdom and glory."
>
> – 1 Thessalonians 2:7–12

224 | ONE Life & Glory

In order to properly raise a family, children need to be cherished and nourished. Additionally, there is also the need to guide and discipline children to become useful people in society. If a person only grows physically but does not know how to work and get things done, that person cannot in the long run contribute to the growth of the family. Therefore, in addition to giving birth, cherishing and nourishing, there is the need for education and coaching so a person can work and contribute to the family and society.

Likewise, a proper minister (servant) of the Lord will do the work of parenting in their ministry. They will cherish, nourish, and disciple believers under their care so those discipled will, in turn, be able to serve the Lord to accomplish God's purpose.

Since Paul cherished and nourished these Thessalonian believers as a nursing mother, he had the standing and stature to exhort them as a father. The word for "exhort" in the Greek, once again, is *parakaleō*, which means, "To call for someone to come alongside." Paul wanted those whom he brought to the Lord — to whom he ministered Christ — to be those who would then come alongside him to do what he was doing in the same way with the same purpose. This is what it means to make disciples, and thus gain more co-laborers to spread the kingdom of God.

The analogy Paul used in this section is clearly of a father and mother rearing their children. Consider how, as a mother, ministers were "nursing" new believers as babies. As those new believers grew, the ministers (as fathers) called these young believers to come alongside to participate in ministry. This is what it means to "exhort" as a father. It is common for fathers when doing a project, whether remodeling, fixing a car, or gardening to call their kids over to work alongside them and to help them. Doing so teaches children how to do things, finish projects, and to help complete the parents' various goals.

In ancient societies, this was a common way for fathers to train their children. When a father worked in a specific trade, his sons were expected to learn and continue in the same trade. The "trade" of every believer is to minister Christ. This is the goal which will build up the ekklesia. This was Paul's ministry and goal; therefore, he exhorted those whom he discipled to serve the Lord as he did.

Comfort Follows Exhortation

Anyone who starts to serve people for the Lord will experience some form of suffering, rejection, or disappointment. That is why comfort follows exhortation. Paul comforted those whom he was exhorting. If ministers do not have the ability to comfort those they are discipling, *those believers* will not last for long in their service; they will become discouraged and give up. That is why comforting is such a critical part of being a father who exhorts. A father who only knows how to exhort, but not comfort, will incite resentment among or between his children. It is the same spiritually. Those exhorting others to serve also need to provide comfort when needed.

Through a minister's cherishing, nourishing, and exhorting with comforting, those being discipled will walk worthy of God's calling. There is only one chapter in the New Testament which explains: "*walk worthy of God.*" It is found in Ephesians 4. In Ephesians 4 Paul says for us to walk worthy of God's calling means for us to keep the oneness for the building up of the Body of Christ. This is done through the participation of every member of the body. This was the apostle's goal in their service to all believers: They would become those who could keep the oneness with all different kinds of believers thereby contributing to the building up of the Lord's ekklesia.

Fathers – Worthy of Being Imitated

There is a need in the Body for more fathers, not more instructors; a begetting father is worthy to be imitated.

> "I do not write these things to shame you, but as my beloved children I warn you. For though you might have ten thousand instructors in Christ, yet *you do* not *have* many fathers; for in Christ Jesus I have begotten you through the gospel. Therefore I urge you, imitate me."
>
> – 1 Corinthians 4:14–16

The difference between an instructor and a father is this: an instructor can only teach; a father can teach and beget. A father's relationship with those he teaches is a *life* relationship, whereas, an instructor can only transfer knowledge. Likewise, a father has innate love and patience not associated with an instructor. Paul said there are "*ten thousand instructors in Christ,*" but not many fathers. In this hour, there is a desperate need for more servants of the Lord who are fathers, with the ability to impart life and equip God's children for His ekklesia. Because of his relationship with the saints in Corinth, it was appropriate for Paul to both warn and ask those he brought to the Lord to imitate him. The word "imitate" here means "to follow," like "exhort" in the previous verses. Paul was asking believers he was shepherding to do what he does by following him.

In context believers were to imitate Paul in the way he served the Lord and ministered Christ to others. In general, when human fathers raise their children, it is common for them to ask their children to follow in their footsteps – in their aspiration, diligence, philosophies, and positive characteristics. Yet, among believers, this kind of "fathering" to other believers is a foreign thought. Believers think only prominent ministers can have followers, but, every believer can and should have a few or at least one newer or younger believer as their follower, imitator, or disciple.

Consider how many prominent ministers have disappointed or led astray millions of their followers because of moral failures or unhealthy teaching. What if there were tens of millions of ministers, rather than a culture of "celebrity" teachers and ministers? That way, failures among these ordinary ministers would only impact a couple of believers at a time. On the positive side, when every believer learns to be a nursing mother or an exhorting father, the scriptural way of building the Lord's assembly will occur – His purpose would then be fulfilled.

> "And Jesus came and spoke to them, saying, 'All authority has been given to Me in heaven and on earth. Go therefore and make disciples of all the nations, baptizing them in [into] the name of the Father and of the Son and of the Holy Spirit, teaching them to observe all things that I have commanded you; and lo, I am with you always, [even] to the end of the age.' Amen."
> – Matthew 28:18–20

After the Lord Jesus resurrected and ascended, all authority was given to Him. He then commanded believers to go and disciple all the nations by immersing people into the Triune God, teaching those who were immersed the entire counsel of God (Acts 20:27). This "sending" to make disciples happens with the Lord's authority. This authority subdues Satan and all his minions. When believers follow the Lord's command to "go," they must exercise the Lord's authority not fearing any of the attacks from the enemy. Making disciples spans the entire process of child-rearing: raising up believers by begetting through faith and baptism, growing them through nourishing teachings whereby they will eventually become functional disciples who will not waver in loving and serving the Lord to further His purpose.

When believers obey and "go" to do this service, the Lord promises He will surely be with them until the end of the age. This promise from the Lord was given in conjunction with commissioning believers. The Lord's presence, and the believer's experience of Him, was more pronounced as the believer followed the Lord's command to make more disciples among the nations. In John 15:8, the Lord said disciples are those who bear fruit. Therefore, all believers, as disciples, are to bring sinners from regeneration all the way into bearing remaining fruit.

Some believers may have special gifts which enable them to excel in a particular service such as evangelism, teaching, giving to the poor, prayer or healing, but taking care of and making disciples one or two at a time throughout the Christian life is a basic call to every believer. One who is especially gifted and enjoys being a prayer warrior should still try and lead another person to the Lord by cherishing, nourishing, and exhorting that person to serve the Lord. This is like a human family. A parent may be a doctor, an entertainer, or a factory worker, but regardless of their prominence or any achievements in their career, they still have a responsibility to raise their family.

Believers tend to fall on one of two sides. On one side, are the gifted and stronger believers, who often want to do something great for the Lord; however, to take care of a couple of people over a long period of time seems too menial to them. They may think this job is beneath their calling and underutilizes their ability. On the other side, there is a majority of believers who do not consider themselves qualified enough to spiritually take care of *any* person. Or, they consider that it is simply not their job. This is the cause of a major deficiency among God's people: the raising up of spiritual families from house to house.

The word for "go" in verse 19 means, "to go on one's way" (Vine's Expository Dictionary). This implies believers do not necessarily have to stop what they are doing and go on a mission to a foreign land. Instead, it emphasizes that as believers "go" from one location to another, living their life, they are to disciple others. Believers need to incorporate the Lord's commission of making disciples into their daily coming and going in life. Only some can go to a foreign land for mission work, but every believer can make disciples as they go about their daily life. There needs to be such an awareness wherein wasted time and opportunities can be seized for making disciples.

Never Force, Coerce or Pressure Others

It is important for ministers to always respect the free will and choices of others — never force, coerce, or pressure others into doing anything.

> "And the Spirit and the bride say, Come. And let him that hears say, Come. And let him that is athirst come; he that will, let him take [the] water of life freely."
>
> – Revelation 22:17, DBY

As believers practice making disciples — begetting, cherishing, nourishing, and exhorting — there is danger of becoming overzealous. Boundaries may be crossed where the person receiving help feels coerced, pressured, or forced to do something they do not wish to do. Free will always has to be honored.

God gave man a free will to choose at the very beginning when He made man; even at the very end of the Bible, in the last chapter of Revelation, free will is active and honored. Jesus calls people to "come" to drink the water of life, but their response depends on whether they desire to come or not when they hear the call. There is still free will on the part of the person hearing the call whether to drink. Therefore, vigilance is needed for those who practice making disciples. They must always respect the free will or choice of others. When care for people is out of true love, then patience and forgiveness will be present, especially when those being shepherded disappoint the shepherd. Once a shepherd either tries to pressure people to follow the Lord or becomes upset with those who do not adequately respond to their discipling, it is no longer the Lord's service.

For example, a ministering believer may challenge a newer believer to study the Bible and regularly pray or share the gospel with friends. Yes, there should be exhortation — calling the believer to come alongside — but there should be sensitivity as well. The minister must guard against coercing others to do these things. Even more, no matter how much a minister may be a spiritual help to someone, it is dishonoring to the Lord Jesus as the Head of all believers if they tell someone what to do or how to live. For example, they should not tell someone how to dress, what movies to watch, or what types of music they cannot listen to. The minister's calling is to feed . . . to be a pattern to others trusting the Spirit to work in the life and conscience of other believers regarding how they will live before the Lord.

Use Opportunities—Anytime and Anywhere—In Twos or Threes

> "For where two or three are gathered together in My name, I am there in the midst of them."
>
> – Mathew 18:20

"In My name" in the Greek should be translated, "*into* My name." "In My name" to most people is understood as "one being a representative of the Lord," such as saying, "I am doing this in the name of the king." That means the king is not actually here, but the representative stands in for the king. A gathering "in" His name, then, would mean the gathering is with a formal intention of representing the Lord's name.

However, "*into*" the Lord's name means the gathering is inside the sphere of or inside the person of the Lord Jesus. That is why the Lord is in their midst — the gathering is *inside Christ*. The gathering envelopes all Who Jesus Christ *is* and *has accomplished*.

The "name of the Lord" is the very person of the Lord Himself. That is why there is no other name given to men whereby they must be saved (Acts 4:12); and why when men call upon the name of the Lord, they are saved (Rom. 10:13). The name can save, because the name of Jesus is the very *person* of Jesus. His name is just Himself; otherwise, the name "Jesus" by itself, separated from the person, means nothing; it cannot save. The gathering into the Lord's name is with the direction or the focus of the gathering to be in the very person, presence, and Spirit of the Lord Jesus. This can and should happen anytime or anywhere when "two or three" believers are together. They, so gathered, should direct their conversation toward the person or work of the Lord Jesus. In doing so, the Lord will be in their midst, and they will be in the Spirit of the Lord with all His riches.

Therefore, in caring for people — begetting (the gospel), cherishing, nourishing, and exhortation — ministers need to take every possible opportunity to bring others *into* the name of Jesus Christ.

The Lord Jesus was a perfect example. He took opportunities to minister at a wedding and as He reclined to eat with people. As He journeyed from one point to another, He ministered at people's houses and taught along the way. Jesus spent much of His time ministering as He went on His way to individuals and small groups of people. In comparison, only a few times in Scripture did He preach to or teach to large crowds. Jesus practiced what He commanded believers to do: to make disciples as they went along their way.

Most Christians only consider going to church, or going to an organized event or meeting, to be a time for "fellowship" with other believers. Ministering or shepherding others also occurs in such venues, but such tradition makes shepherding and ministering to others limited and inefficient. If Christians would consider ministry to occur "where two or three" are gathered into His name, all sorts of opportunities throughout the day and week would open! Fellowship can occur for a short period of time, even for five-minutes. It can happen while commuting to work. It can transpire over a coffee break, at a restaurant, or even while shopping with another person. Understanding this, every believer can find opportunities to minister Christ by meeting with another person or two, during the normal activities of life.

This verse cannot be emphasized enough. Practicing this verse will liberate believers to meet others anywhere, anytime, and for any length of time. There is no need for set events, or a special place like a church. No agenda, schedule, or material is required. What freedom to be able to gather and have the Lord Jesus in one's midst, wherever they are! Practicing this brings freedom for every believer to serve and minister Christ. Without this understanding, believers may always think they need to be somewhere or do something special in order to do the work of their ministry. This exercise is also the way to fulfill Paul's charge in Romans 16 to greet other Christians who are not in the same church. Here is the simplicity of obeying Paul's command to go greet and fellowship with unfamiliar believers — anytime, anywhere . . . *into* the Lord's name.

Houses (Homes): The Preferred Place for Ministry

Jesus Himself regularly practiced visiting people in their homes. A person's own home is where they can truly be who they are. It expresses their personality and where they feel the most comfortable and most protected. It is their place of living, and the place where all family members gather.

It is significant God's eternal purpose — the ekklesia — would be right inside a believer's home. Just as God Himself wants to live inside His people, His ekklesia is also in His people's homes. God wants to be in the center of His children's life and family. Instead of going to a religious building such as a temple or a church to have a relationship with God, God comes to His people's homes to have a relationship with them. Since the homes of people are so central to God's assembly (His eternal purpose), then it makes sense why homes were the very place where Jesus Christ ministered when He was on the earth.

Matthew's House

> "After these things He went out and saw a tax collector named Levi, sitting at the tax office. And He said to him, 'Follow Me.' So he left all, rose up, and followed Him. Then Levi gave Him a great feast in his own house. And there were a great number of tax collectors and others who sat down with them. And their scribes and the Pharisees complained against His disciples, saying, 'Why do You eat and drink with tax collectors and sinners?' Jesus answered and said to them, 'Those who are well have no need of a physician, but those who are sick. I have not come to call the righteous, but sinners, to repentance.'"
>
> – Luke 5:27–32

Matthew (Levi) wrote the gospel of Matthew — he was a tax collector. Matthew was working at his tax-collecting office when Jesus came to call him to be a disciple. The first place Jesus went after Matthew was called was his house; they had a "party" with all of Matthew's fellow tax collectors and sinners. It would have been normal for Matthew to gather those in his same social circle to meet Jesus. At Matthew's home, the Lord was with those who were comfortable with each other where they were enjoying food and drink together. After calling Matthew, the Lord didn't bring him to the temple or the synagogue to pray or to worship; rather, he went to his house to feast. The religious people were offended because Jesus was eating and drinking with tax collectors and sinners, but Jesus said this was exactly where He should be: as a physician hanging out with those who needed Him. Where did he find the "sick" who needed Him? Not in the temple, but in a home.

It is the same today. The "tax collectors and sinners" of today likely won't be going to church. They will be hanging out with friends and fellow "sinners" in each other's apartments or houses. If a person is willing to invite a ministering believer to eat in his or her house, it shows such a person is open to receive them as a friend.

It is clear Jesus specifically intended to minister in homes. Let's look at a couple more examples to see how Scripture affirms this.

Zacchaeus' House

Jesus visited and lodged at Zacchaeus' house, bringing salvation to his household.

> "Now behold, there was a man named Zacchaeus who was a chief tax collector, and he was rich. And he sought to see who Jesus was, but could not because of the crowd, for he was of short stature. So he ran ahead and climbed up into a sycamore tree to see Him, for He was going to pass that way. And when Jesus came to the place, He looked up and saw him, and said to him, 'Zacchaeus, make haste and come down, for today I must stay at your house.' So he made haste and came down, and received Him joyfully. But when they saw it, they all complained, saying, 'He has gone to be a guest with a man who is a sinner.' Then Zacchaeus stood and said to the Lord, 'Look, Lord, I give half of my goods to the poor; and if I have taken anything from anyone by false accusation, I restore fourfold.' And Jesus said to him, 'Today salvation has come to this house, because he also is a son of Abraham.'"
>
> – Luke 19:2–9

In this story, Jesus didn't preach to Zacchaeus. He simply invited Himself to Zacchaeus' house. It is certain that Zacchaeus already knew what Jesus was about – he was attracted to Jesus. As a result of Jesus' offer to go to Zacchaeus' house, Zacchaeus came to salvation.

The religious people, however, were upset because Jesus had the audacity to go to a sinner's house. Religion cares for their places of worship where people perform religious duties, but Jesus cared for people in their homes. It was not possible to perform a religious ritual at table with a bunch of sinners, but it was easy for Jesus to be Himself in the homes of people – caring for people and enjoying eating and drinking with them. This is the best environment for salvation: in a sinner's home, rather than in a religious place. Zacchaeus received transforming salvation, so much so that he was willing to make restitution for his past wrongs, and to help those who were less fortunate.

One cannot be a good minister — a servant of the Lord — if one doesn't know how to visit the homes of people. Very few believers have the ability or the opportunity to preach to hundreds or thousands, but every believer can visit someone's home. Believers need to learn to invite themselves to a person's home for Christ to be ministered so salvation can come to that household.

A Leper's House in Bethany

Another home Jesus visited was the leper's house in Bethany, where Jesus would also be anointed.

> "After two days it was the Passover and *the Feast* of Unleavened Bread. And the chief priests and the scribes sought how they might take Him by trickery and put *Him* to death. But they said, 'Not during the feast, lest there be an uproar of the people.' And being in Bethany at the house of Simon the leper, as He sat at the table, a woman came having an alabaster flask of very costly oil of spikenard. Then she broke the flask and poured *it* on His head."
>
> "Assuredly, I say to you, wherever this gospel is preached in the whole world, what this woman has done will also be told as a memorial to her."
>
> ~ Mark 14: 1–3, 9

What a contrast between religion and the Lord's way of relaxing and enjoying people in their home! In Mark 14:1–3, the religious leaders were planning to trick Jesus so they could kill Him while Jesus was enjoying fellowship with believers in a leper's house. In ancient biblical times, people with leprosy were to be shunned and avoided due to the fact they could spread the disease. Yet, Jesus ignored the disease, and entered the leper's home where he was welcomed and comfortable. There was no home so sinful and worldly where Jesus would not visit. He enjoyed a meal there, and a woman came to anoint Him with precious ointment. This was not in the temple or a religious meeting place, but in a home where Jesus was served and loved. Jesus Himself chose to take refuge there. Homes became the place where those who love Him could serve Him and have fellowship with Him.

The woman's act of pouring out costly oil on the Lord Jesus was most endearing to the Lord, because it reflected a responsive and sacrificial love. The preaching of the gospel speaks of the Lord's love for man while her "pouring out" testifies to the believers' love for the Lord. Jesus poured Himself out for man. Man's response to Jesus should be a "pouring out" upon Him. Thus, this story concerning the woman who poured out her expensive ointment on the Lord should be shared whenever the gospel is preached. This was the only instance of an action performed by a person where the Lord said should be a memorial . . . and it happened in a home. The woman didn't go out to do anything great in the sense of traveling the world to preach the gospel or feed the poor. She did something simple which touched the Lord's heart, right in a home. This didn't happen at the temple, at any preaching event, or at a "revival" meeting, but at a leper's home while having a meal.

Every believer can do something extraordinary in a home fellowship with Jesus. Visiting homes to bring salvation and nourishment can open the opportunity for anyone, both believers doing the visiting and those being visited, to become remarkable lovers of the Lord Jesus.

Jesus Commissioned Believers and Sent Them to Peoples' Houses

Jesus sent the twelve disciples, then seventy others, and all subsequent workers to go out and spread the gospel in the exact same way.

> "Then He called His twelve disciples together and gave them power and authority over all demons, and to cure diseases. He sent them to preach the kingdom of God and to heal the sick. And He said to them, . . . 'Whatever house you enter, stay there, and from there depart.'"
>
> – Luke 9:1–3a, 4

> "After these things the Lord appointed seventy others also, and sent them two by two before His face into every city and place where He Himself was about to go. Then He said to them, 'The harvest truly [is] great, but the laborers [are] few; therefore pray the Lord of the harvest to send out laborers into His harvest.

Go your way; behold, I send you out as lambs among wolves. Carry neither money bag, knapsack, nor sandals; and greet no one along the road. But whatever house you enter, first say, 'Peace to this house.' And if a son of peace is there, your peace will rest on it; if not, it will return to you. And remain in the same house, eating and drinking such things as they give, for the laborer is worthy of his wages. Do not go from house to house. Whatever city you enter, and they receive you, eat such things as are set before you. And heal the sick there, and say to them, 'The kingdom of God has come near to you.'"

– Luke 10:1–9

In Luke 9, the Lord first sent the twelve disciples into the homes of people. Then in the very next chapter, He increased the "sending" to seventy others. In fact, the Lord asked them to pray for more workers to be sent forth into the harvest. That means if the Lord has more workers (which would include all the Lord's workers since then), He will send them in exactly the same way.

This is significant to consider: This is how the Lord wants believers to serve Him in the harvest. With all power and authority, He has given to the workers, one would think Jesus would have told them to hold a big meeting, or a conference, in order to preach the gospel and perform healings. No, they were commanded to go to people's houses — so insignificant, with a limited audience to witness their works of power if they were performed. This is counter-intuitive to how people often think ministers should work! Typically, people think the bigger the audience, the better; it is much more efficient this way. But that was not the way the Lord commanded the disciples. His way and direction, which is consistent with His eternal purpose for the ekklesia is in homes — His way is to go from house to house.

Note also how the Lord specifically directed them to "*greet no one along the road*." It seems He didn't want them distracted by those along the road. Surely there are needy people along the road, but the Lord's desire was homes, households. People "along the road" can be defined as anyone who cannot be tracked or followed back to their homes. Since the Lord's goal here was households, He wanted His disciples to spend time in people's homes rather than with random people "along the road." Certainly, there is nothing wrong with helping and preaching to people along the road, which

Jesus and the apostles did. But in the Lord's instruction to His workers here, He specifically excluded those people so that they could spend time to find a "son of peace" and focus on households in homes.

Gaining the Entire Household

"Harvesting" takes place in peoples' homes. So, the Lord Jesus thrust workers to go into homes, going house by house, looking for "sons of peace." He instructed workers to bring the peace of the Lord into a house; if the household accepted this peace, it meant there was a person of peace there. This peace included not just the words concerning the Lord Jesus as the gospel, but also the minister's care, cherishing, and love.

When there is a person of influence in the house who welcomes the Lord's worker bringing such peace, a person of peace is present. When such a person is found, the Lord instructs disciples to remain in that house. The worker is to stay and cultivate that house — to beget, cherish, nourish, and make disciples of those in the household. That household, along with all its friends and relatives connected with it, is the "field" for harvesting — the place to bear remaining fruit. It is from such a house an assembly (ekklesia) can be raised.

It is important to note a house represents the entire city. One house receiving the Lord's peace means the entire city has favor with God. If no house receives the Lord's peace, then the entire city is condemned. How significant it is to work in the way the Lord has directed — finding a house with a person of peace, and from that household, continuing to disciple and shepherd in order to gain all those connected to that house. As ministers work from such a house, they will find the connections from that house will spread throughout the entire city. So, from one house, more and more houses will be gained — people will come to salvation and will grow to serve the Lord as remaining fruit with the Lord's ekklesia being manifested.

This is contrary to the typical way Christians practice ministry today. The method most Christian workers use is to gain one person at a time through various venues: at church, open air, or TV for example. After individuals believe through this method of gospel outreach, they are directed to leave their home environments to go to church to meet with other Christians to hear more teachings and ministry of the Word. The person's household is basically neglected. It is not necessarily that today's methods are wrong; they are just completely different from the way the Lord outlined in this portion of Scripture, which is to work right inside the house until the entire household is won over to the gospel and discipled.

Gathering people only into churches builds up the ministries which own those buildings; whereas, the Lord's way of directing believers to work is for building His heart's desire, which is the ekklesia, in house after house.

The Lord's way is available for every believer who wants to serve Him (which should be every believer) as a "worker." Every believer today, if they would follow what has been outlined in these chapters, will find a "son of peace" in their community — even within their social circles. If one cannot be found, then a believer can join with another fellow worker who has found someone in the community who has accepted the Lord's peace. Once such a person of peace is located, then over time, through visitations to this person's house, the ministry of begetting, cherishing, nourishing, and exhortation can take place. With the faithfulness of a farmer, the "harvest" will spread to relatives and friends networked to that house.

When there is an opening for a co-worker of Jesus to stay connected to a home with regular visits, discipling can commence in earnest, such as: Bible studies to know God's Word as truth, discourse concerning applying and experiencing Christ in the midst of the joy and challenges of life, praying for others, making requests known to God, testifying, and speaking about Jesus to their relatives and friends, making commitments to serve God and people, fellowshipping with other Christians, participating and building up the Lord's ekklesia.

An effective worker will continue cherishing, nourishing, and comforting as spiritual parents; nevertheless, don't make it into the worker's "church." Those discipled are not to be a "house church" which becomes another defined group under this laboring minister. There is a strong temptation for a worker who has been effective to regard those served by him as his people and are expected to be loyal to his ministry. Just as parents raise their children expecting them to be free and independent when mature, a co-worker of the Lord must have the same heart and direction. Fellowship between those who labored in ministry and those served shouldn't be broken, but a minister must work toward the independence of those served that they too would have their own ministries. No matter the efforts expended, those discipled will be able to build the Lord's ekklesia and gather with other Christians without the minister who served them.

If believers would heed the Lord's sending out in His way, they would find they indeed have authority over all evil forces having the ability to heal the sick. It is certain believers going out to make disciples in the power and authority of the ascended Christ have nothing to fear. Those spiritually sick and psychologically struggling will be healed in accordance with the Lord's will; moreover, physical healing will transpire.

A person of peace can be both an unbeliever who is open to the gospel of the grace of God, or one who, already a Christian, is open to the gospel of peace. God's peace is both personal and corporate. Personal peace is between a believer and God (Rom. 5:1). The corporate peace is between divided people. It is this corporate peace which unites previously divided and hostile people together (Eph. 2:14-17). Therefore, finding a person of peace can be of either category: An unbeliever seeking peace with God or a Christian seeking peace with other believers to enjoy unity in the fellowship of Jesus Christ. As workers of the Lord, we need to be ready to serve and minister to both kinds of "sons of peace."

In localities where the population are already Christians, it is just as critical to seek for the "sons of peace" among believers. Even though there may be many Christians and Christian activities, the Body of Christ may be so divided that there is a scarcity of the reality of His ekklesia; moreover, the manifestation of oneness is most likely non-existent. In such a state, the Lord would be preparing "sons of peace" among His people who are seeking for fellowship regarding the oneness of the Body of Christ. It is just as essential to find such "sons of peace" and serve their households for the building up of the Lord's ekklesia. Paul, as an apostle, did such a service. To establish the Lord's ekklesia in a home is certainly within the function of an apostle. More concerning this matter will be revealed later in this chapter.

The First Gentile Assembly

After Jesus' death, resurrection and ascension, His apostles continued to spread His ekklesia from house to house, expanding to the Gentiles. The book of Acts tells how Peter went to Cornelius' house, where Cornelius gathered his relatives and friends.

"And they said, 'Cornelius [the] centurion, a just man, one who fears God and has a good reputation among all the nation of the Jews, was divinely instructed by a holy angel to summon you to his house, and to hear words from you.'"

"And the following day they entered Caesarea. Now Cornelius was waiting for them, and had called together his relatives and close friends."

". . . how God anointed Jesus of Nazareth with the Holy Spirit and with power . . . whom they killed by hanging on a tree. Him God raised up on the third day, and showed Him openly."

"'To Him the prophets witness that, through His name, whoever believes in Him will receive remission of sins.' While Peter was still speaking these words, the Holy Spirit fell upon all those who heard the word."

– Acts 10:22, 24, 38–40, 43–44

The very first preaching of the gospel to the Nations (i.e., the Gentiles) was divinely orchestrated to be in a house, in Cornelius' home. This meeting could have been arranged anywhere, but the divine arrangement sent an unmistakable message concerning God's move in initiating the building up of His ekklesia among the Gentiles by starting in a home. Cornelius invited all his relatives and intimate friends. This was his extended "household." While his household was listening to the good news of Jesus Christ, the Spirit filled them as they were saved by faith. What a wonderful sight! Everyone in Cornelius' household was filled with the Spirit. Cornelius was a "son of peace," and through him his entire household, relatives, and friends, were saved . . . the first Gentile assembly began in a home. How significant! This is God's way of salvation: His salvation is for the entire household.

Isn't it a relief not to worry about which family member or friend is "chosen" by God for salvation? How sad it would be if the Spirit came to save a couple of relatives and friends but not others in the same household. Believers need to have faith in God's salvation for their entire household. Today, some may be quicker to believe and others slower, but it is important to believe God's heart of love is for the entire family. Although it is still up to each individual to choose the Lord, it may not ultimately work out for every family; nevertheless, it is *not* God's choice to break up families; He treasures the family unit, and desires the entire family would be saved.

Fulfilling the Apostle Paul's Command to Greet

> "And when you go into a household, greet it."
> – Matt. 10:12

> ". . . and entered the house of Zacharias and greeted Elizabeth."
> – Luke 1:40

In Romans 16, Paul, at the end of his letter to "all those called to be his holy people" in Rome (Rom. 1:7), charged them to go greet one another. In the book *One Ekklesia*, much discussion and emphasis was on the subject of "greeting." In short, it was Paul's way of bringing believers who normally gathered in divided groups to mix it up — fellowship together and become one ekklesia. The greetings among the saints brought peace between segregated groups of believers. It was after this greeting, at the end of this chapter where Paul declared: *"the God of peace shall soon crush Satan under your feet."* This punctuates the importance for believers to go greet one another.

Greeting in the days of the New Testament normally took place by visiting a home or by receiving someone into a home. It is in the environment of a comfortable home where the guest and host have time to get to know each other's welfare. This is another highlight showing it is critical to visit and have fellowship in homes.

Greeting in homes among believers; especially, with those who may be unfamiliar with each other has to be practiced if there is a heart to build up the oneness of the Body. It is so easy and comfortable to stay in one's own home. This is where bearing the cross and denying self is needed. The glory of Jesus is needed to strengthen a believer's resolve to get out of their comfort zone to visit or greet others in homes for fellowship. This is for the building up of the Lord's ekklesia resulting in glory to God and crushing of Satan.

Paul's Gospel Preaching Gained Households

> "Now a certain woman named Lydia heard *us*. She was a seller of purple from the city of Thyatira, who worshiped God. The Lord opened her heart to heed the things spoken by Paul. And when

she and her household were baptized, she begged *us*, saying, 'If you have judged me to be faithful to the Lord, come to my house and stay.' So she persuaded us."

– Acts 16:14–15

Remember the Philippian jailer who nearly killed himself after he discovered the jail doors were opened and everyone's chains were loosed – but no prisoner had left, including Paul and Silas. Then the jailer cried out: *"Sirs, what must I do to be saved?" Paul and Silas said: "Believe on the Lord Jesus Christ, and you will be saved, you and your **household** . . . Then they spoke the word of the Lord to him and to **all who were in his house** . . . Now when he had brought them into **his house**, he set food before them; and he rejoiced, having believed in God with all **his household**"* (Acts 16:25-34, excerpts).

The apostle Paul followed the Lord Jesus' way in Luke 10 by gaining households and abiding in the house of the person of peace. In fact, according to these verses, it seems as soon as one believed, the entire household followed. In both stories in Philippi we've related. Paul gained whole households, not just one person at a time. Both Lydia and the jailer were persons of peace, and through Paul, their entire households were gained. Paul then took hospitality and stayed in their homes following the pattern given by the Lord in Luke 10. A person of peace, in his or her house, we discover that the whole household is inextricably linked – connected to one another, accomplishing God's purpose for salvation.

Man's need is for salvation and God's need is for His ekklesia are both focused in the homes from house to house.

Paul Opened His Own Hired Dwelling for Shepherding

"Then he stayed two whole years in his **own rented house**. And he welcomed all who visited him, proclaiming the kingdom of God and teaching the things concerning the Lord Jesus Christ with full boldness and without hindrance."

– Acts 28:30–31, HCSB

Paul's narrative in the book of Acts ends with two verses describing Paul fellowshipping in his house, declaring Jesus Christ. The greatest apostle purposely left this impression in the record of his acts. He was not preaching to thousands, teaching in synagogues, doing a healing or deliverance ministry, or feeding the poor; rather, he was having home fellowship. He was teaching and preaching in his humble, rented house.

Remember, Paul was the same person who persecuted the ekklesia in Jerusalem by going from house to house. The memory of going into each house to drag away believers was likely an unforgettable image in Paul's mind. Those fellowshipping in homes may have been having a meal, singing, or praying. Each house Paul entered likely was doing something different at the time he arrived to arrest them. It is significant this persecutor who went from house to house persecuting believers was now ending his story in Acts in a rented house having fellowship.

What a contrast between the beginning and the end of Acts! In the beginning of Acts at the day of Pentecost, Peter preached to thousands at the temple where 5000 people were saved. Miracles became normal occurrences. At the very end of Acts, Paul is seen having fellowship in his home with a few people at a time. This may seem insignificant, but it is profound. Though this was the end of the Acts of the Apostles so recorded, we must understand that all the apostolic ministering wrought by believers sent by the Lord will not end until the Lord's return. In other words, the record must continue in our days.

An apostle literally means "one sent forth" (Vine's Expository Dictionary), as in Matthew 28:19 when the Lord Jesus charged His disciples to "*go therefore to make disciples.*" There may not be many prominent apostles such as Paul or Peter, but every believer should be an apostle since each believer is sent by the Lord Jesus to go and bear remaining fruit (John 15:16). As a sent one, not every believer can preach like Peter to thousands and do miraculous work as in the beginning of Acts. However, every believer can be an apostle in a house while teaching and experiencing fellowship as Paul did at the end of Acts. The conclusion found in Acts opens the door for every believer to continue the writing of the book of the Acts of the Apostles by visiting homes and opening their own houses to build the ekklesia. How wonderful it would be if each believer learned to share the good news of Jesus Christ? What if believers taught the truth in their own homes or in someone else's home?

The greatest minister, apostle and worker for the Lord Jesus, left us this pattern for all believers to follow. Homes is where the gospel and teaching can continue boldly without hindrance. In many places around the world today, the gospel cannot be publicly preached because churches are either closed or monitored. Yet people are being saved in their homes because the gospel is preached there. For example, the number of Christians dramatically increased in China after prominent leaders were imprisoned. Christian gatherings held in public places or churches were banned. Believers rose up to function by starting meetings from house to house. It was a blessing in disguise; forcing believers to meet in homes brought boldness to believers advancing the unhindered spread of the gospel. The same is going on in many Muslim countries today.

Therefore, all believers desiring to serve the Lord by being a minister of Christ to people around them should learn both to open their own homes to teach and fellowship, and to visit other homes for ministry. This is critical to any minister with a goal of building up God's ekklesia going from house to house. It is in these homes the gospel is preached for begetting; where love is expressed for cherishing, where Christ is unveiled for nourishing, and the place where disciples are raised up through exhortation and comforting for the building up of the Lord's ekklesia.

This author has no intention to disparage all the various ways and methods of preaching the gospel and teaching the truth. We find in Philippians 1:18 wherein believers should rejoice whenever and however the gospel is preached. The intention here is to bring to light what the Lord Jesus Himself commanded His disciples to do and how the early apostles followed that pattern. Believers today should follow as well.

Practice: Visitation

A little practicum now . . . Go out to visit neighbors, friends and family, even for a very short time. Be warm and hospitable. Have no religious forms or set ways. Hold to a view of cherishing and nourishing. At the same time open your home and regularly invite people over or on a semi-regular basis.

List a few names placed on your heart: _____

_____

_____

_____

Contact them to arrange a time for a visit.

Suggestions:
1. A meal or at least dessert together as preferred.
2. Today, there's great opportunity in sharing the gospel at coffee houses and shops — sometimes you can take a friend and, while there, meet new people who might be overhearing your conversation about the Lord . . . use every opportunity!
3. Depending on the situation, nothing spiritual needs to be brought up.
4. The easiest way to bring in Jesus Christ or the spiritual realm is to ask if there is anything you can pray for them. This could open a person's heart.
5. If there is an opening, reading a few verses together and having a short discussion will bring in spiritual nourishment. This can be done in 5–10 minutes.

12

Building: Ekklesia in Oneness and Mutuality (Section A)

The Ultimate Goal of Workers

The goal of any worker is to build up the Lord's ekklesia from house to house — the Body of Christ.

> "And I also, I say unto you that thou are Peter, and on this rock I will build my assembly [ekklesia], and hades' gates shall not prevail against it."
>
> – Matthew 16:18, DBY

> "Now, I rejoice in sufferings for you, and I fill up that which is behind of the tribulations of Christ in my flesh, for his body, which is the assembly [ekklesia]; of which I became minister, according to the dispensation of God which [is] given me towards you to complete the word of God."
>
> – Colossians 1:24–25, DBY

The book, *One Ekklesia,* shows clearly the Lord's ekklesia (assembly) is God's eternal purpose. It is for the ekklesia Jesus Christ entered humanity, died on the cross, and resurrected. His entire purpose for redemption and salvation was designed so He could build up His ekklesia, His Body. Therefore, any co-worker with the Lord, any minister or servant of the Lord, should have the same goal: to build up the ekklesia, His Kingdom. It is critical for all ministers of Christ to have this same vision and to understand it as the goal of the multiplicity of their labors — the building up of this eternal, yet practical, ekklesia from house to house. If the ekklesia is not a minister's goal, their ministry is deficient at best; likewise, at worst it could be dividing the Body of Christ.

Just as Jesus Christ suffered for the building up of His ekklesia, Paul declared it was his rejoicing in suffering for His one body, the ekklesia. It was for her he became a minister. The Word is concise concerning the purpose for which Paul became a minister and why he endured suffering in his ministry: it was for the Body of Christ, the ekklesia. Preaching the gospel to bring forth sons of God through the new birth, caring and nourishing new believers to help them grow, and exhorting believers to disciple them towards being mutually participatory members are all for the assembly. Each service provided by a myriad of ministers to people around them is for the building up of the ekklesia. If their services are for any other reason, even their best efforts will come short of God's goals.

The first two elements of service in the previous chapters — begetting and nourishing — have been generally practiced by ministers for centuries. Furthermore, exhorting and comforting for discipling to equip more ministers in homes has been to some extent taught and practiced. There are many other helpful books for equipping believers for these services. However, these three services without the last one still will not build up the Lord's ekklesia, His body will remain splintered and divided.

The reason for this is a shortage of understanding concerning the Lord's ekklesia. Without proper knowledge, gifted ministers will use their services to build up their own ministries instead of the Lord's ekklesia. When believers are congregated around ministries or churches, they are segregated without opportunities to serve according to their God-given gifts to build up the Lord's ekklesia. Now is the time for every believer to be equipped — to participate in services specifically designed for the building up of His ekklesia.

Referring to discussions in the book, *One Ekklesia*, there are three developments of the Lord's ekklesia: Constituents, reality, and manifestation. The *constituents* of the Lord's ekklesia consist of all His regenerated (born again) children. All believers are members of His ekklesia, stones for His building. The *reality* of His ekklesia is found in the fellowship of the Holy Spirit among all believers. Whenever and wherever, fellowship takes place between two or three (a few) people, the Lord is in their midst, His ekklesia becomes real.

Finally, there is the *manifestation* of His ekklesia which is uniquely described in 1 Corinthians 11:17 through 1 Corinthians 14. Although the Lord's ekklesia in the New Testament met in homes, house after house, a clear distinction must be made between the descriptions proffered in 1 Corinthians 11-14 and what may be known as "house churches." House churches can easily be another defined group not open to having fellowship with believers in other churches; they can be a place where a dominating personality prevails; or an extension of a bigger ministry under its control. However, God's ekklesia is manifested when diverse believers who may normally not be in fellowship come together for "spiritual democracy" where they become unified by remembering and lifting up Jesus alone, where everyone speaks, and shares their revelation and experience of Christ; where they do not let any one person dominate the assembly, and where each is encouraged and comforted — a place where unbelievers are convicted, and the ekklesia is built up. The ekklesia, in sum, is an assembly of diverse believers and NOT a one-man or woman show nor a cabal of speakers who dominate — "*all can prophesy one by one*" for "*each one has*" (1 Cor. 14).

Gathering Material for the Building

"Thus says the LORD of hosts: 'Consider your ways! Go up to the mountains and bring wood and build the temple, that I may take pleasure in it and be glorified,' says the LORD. '[You] looked for much, but indeed [it came to] little; and when you brought it home, I blew it away. Why?' says the LORD of hosts. 'Because of My house that [is in] ruins, while every one of you runs to his own house. Therefore the heavens above you withhold the dew, and the earth withholds its fruit. For I called for a drought on the land and the mountains, on the grain and the new wine and the oil, on whatever the ground brings forth, on men and livestock, and on all the labor of [your] hands.'"

– Haggai 1:9–11

"... but if I delay, in order that thou mayest know how one ought to conduct oneself in God's house, which is the assembly of the living God, the pillar and base of the truth."

– 1 Timothy 3:15, DBY

God's house in the OT is a type or prefigure of His ekklesia — the real house of God for eternity. Any person among God's people who are not building up His house, will not be satisfied with their Christian life. They will sense a lack of blessing from the Lord; moreover, lack of joy and supply of the Spirit will afflict them. When believers sense this lack, the Lord asks: "*Consider your ways. Are you building up God's house, or are you just caring for your own house?*"

This "caring for your own house" certainly can be the believer's physical house — which relates to selfish care afforded their physical and psychological well-being on earth. However, from a spiritual application, "your own house" can be the believers' own church or ministry. Is the worker's goal to build up his own ministry — his own house (church) — or is it indeed for the building up of the Lord's house?

All believers (who should be workers for the Lord) need to consider their ways and arise with renewed hearts to take action for the building up of God's house. All the people who are raised up through the labor of ministers are material for the building of God's house, or "wood." The minister's goal should not be to gather material for his own church or ministry, but for the Lord's house.

> "... as newborn babes desire the pure milk of the word, that you may grow thereby, if indeed you have tasted that the Lord [is] gracious."
>
> "... you also, as living stones, are being built up a spiritual house, a holy priesthood, to offer up spiritual sacrifices acceptable to God through Jesus Christ."
>
> – 1 Peter 2:2-3, 5

In Matthew 16:18, the Lord called Simon "Peter," which means "a stone." Then when Peter wrote his letter, he told all believers they too were "living stones" for the building of God's spiritual house. Peter was not unique but was a stone just like all other believers. They were all stones for God's building. In the OT the physical temple was built with physical stones, but for the eternal house of God (which is spiritual), people are needed as living stones. Therefore, all the services of believers rendered to people surrounding them are to transform them from lost sinners through regeneration (newborn babes) through to maturation — feeding them so they will become living stones for the building of God's eternal assembly.

In the OT only Israelites from one specific tribe were chosen to be priests (viz., the Levites). A priest was one who brought people to God — one who could offer sacrifices so people could be brought into fellowship with God. In the New Testament, Peter stated: believers — living stones — are also a holy priesthood. This means every believer today is a member of the New Testament priesthood, qualified to serve God, to bring people to have fellowship with Him.

Characteristics of God's Ekklesia

"For, in the first place, when you come together as a church [ekklesia] . . . for there must be factions among you in order that those who are genuine among you may be recognized."
                                              – 1 Cor. 11:18-19 ESV

"The one who speaks in a tongue builds up himself, but the one who prophesizes builds up the church [ekklesia]."
                                              – 1 Cor. 14:4 ESV

We recall how the word *ekklesia* literally was the practice of Greek democracy — an assembly of people from various factions, where everyone had the right to speak . . . no one could dominate the discourse. Therefore, there must be freedom for every believer to contribute according to their capacity when there is diversity gathered in unity.

There is only one portion in the epistles which speaks of an assembly where the Lord's ekklesia was manifested. It is found in 1 Corinthians 11:17 to the end of 1 Corinthians 14. The book, *One Ekklesia,* has an in-depth discussion on 1 Corinthians 11-14. In brief, these are the practical characteristics and activities described concerning the Lord's ekklesia:

1. It was a physical assembly at someone's house (Gaius: Rom. 16:23)
2. They had "pot-luck" meals together (1 Cor. 11:21)
3. Believers from factions were represented (1 Cor. 11:19)
4. The approved or genuine ones were needed (1 Cor. 11:19)
5. The Lord's supper with bread and cup to remember and uplift Jesus was present (1 Cor. 11:24-26)
6. Everyone was equally appreciated, accepted, and honored (1 Cor. 12)
7. Love for one another was expressed (1 Cor. 13)

8. Everyone contributed by prophesying to unveil and uplift Jesus
    Christ through praying, singing, teaching (*didache*), and testifying
    (1 Cor. 14:15, 26, 31)
9. Not one person could dominate (1 Cor. 14:30)
10. Unbelievers and novices (the "unlearned") were present — and
    could readily become worshippers of God (1 Cor. 14:24-25)

Since this unique pattern has been presented in Scripture for the
building up of the Lord's ekklesia, it is best to follow and practice all 10
items. Don't be distracted by the questions of how or how long these things
were done: such as, how many songs they sang, how long they prayed, or
was wine or juice used for the cup, etc. Focusing on these details has caused
many divisions.

In principle, the aim here is to include as many of these 10 items as
possible. If these characteristics or practices diminish, the less there is the
practical building up or the manifestation of true ekklesia. When less and
less of these elements are consistently omitted, then after a short period this
gathering will either fade away or resemble another person's ministry . . . no
longer the Lord's ekklesia.

The Lord's ekklesia in its manifestation is more than simply 2 or 3
believers who are gathered into the Lord's name. This was seen in Matthew
18 where the 2 or 3 still were deferred to the ekklesia for unsolved issues.
Since the Lord's ekklesia gathered in homes during the times of the apostles,
the number of people able to fit into a typical house would probably be in
the range of 12-25 people. Some of the larger homes probably would be able
to fit up to 50 or so people. This is not to say for believers today, ekklesia
cannot take place in a park or a public venue such as a community center or
a hotel conference room. Nevertheless, since one of the goals is for everyone
to have the opportunity to speak and participate, the number of people
cannot be too large. Keeping ekklesia in homes as in the New Testament
would insure ekklesia stays within the number of people where all 10 items
can be practiced.

Let's cross reference the 10 items in 1 Corinthians with how Acts
recorded the activities of the Lord's ekklesia.

Five Key Activities of the Ekklesia in Acts

"And they devoted themselves to the apostles' teaching and the fellowship, to the breaking of bread and the prayers."

"And day by day, attending the temple together and breaking bread in their homes [from house to house], they received their food with glad and generous hearts, praising God and having favor with all the people. And the Lord added to their number day by day those who were being saved."

– Acts 2:42, 46–47, ESV

"And every day, in the temple and from house to house, they did not cease teaching and preaching that the Christ [Messiah] is Jesus."

– Acts 5:42, ESV

"But Saul ravaged the assembly [ekklesia], entering into the houses one after another, and dragging off both men and women delivered them up to prison."

– Acts 8:3, DBY

As soon as people became believers in the Lord Jesus Christ, His ekklesia started meeting in homes. In Jerusalem, the apostles taught and ministered openly in the temple, but the ekklesia took place from house to house in the homes of various believers.

Based on these verses in Acts, let's consider the five activities were common for the Lord's ekklesia. These activities consisted of the teaching of the apostles, the fellowship of the apostles, the breaking of bread, prayers, and the gospel.

In Acts 2:42, the apostles' teaching and fellowship were a unique pair. There was only one teaching of the apostles and one fellowship of the Holy Spirit; therefore, this same pair existed in all the assemblies no matter when they took place or where they were around the globe. Whereas, the breaking of bread and prayers can be flexible depending on the situation and location. The timing of a meal and how to break bread may very well be different from house to house. The subject of prayer and how to pray may also be different. It is unreasonable and illogical to assume what one eats and what one prays would be uniform in every home; however, the apostles' teaching and fellowship cannot be altered. They should be the unique focus of every ekklesia in every home, everywhere, throughout time. Let's look at each one in more detail.

Teaching of the Apostles

This portion is the very first preaching or teaching done by Jesus' apostles. It was completely on the topic of Jesus Christ — His Person and His work. Peter used the Scriptures to expound on and describe Jesus Christ without deviating, setting an example for the teaching of Jesus Christ.

> "Men of Israel, hear these words: Jesus of Nazareth, a Man attested by God to you by miracles, wonders, and signs which God did through Him in your midst, as you yourselves also know — Him, being delivered by the determined purpose and foreknowledge of God, you have taken by lawless hands, have crucified, and put to death; whom God raised up, having loosed the pains of death, because it was not possible that He should be held by it."
>
> "Therefore let all the house of Israel know assuredly that God has made this Jesus, whom you crucified, both Lord and Christ."
>
> – Acts 2:22–24, 36

It is critical to understand the two Greek words translated for "doctrine" or "teaching": *Didachē* (Strong's #1322) and *Didaskalia* (Strong's #1319). According to Biblehub.com, *Didachē* means: Established teaching, especially a "summarized" body of respected teaching (viewed as reliable, time-honored). However, *Didaskalia* means: Applied teaching; systematic theology; Christian doctrine (teaching) as it especially extends to its necessary lifestyle (applications). These two important distinctions were discussed in depth in our text, *One Truth*.

In brief, the Greek word used for the apostle's teaching is *Didachē*, which is also the same word used for the doctrine of Jesus Christ which brings people the Father and the Son (2 John 1:9). For the same Greek word, Scripture sometimes uses *teaching* and other times, *doctrine*. Notice the believers devoted themselves to the apostles' teaching (singular). Just as there is only one doctrine of Jesus Christ, there is only one teaching of the apostles. This is the doctrine in which believers should steadfastly continue. This teaching is the unique truth of the New Testament given to all believers in John 17. All the apostles focused on only one teaching or doctrine: The person and work of Jesus Christ. It is critical for all the Lord's assemblies to focus on this essential teaching of Jesus Christ. Without this doctrine, the assembly is missing the heart of true ekklesia.

It is this teaching which brings believers into the unique fellowship of the Father and the Son (1 John 1:3). After believers heard the teaching of Jesus Christ from the apostles, it became their topic of fellowship in the ekklesia in many homes. Acts chapters 3 and 4 continue with more of the teaching of Jesus Christ. The teaching of Jesus Christ is not only in the New Testament, it likewise includes the entire OT, since Jesus Himself said the Scripture was all about Him (John 5:39; Luke 24:27). And, by the way, the early ekklesia only had the Hebrew Scriptures! The topic of Jesus Christ is unending and unsearchably rich. To build up the Lord's ekklesia, believers — as ministers — need to keep the focus and topic on Jesus Christ. Is this not amplified by the resurrected Christ with the two on the road to Emmaus where we read: *"And beginning at Moses and all the Prophets, He expounded to them in all the Scriptures the things concerning Himself"* (Luke 24:27).

There is a differentiation between the doctrine of Jesus Christ and many other doctrines (*didaskalia*) in the Bible. Many applications are designed which influence lifestyle; these teachings can be taken from the Bible. The Bible speaks of morality, head coverings, foot washing, giving to the poor, clothing, paying taxes, eldership, predestination, tongue speaking, end times, and so on. Applying these various teachings in order to influence ways to live and worship can become a distraction from the nexus of our gathering: Jesus Christ. These topics may be related to healthy Christian living and practice, or they may be items which are mentioned in passing, but they are not the primary doctrine of Jesus Christ, the heart of the assembly. These doctrines (*didaskalia*), if not used correctly, can be utilized by the enemy to toss babes to and fro carrying them into various religious schemes (Eph. 4:14).

Using the Bible, one can quote verses and support a liberal political agenda, but from the same Bible another can advocate a conservative agenda. Just about any cause, ways to live, and worship can be supported by using the Bible. However, only the doctrine of Jesus Christ can bring liberals, conservatives — those with differing opinions — into the same mind concerning Him. Therefore, how well a person can minister depends on how skillful he or she is in bringing the focus around to Jesus Christ thereby facilitating the ecclesia's quest to explore and enjoy all the riches of Christ manifested in fellowship.

> "For many deceivers have gone out into the world who do not confess Jesus Christ [as] coming in the flesh. This is a deceiver and an antichrist."
>
> "Whoever transgresses and does not abide in the doctrine of Christ does not have God. He who abides in the doctrine of Christ has both the Father and the Son."
>
> *– 2 John 1:7, 9*
>
> "And without controversy great is the mystery of godliness: God was manifested in the flesh, Justified in the Spirit, Seen by angels, Preached among the Gentiles, Believed on in the world, Received up in glory."
>
> *– 1 Timothy 3:16*

Believers have only one essential and critical doctrine – the doctrine of Christ – that Jesus Christ is God come in the flesh. This doctrine is not just related to the incarnation of Jesus (God born in the flesh), but also His sinless living, His crucifixion, His resurrection, His ascension as a Man, His crowning as Lord and Christ, the outpouring of His Spirit, His indwelling believers, His continuing work in believers, the building up of His ekklesia, and the bringing of His people into glory. This is the doctrine of God manifested in the flesh.

As the apostles taught this doctrine in the Acts and throughout the epistles, it became the all-inclusive spiritual food which is the truth for believers to eat and enjoy in the Lord's ekklesia today. Any other topic can become a controversy and a source of contention, such as how to baptize, how to have communion, whether speaking in tongues is allowed, and on and on. Believers, as ministers, need to bring any discussion and focus back to Jesus Christ. Without anyone feeling they were ignored or corrected. A skilled and mature believer will be able to relate any topic back to Jesus Christ helping everyone in the assembly to see Jesus only. These are the "approved or genuine ones" – the peacemakers as described in 1 Corinthians 11:19.

Fellowship of the Apostles

> "That which was from the beginning, which we have heard, which we have seen with our eyes, which we have looked upon, and our hands have handled, concerning the Word of life — the life was manifested, and we have seen, and bear witness, and declare to you that eternal life which was with the Father and was manifested to us — that which we have seen and heard we declare to you, that you also may have fellowship with us; and truly our fellowship [is] with the Father and with His Son Jesus Christ."
>
> — 1 John 1:1–3

The fellowship of the apostles comes from the teaching of the apostles. The fellowship and teaching of the apostles go together as a pair. The teaching brings fellowship, and the fellowship is the enjoyment (sharing) of Jesus Christ Who is the content of the teaching. John declared Jesus Christ coming in the flesh, and through which the hearers were brought into fellowship. This fellowship was not just with the apostles — it was also with the Father and His Son Jesus Christ. This is the one fellowship of the Spirit. In this fellowship believers find love, joy, peace, comfort, and strength — everything from the Spirit which is common and shared among believers. It is in this fellowship Jesus Christ is realized. Fellowship is not unilateral. It is not just listening to someone talk; it is reciprocal — multiple ways — depending on how many believers are present. Every believer is a giver and a receiver in fellowship. Through this sharing, believers experience the Father and the Son. How wonderful!

Fellowship means mutuality. It is not dictation or a one-way contribution, but a sharing from each member based on something they all have in common, which is Jesus Christ. This mutuality is expressed in the phrase "one another." There are about fifty-six incidences of "one another" in the New Testament in relation to members being in the Body. This term means believers should not only wait for someone to help them or to do something for them, but each believer has the responsibility to help and do something for another. This is considered mutual giving and receiving in the Body. This is true Body Life where each member functions in the Body. This is the Body building itself up in love as described in Ephesians 4:16.

The fellowship of the Spirit is the functioning of the Body. No matter how little or how much, every believer needs to do their part to support and supply other members in the Body; otherwise, the Body is handicapped or crippled. Listed below are just a few samples in Scripture where the fifty-six uses of "one another," revealing activities needed in Christ's body, can be found:

1. Love one another (John 13:34)
2. Same care for one another (1 Cor. 12:25)
3. Serve one another (Gal. 5:13)
4. Speaking, singing and submitting to one another (Eph. 5:18-19, 21)
5. Considering, inciting, and exhorting one another (Heb. 10:24-25)
6. Teaching and admonishing one another (Col. 3:16)
7. Prophesying, listening, and discerning one another (1 Cor. 14:29-31)
8. Bearing and forgiving one another (Col. 3:13)

This fellowship expressed in these above activities of "one another" is both the reality and the manifestation of the ekklesia. If this fellowship is missing, then there is just an empty shell with religious rituals when believers are gathered.

> "Finally, brothers, rejoice. Aim for restoration, comfort one another, agree with one another, live in peace; and the God of love and peace will be with you."
>
> "The grace of the Lord Jesus Christ and the love of God and the fellowship of the Holy Spirit be with you all."
>
> ~ 2 Corinthians 13:11, 14

When the teaching of Jesus Christ — the truth — is our focus, then the fellowship of the Holy Spirit is the believers' experience. In the fellowship of the Holy Spirit, the grace of the Lord and the love of God are found, as well as restoration, comfort, harmony, and peace. When these items are present, this is the fellowship of Jesus Christ. If discussions among believers lead in the opposite direction — disharmony, suspicion, condemnation, arguments, and unhappiness will result — this then is not the fellowship of Jesus Christ. In this chapter, practical points will be shared to help facilitate fellowship.

Questions Are Good Openings to Unveil Christ

> "He [Jesus] said to them, 'How then does David in the Spirit call
> Him 'Lord,' saying: 'The LORD said to my Lord, 'Sit at My right
> hand, Till I make Your enemies Your footstool'"?
> – Matthew 22:43-44

Jesus asked this question so people would consider Who He is: He is
the Son of God. Genuine questions are the best opening for fellowship
concerning the truth. Most people hear lectures at church with no room
for questioning; the environment is generally not open to challenge what
is being said. As a result, there is little fellowship – the more thoughtful
people are left unsatisfied. In fellowship, however, it is important people
are encouraged to ask questions. It is through various questions participants
start to consider not only the truth, but also how the truth is applied in
people's daily lives. Believers should not fear questions, but rather welcome
them since it can lead to more fellowship.

When questions arise about teachings, practices and life choices, it is best
the most knowledgeable, mature, or talkative person *does not answer* first. If
they do, they may communicate a terminal answer or dominate the time;
therefore, obstructing fellowship. The less mature or knowledgeable people
will automatically think they can no longer contribute since the "correct"
answer has been given. So, it is important for those more knowledgeable
folks to remain quiet and allow those who are the least knowledgeable to
speak first. In fact, the more knowledgeable believers should encourage
others to speak first by asking things like, "So John, how would you answer
that question?" Remember, the definition of fellowship is "participation,"
and "contribution." Everyone needs to participate and contribute.

Contributions from the least knowledgeable may present a "wrong"
answer according to the Scriptures, but that is okay because they are learning
to participate. This is like a baby learning to speak, who will say things not
all that intelligible; syllables may not be clearly enunciated. However, it is
through this learning process they eventually talk. If babies had to remain
silent until they could form a perfectly composed sentence, they would
never speak!

Let the "unbelievers" or novices regarding the Bible speak. Many
times, their answers may be surprising. They may share exactly what the

questioner or someone else in the room needs to hear. Their contribution can turn out to be more helpful than the more mature believer with all their scriptural references. The beautiful thing about fellowship is when all the contributions are added up in their aggregate, even with some wrong answers, the Spirit moves and brings light to both the questioner and the entire fellowship with love, joy, and peace. So, by focusing on fellowship rather than the "correct" answer, the goal of fellowship is reached.

All believers when answering sundry questions should learn how to apply the truth of Jesus Christ as the answer. For example, let's say someone asks, "Can someone explain the matter of a wife having to submit to her own husband? I think it is sexist." A question like that can quickly spiral downward if, for example, the discussion is centered on whether submitting to one's husband is true according to the authority of Scripture, or whether society has changed so that this Scripture is no longer valid. Those who are clear about the truth will bring up the fact that the portion in Ephesians is talking about Christ dying for His Body, the ekklesia which includes both male and female — being the real wife. Bringing up Jesus Christ in context will steer the fellowship to appreciate Christ, His work, and the real eternal marriage of the universe.

Another example would be a question about baptism by immersion. The discussion could focus on whether believers should practice this or not; why immersion is more scriptural than sprinkling, or who is qualified to baptize or be baptized. All these points can be part of the conversation, but if the overall focus is not on the truth, then arguments and lingering questions may result. Eventually, the spotlight must shift from the *practice* of baptism to the *reality* of baptism: believers are immersed into Christ. Jesus Christ is the entire universe for believers. They are in Him and will never be able to get out of Him. In Him they are a new creation. It is of God that they are in Christ Jesus. The practice of baptism itself is only a symbol for the reality a believer shares in Christ. This fellowship would then exalt Jesus Christ based on the teaching of the apostles, the truth.

In some cases, some questions just cannot be answered or at least those participating in that group cannot answer them. It is humbling to admit either there is no answer, or one simply doesn't know *how* to answer, which is perfectly fine. After trying to answer a question, if a satisfactory answer is simply not available, it is good to just say, "Let's pray and give this to the Lord, and let Him give us the answer in due time." Those hard-to-answer questions can also be brought before more mature believers not present afterwards for further fellowship. In this way the network and circle of fellowship increases to include others — their contribution may be exactly what is needed.

Fellowship should be open and non-judgmental so whoever is sharing does not feel rejected; this would cause not only the rejected person to shrink back and be withdrawn, but it would cause those observing the rejection likewise to withdraw. "I could be rejected next if I say something incorrectly," they might think. Even if someone says something obviously unscriptural, great care needs to be taken whether to openly correct that person. It is much better to have a further discussion privately with that person privately.

Be Open to Share Experiences and Difficulties

"O Corinthians! We have spoken openly to you, our heart is wide open."

– 2 Corinthians 6:11

". . . that there should be no schism in the body, but [that] the members should have the same care for one another. And if one member suffers, all the members suffer with [it]; or if one member is honored, all the members rejoice with [it]."

– 1 Corinthians 12:25–26

In home assemblies there is real and genuine fellowship, which means believers have open hearts and openly speak. If believers cannot openly speak what is in their hearts, fellowship will be hindered; everyone may be putting on a façade, putting on an act, without really knowing each other.

An ekklesia is different from going to church. One can go to church for years, listen to the sermons or messages, shake everyone's hand after the service, and maybe serving in their Sunday school program, but still not really know anyone. The reason? There is no openness to really know what is going on and what others are thinking or experiencing.

How can all the members rejoice or suffer with one another if open sharing of what each is going through, either in victory or in trials, is not presented? So, in fellowship, space must be allowed for people to openly speak from their heart.

An open environment makes the truth of Jesus Christ practical. Many times, the doctrine of Jesus may seem theoretical, only affecting what may be in the future or in the abstract. A disconnect between doctrine and present experiences may exist; therefore, believers simply don't know that the teaching of truth is very applicable in daily life, affecting practical challenges a person may be facing. When someone opens about their difficulties, those who have been comforted and have overcome similar situations, can share their experiences. Others may bring up Scriptures to apply the teaching of Jesus Christ to the situation. This is the same care given to one another. In doing so believers will see truth is applicable and experiential – grace, peace, and joy are supplied to all in the fellowship.

In an open, loving, and caring fellowship where judgment and fear do not exist, and the truth is its substance, the oneness of the Body is expressed. There is no division; moreover, mutual caring for one another is manifested. This is the apostles' doctrine and fellowship that early believers started and steadfastly continued from house to house.

An increased familiarity in a home gathering has its ups and downs – its joys and even its difficulties . . . some would even say its "dark side" in that such familiarity among believers can lead to all sorts of issues which can fester and even explode – that's why 1 Corinthians 13, the "love chapter," is inserted in the practice of ekklesia. Without this eternal-divine love, the Body of Christ will not express its reason for being – how we need the love of Jesus to keep His people together in fellowship!

Breaking of Bread

Sharing meals with believers (the "breaking of bread") and the practice of the Lord's table are important in the assembly.

> "So continuing daily with one accord in the temple, and breaking bread from house to house, they ate their food with gladness and simplicity of heart, praising God and having favor with all the people. And the Lord added to the church [assembly] daily those who were being saved."
>
> – Acts 2:46–47

> "Now in giving these instructions I do not praise [you], since you come together not for the better but for the worse. For first of all,

when you come together as a church [ekklesia], I hear that there
are divisions among you, and in part I believe it. For there must
also be factions among you, that those who are approved may be
recognized among you. Therefore when you come together in
one place, it is not to eat the Lord's Supper. For in eating, each
one takes his own supper ahead of others; and one is hungry
and another is drunk. What! Do you not have houses to eat and
drink in? Or do you despise the church [ekklesia] of God and
shame those who have nothing? What shall I say to you? Shall
I praise you in this? I do not praise you. For I received from the
Lord that which I also delivered to you: that the Lord Jesus on
the same night in which He was betrayed took bread; and when
He had given thanks, He broke it and said, 'Take, eat; this is My
body which is broken for you; do this in remembrance of Me.' In
the same manner He also took the cup after supper, saying, 'This
cup is the new covenant in My blood. This do, as often as you
drink it, in remembrance of Me. For as often as you eat this bread
and drink this cup, you proclaim the Lord's death till He comes.'"

– 1 Corinthians 11:17–26

During the time of the apostles, the breaking of bread was typically
accompanied with a meal. When the Lord Jesus first introduced the bread
and the cup, for example, it was after a meal (Matt. 28:16). As previously
pointed out, the breaking of bread can vary from house to house depending
on what is practical for that home. Keeping this in mind, below are principles
relating to this practice.

As a Meal among Believers – Satisfaction, Relaxation, and Enjoyment

A meal at the end of the day is the focal point of most households. It is the
optimum time to relax with family and friends. Eating and drinking together
always brings satisfaction; being filled up with good food and drink is about
the best experience of human life. It is also a time of enjoyment, providing
entertainment, especially back in the days when there was no television or
video games. A meal with family and friends is what a party is all about!

It is reasonable, then, the verse that follows right after the phrase they
"ate their food with gladness" says the believers were praising God, and

finding favor with all their neighbors, family, and friends. Salvation could be brought to all. Thus, many were added daily to the ekklesia.

Who wouldn't be attracted and desire salvation when invited to a meal where believers can be seen eating and drinking together, full of peace, love, and joy? During a meal is when hearts are open in which there is time to really get to know one another. It may be like a "potluck" - "brunch" – or BBQ where a few people are gathered here and there conversing, some discussing meaningful topics of life, while others laugh and engage in lighter topics. Children and young people might play and happily chat. There is no hint of any religious rituals, but the name of Jesus is mentioned and lifted up; there, God is glorified.

A meal together will manifest either harmony as in Acts 2 or division as in 1 Corinthians 11. In 1 Corinthians 11 rich believers brought their food and ate together, while poorer believers didn't have enough to eat. Instead of sharing in harmony, there was division between those who had abundance and those who did not. Due to this division, Paul said it was not the Lord's Supper they were celebrating. The Lord's Supper (or the Lord's table) – the partaking of the bread and cup commonly known as "communion" – declares the Body of Christ is one without any divisions. If there is division, it is no longer the Lord's Supper. Therefore, mutual care for one another in the oneness of the Body during a meal determines whether believers are truly practicing the Lord's Supper. If believers' practice the bread and cup for the Lord's Supper, and there is division, instead of partaking of blessings, they will be partaking of judgment.

This is a warning for believers. When gathering for a meal as the assembly there should be different factions represented; however, factiousness or divisiveness cannot exist. It is so easy for believers to congregate with people with whom they are familiar — not extending themselves to others with whom they are less familiar or contrary. It is also easy to gravitate towards others with similar ethnic backgrounds or towards those in the same age group who share in similar political leanings or doctrinal understanding. However, believers need to proactively reach out to everyone in the assembly. Again, the best time and place to do so is during a meal.

As a Symbol to Remember the Lord Jesus

When it comes to partaking of the bread and the cup, it is a symbol wherein believers partake of the Lord Jesus Himself. There are many ways to practice this. Sadly, Christians have argued and divided over these symbols for centuries. Opinions differ whether to use wine or grape juice, whether the bread must be unleavened, whether female believers can break the bread and pass it, and many other points of potential arguments. The irony is (lost in all these ritualistic concerns) the entire symbol of breaking bread is for remembering the Lord Jesus — His person and His work, producing His one corporate Body.

Believers need to keep their attention on the various points of the truth shown by the symbol and not on the formality of the symbol itself.

The Bread is God Who Became Flesh to Be Eaten for Life

> "Now as they were eating, Jesus took bread, and after blessing it broke it and gave it to the disciples, and said, 'Take, eat; this is my body.'"
>
> — Matthew 26:26, ESV

Jesus as the "bread" is the bread from heaven (John 6:33, 51). When the bread as a symbol is presented, it is a clear reference Jesus is God who became flesh so that man may have eternal life through Him. God in the flesh (Jesus) came to give life to man, and if man would be nourished by Him, man would live by Jesus (John 6:57). Therefore, the symbol of eating the bread, which is the Lord's body, is a declaration that believers eat Jesus (God) Who became flesh for man's life.

The Cup is the Death of Jesus for the Forgiveness of Sins

> "And he took a cup, and when he had given thanks he gave it to them, saying, 'Drink of it, all of you, for this is my blood of the covenant, which is poured out for many for the forgiveness of sins.'"
>
> — Matthew 26:27–28, ESV

The "cup" is the blood separated from the bread — the body — meaning death. It was through the shedding of the blood of Jesus, the sinless God–Man wherein the sins of the world were taken away: God forgave man. Although God's original intent was for man to receive God's life, sin came into man and separated him from God; man was thus prevented from partaking of God. The death of Christ was needed for the forgiveness of sin in order that man could come to God with boldness to receive Him.

The New Covenant: God Did Everything for Man

> "And likewise the cup after they had eaten, saying, 'This cup that
> is poured out for you is the new covenant in my blood.'"
> – Luke 22:20, ESV

The old or first covenant was conditional, based on whether man followed God's laws; if man could abide by God's laws, there would be blessing; if man broke God's laws, there would be death and God's people would be cursed. The New Covenant, however, is based on faith wherein God did everything for man — unconditionally. All man needs to do is to receive all He has done by eating and drinking Him. This symbol declares man's portion is to eat and drink of Jesus. Jesus, as divine food for man, will automatically transform man into a New Creation (Gal. 6:15), into the image of Jesus Christ.

The Mystical Corporate Body of Christ

> "The cup of blessing which we bless, is it not the communion
> of the blood of Christ? The bread which we break, is it not the
> communion of the body of Christ? For we, [though] many, are
> one bread [and] one body; for we all partake of that one bread."
> – 1 Corinthians 10:16–17

Because the word "communion" is used in the popular King James Version translation of the Bible, communion is commonly associated with the symbol of the bread and cup. So, when people say, "Our church is having communion this Sunday," it typically means the service will include the bread and cup in its liturgy.

However, the word for "communion" in the Greek, *koinónia*, which is exactly the same word translated as "fellowship." Consider the phrases in 1 Corinthians 10:16–17 as "*the fellowship* (communion) *of the blood of Christ*" and the "*fellowship* (communion) *of the body of Christ.*"

The bread is no longer just the body of Jesus; it is the corporate Body of Christ. The physical body of Jesus, through His death and resurrection, has produced many "grains" (believers). These "grains," grounded and blended, are baked into one bread — the Body. It is out of the physical body of Jesus, buried and "broken" for believers, where His Body has expanded and increased to include all His believers as members of the one corporate Body of Christ. They share in the same life, nature, and expression as Jesus, the original grain. Therefore, when believers partake of the bread, they are also declaring there is only one Body of Christ – all believers are part of that one Body. There is only one fellowship in this Body. The fellowship of the Body of Christ is one. That is why 1 Corinthians 11 indicates God's people could not possibly be partaking of the Lord's table because there was division during the meal the believers in Corinth were having. As a result, judgment descended instead of blessing.

The Return of Christ

> "'I tell you I will not drink again of this fruit of the vine until that day when I drink it new with you in my Father's kingdom.' And when they had sung a hymn, they went out to the Mount of Olives."
>
> – Matthew 26:29–30, ESV

Finally, the symbol of the bread and cup reminds believers Jesus Christ is coming again to bring forth the Father's kingdom. Believers are prompted to remember this every time they partake of the cup; the world today is *not* God's kingdom. It is still the kingdom of the evil one.

As believers eat and drink Christ in the one fellowship of the Body, they express a glorious hope – the hope of the Lord's second coming, the hope of a glorious and transfigured physical body, and the hope of a kingdom where love and righteousness reign. Since believers live and work in this world today, they are often caught up and distracted with a multitude of worldly enticements: money, politics, sports, entertainment, fashion, sins and unrighteousness. But the Lord's table recalibrates believers and turns them back to Jesus Christ focusing them on His eventual and soon return. The world we are in today will end – the Kingdom of His dear Son will be manifested in glory.

As a minor point, notice the singing of hymns is clearly related to the practice of the Lord's table.

The focus revealed in examining the Lord's table exactly match the teaching of the apostles. The teaching (doctrine) of the apostles, which is the truth of the New Testament, is fully unveiled and enjoyed in the participation of the bread and cup.

Therefore, the practice of the Lord's table keeps believers centered on the apostles' teaching and fellowship — to remember Him. The teaching and fellowship take the practice of the Lord's table out of the realm of religious ritual, into the realm of praise and enjoyment, and into an appreciation of the reality of all God is and is doing today.

It is a tragedy for Christians to have created so many divisions over this symbol of the bread and cup — to have reduced it to a mere religious ritual. Due to these confusions, most Christians, other than an official communion in a church, have completely given up this marvelous practice. The Lord's intention was that the bread and the cup representing His table was to be observed with full appreciation and knowledge of Him. In remembrance of Him. It was to be a time of joy, rejoicing, and fellowship. This is a table of blessing to bring divided believers together into one ekklesia for the Father to be glorified. It is time to practice genuine ekklesia of the Lord and to enjoy the riches displayed by this supper of the Lord as we partake of His body and blood.

Paul warned believers in Corinth: Due to their divisions, they were not partaking of the Lord's supper; rather, they were partaking of God's judgment. When believers do not discern the Lord's Body and partake of the bread and the cup unworthily, judgment comes upon them. God's purpose and desire is for the oneness of His people; therefore, when Christians stay in their factiousness instead of receiving each other in fellowship, they come under judgment. Yes, partaking of Jesus Christ in the fellowship of His ekklesia is a great blessing; conversely, remaining in divisiveness brings judgment.

Prayer of the Ekklesia

In a previous chapter, the matter of unceasing prayer for personal life and fellowship with the Lord was highlighted. In this section, the focus will shift to the prayer of the ekklesia — a normal activity in His ekklesia. As ministers desire the building up of the ekklesia, prayer should be encouraged

> "So then Peter was kept in the prison; but a prayer was being made fervently by the church [ekklesia] to God concerning him."

"So, when he had considered [this], he came to the house of Mary, the mother of John whose surname was Mark, where many were gathered together praying."

– Acts 12:5a, 12

When Peter was arrested and kept in prison, the ekklesia in Jerusalem offered prayer to God concerning him. Due to the prayer of the assembly, Peter was miraculously released from prison. After his release, he went to Mary's house, where many were gathered praying. This shows the assembly was praying in houses. One of the functions of the ekklesia is to pray from house to house. They prayed for whoever and whatever needed prayer at that time. Since Peter was put into prison, they prayed for him to be released. There was no human way for these believers to release or help him, but through prayer, the Lord answered and released Peter.

"And when they had prayed, the place where they were assembled together was shaken; and they were all filled with the Holy Spirit, and they spoke the word of God with boldness."

– Acts 4:31

On one hand, prayer petitions the Lord to do something believers cannot do. On the other hand, prayer does something to believers. When believers pray, they are filled with the Holy Spirit. In this case the apostles were threatened by religious leaders to stop preaching Jesus. Hearing this, the saints prayed. While they were still praying, the place was shaken, the Spirit came, and filled them so they were energized with boldness, and with such boldness they went out to preach the good news of Jesus Christ. Those in the assembly were not praying for personal or material needs. They were motivated to pray because they wanted the Word to go out concerning Jesus Christ. They prayed when they were threatened to stop preaching. After they prayed, they were strengthened to speak all the more.

". . . meanwhile praying also for us, that God would open to us a door for the word, to speak the mystery of Christ, for which I am also in chains."

– Colossians 4:3

The primary burden prayer has within the ekklesia relates to the Lord's purpose. Prayer purposefully is designed for the release of the rich Word of Christ. All those ministers (which should be every believer) would have an open door of utterance, through prayer, to declare the riches and mystery of Christ. The mystery of Christ is His One Body, the ekklesia (Eph. 3:4–6). Prayers are needed not just for the gospel concerning Jesus Christ to have an unhindered outlet, but for the Lord's purpose concerning the oneness of the Body of Christ.

This Word concerning God's ekklesia, His eternal purpose, is needed even more than the gospel for salvation. Today there are millions of Christians, but there is a real deficiency relating to the oneness of believers. Where is the oneness among those for whom Christ died? There are millions upon millions of Christians, but most are divided by various teachings and practices. Therefore, prayer is desperately needed for the unveiling of the oneness of His Body. Concerted prayer on behalf of genuine ekklesia, where diverse believers are one in the same faith of Jesus, enjoy the oneness in the fellowship of the Body.

Prayer and Care in Mutuality

"Be anxious for nothing, but in everything by prayer and supplication, with thanksgiving, let your requests be made known to God."

– Philippians 4:6

"Therefore I exhort first of all that supplications, prayers, intercessions, and giving of thanks be made for all men."

– 1 Timothy 2:1

When believers fellowship and share meals together with open hearts, various needs will surface: troubles relating to work, finances, family situations, and health will be made known. Burdens for various friends and relatives to receive salvation will also be shared. All these situations with the needs of the brethren should be lifted up to the Lord in prayer. Many situations today cause saints anxiety. It seems there is no way to be trouble free. So, there are many opportunities and requests believers can make known to God. Home assemblies are also where these prayers can be offered after hearing people's various needs.

"If a brother or sister is naked and destitute of daily food, and one of you says to them, 'Depart in peace, be warmed and filled,' but you do not give them the things which are needed for the body, what does it profit? Thus also faith by itself, if it does not have works, is dead."

– James 2:15–17

"My little children, let us not love in word or in tongue, but in deed and in truth."

– 1 John 3:18

Along with prayers, consideration should be given as to whether a situation could use practical follow-up help. In many situations, practical help can be rendered to lighten the load of those burdened. As prayers are being offered to God, there should also be, if possible, opportunities for those praying to help in some tangible way. Believers shouldn't just pray without doing anything practical to help, if they can. It can be simple things like visiting someone, offering a monetary gift, helping to "babysit," or helping to clean a house; even help clean up after a gathering in a host's home. The point is there should be an awareness to bear each other's burdens, not just spiritually, but practically. If the need is not confidential, discussions can even take place in fellowship to consider how to render help as a group or someone may volunteer to help . . . "we're all in this together!"

Preaching of the Gospel

"And every day, in the temple and from house to house, they did not cease teaching and preaching that the Christ is Jesus."

– Acts 5:42, ESV

The gospel preached and taught concerning Jesus Christ should publicly take place everywhere, and in the ekklesia from house to house. Here the emphasis is on the miraculously normal gospel in the ekklesia: preaching and teaching Jesus Christ. The element of excitement and joy is present when unbelievers are saved by grace through faith in Christ. In Acts 2, people were coming to salvation daily as they witnessed the activities taking place in the Lord's ekklesia from house to house (Acts 2:47). Likewise, there were unbelievers and the "uninformed" in the ekklesia in 1 Corinthians 14:23-24.

As they witnessed the variety of the saints enjoying the Lord together in oneness, they literally fell down to worship God — they believed: "*God is truly among you!*"

Both these portions of Scripture show unbelievers were present in the ekklesia witnessing Christians enjoying the breaking of bread and prophesying to build up one another. There has been a general tradition among most churches which says communion services are not for unbelievers, only for members or believers. Yet, the pattern given in Scripture is contrary to tradition. In actuality, the ekklesia is the best presentation of the gospel: Jesus is uplifted and unveiled by the remembrance at His table where speaking and testimony is shared from all sorts of believers. Here, the love and care for each other is shown in practicality.

Christians should proactively invite their relatives and friends to the Lord's ekklesia where they can observe for themselves the Body of Christ in action: diverse individuals comfortable with their own identity in Christ; yet, they are in unity displaying true love and care for one another. This is the desire of all people: no pressure to convert or be someone else; yet, fully accepted, respected, appreciated, and loved in the joy and fellowship of the Holy Spirit. In this atmosphere of the Lord's ekklesia, those without faith, after observing this genuineness of joy, will eventually come to faith. I have a friend who calls this "osmosiating" into the Kingdom of His Dear Son."

Without the presence of unbelievers and those "unlearned" (viz., novice believers in the ekklesia), the gathering will become stale; people will settle into a routine. They are the ones who keep questions and answers real. Their company will retain the environment of the gathering fresh in the Spirit — and believers will be full of anticipation to witness the work of the Spirit in bringing the lost to salvation and the growth for the young in Christ.

It is unhealthy to have the same Christians gathering week after week and month after month. In Ezekiel 47:9-11 we see a river flowing — "*everywhere the river flows there are fish!*" Once the river no longer flows — the fish cease. Unbelievers and those novices concerning the things of Christ should be asked to "come and see" — to enjoy the meals and fellowship. Especially, those being visited in their homes for cherishing, nourishing or discipling should be there. The Lord, who loves all men and desires all men to be saved and come to the full knowledge of the truth, wants the unbelieving and uninformed to be included in His ekklesia. Here they can witness the love and oneness of believers, the living testimony from each, and the unveiling of Christ and His Body in an understandable message through singing, praying, and speaking. Oneness in the ekklesia fulfills the Lord's Prayer in John 17 and causes unbelieving and uninformed men and women to see the practical manifestation of God. Witnessing this will lead them to believe and worship God, who is real and expressed in the ekklesia. This is how the Lord was able to add to the assembly day by day those who were being saved.

Practice: Speaking Hymns to One Another

One of the easiest ways to participate and function in a gathering of believers is the practice of speaking songs and hymns to one another.

> "And do not be drunk with wine, in which is dissipation; but be filled with the Spirit, speaking to one another in psalms and hymns and spiritual songs, singing and making melody in your heart to the Lord."
>
> – Ephesians 5:18–19

In verse 18 above, Paul charged believers to be filled with the Spirit. Although being drunk with wine is a waste, Paul still used it to compare and contrast being filled in Spirit. The similarity may lie in the fact that both bring a sense of freedom from self-consciousness and a release from burdens, as well as joy and pleasure. Being drunk is a complete waste and harmful, whereas being filled with the Spirit accomplishes God's will (Eph. 5:17).

Paul, in these verses, told Christians how to be filled with the Spirit. The first way is by "*speaking to one another in Psalms and hymns and spiritual songs.*" This came even before singing and making a melody to the Lord. Even though "speaking songs and hymns" was clearly instructed by Paul, this is rarely practiced among believers. Typically, in the gathering of Christians where hymns are sung, they are sung successively without a break between songs; Hymns are sung looking down at a hymn book, looking toward the front, or looking up to heaven. They are not sung to one another; moreover, it is all the more rare when there is speaking to one another using the lyrics of the songs. This speaking to one another means there is communication directed at one another — I speak to you and you speak to me using the lyrics of the songs.

When there is no designated speaker in a gathering, many times Christians don't know what to speak to one another. The songs and hymns provide the words necessary to easily start speaking to one another the things of Christ.

Let's practice using Amazing Grace:

Amazing Grace how sweet the sound
That saved a wretch like me
I once was lost, but now I'm found
Was blind, but now I see.

There is no standard or correct way to do this other than according to your initiative and the Lord moving in you.

Person 1: "I want to say something about grace, God's grace, the grace of the Lord Jesus Christ. It is amazing and sweet. The Lord's grace is absolutely amazing, and I can't have enough of it."

Person 2: "Why is it amazing?"

Person 3: "It is amazing because grace was able to save a wretch like me. I was really in a wretched condition. I was so wretched that I thought God gave up on me, but one day, Jesus came to touch me and saved me."

Person 2: "That reminds me of a verse in John 1:18 that the law was given by Moses, but grace came through Jesus Christ — the contrast is between law and grace. With law there is a demand on people, and with that demand, since we can't fulfill it, is condemnation. But with Jesus Christ came grace."

Person 1: "Do you guys know that grace in the Greek literally means pleasure, joy, rejoicing and enjoyment? So that means it is the joy, the enjoyment of the Lord Jesus that saves us."

Person 3: "I can definitely testify that I got saved through enjoying Jesus. It wasn't my trying to keep the law that saved me. In fact, in my wretched condition it was impossible to keep God's law. I didn't want to have anything to do with it, but then I found pleasure in the Lord Jesus. He is so enjoyable. He is joy and rejoicing to me. He gives me more pleasure than alcohol and worldly entertainment. He saved me."

Person 2: "Now I see. I was blinded to Jesus, but now I see Jesus."

This is just a simple example, but this kind of speaking before or after singing will make the singing come alive. Singing will have more meaning with a greater appreciation of the Lord Jesus. Again, there is no correct way to do this! Just start practicing speaking songs and hymns. The only caution is not to speak too long. By each speaking only a few seconds or a minute, much can be conveyed one to another.

13

BUILDING: EKKLESIA
IN ONENESS AND
MUTUALITY (SECTION B)

The description of the Lord's ekklesia started from 1 Corinthians 11:17, and in verse 19, it shows how believers from various "factions" not only show up at an ekklesia, but are necessary for ekklesia; notwithstanding, they should not be factious. Those in an ekklesia need to receive and love each other no matter the differences. Now in 1 Corinthians 14 the building up of the ekklesia is described by the functioning of each member. It is significant, for in the ekklesia God's eternal purpose is practically built up in a place so insignificant — a common home.

Prophesying – The Most Profitable Gift for Building Up the Body

Every believer can prophesy; this is the most profitable gift for the building up of the assembly.

> "Pursue love, and earnestly desire the spiritual gifts, especially that you may prophesy. For one who speaks in a tongue speaks not to men but to God; for no one understands him, but he utters mysteries in the Spirit. On the other hand, the one who prophesies speaks to people for their building up and encouragement and consolation. The one who speaks in a tongue builds up himself, but the one who prophesies builds up the church [ekklesia]. Now I want you all to speak in tongues, but even more to prophesy. The one who prophesies is greater than the one who speaks in tongues, unless someone interprets, so that the church [ekklesia] may be built up. Now, brothers,

if I come to you speaking in tongues, how will I benefit you unless I bring you some revelation or knowledge or prophecy or teaching?"

"So with yourselves, since you are eager for manifestations of the Spirit, strive to excel in building up the church [ekklesia]."

"For if I pray in a tongue, my spirit prays but my mind is unfruitful. What am I to do? I will pray with my spirit, but I will pray with my mind also; I will sing praise with my spirit, but I will sing with my mind also. Otherwise, if you give thanks with your spirit, how can anyone in the position of an outsider say 'Amen' to your thanksgiving when he does not know what you are saying? For you may be giving thanks well enough, but the other person is not being built up."

"Nevertheless, in church [ekklesia] I would rather speak five words with my mind in order to instruct others, than ten thousand words in a tongue."

"If, therefore, the whole church [ekklesia] comes together and all speak in tongues, and outsiders or unbelievers enter, will they not say that you are out of your minds? But if all prophesy, and an unbeliever or outsider [uninformed] enters, he is convicted by all, he is called to account by all, the secrets of his heart are disclosed, and so, falling on his face, he will worship God and declare that God is really among you. What then, brothers? When you come together, each one has a hymn, a lesson, a revelation, a tongue, or an interpretation. Let all things be done for building up."

"Let two or three prophets speak, and let the others weigh what is said. If a revelation is made to another sitting there, let the first be silent. For you can all prophesy one by one, so that all may learn and all be encouraged, and the spirits of prophets are subject to prophets. For God is not a God of confusion but of peace. As in all the churches [ekklesia(s)] of the saints."

– 1 Corinthians 14:1–6, 12, 14–17,
19, 23–26, 29–33, ESV

The use of the words "build up" and "ekklesia" together occur in only five verses in the New Testament. The first and most importantly was when Jesus Himself said He would build up His ekklesia (Matt. 16:18). That was His stated purpose as the anointed one, the Christ (Messiah). Then, Paul said in Acts 9:31 the ekklesia throughout all Judea was being built up; it was multiplying. The remaining three verses which use the words "build up" and "ekklesia" are found in 1 Corinthians 14, which is the last chapter describing the gathering of the ekklesia starting from 1 Corinthians 11. We find in 1 Corinthians 14 the way believers from various factions, being different, yet honoring one another in love, can practically build up the Lord's ekklesia while on earth. Therefore, any believer who desires to serve the Lord needs to understand the pattern laid out in this chapter in order to have a clear direction in their ministry to build up God's eternal purpose.

The Building Up of Individual Believers is the Building Up of the Ekklesia

The building up of the ekklesia is not building up any specific group of Christians, as if that group has an identity separate from other groups of believers. All believers are, individually, part of the ekklesia, the Body of Christ (1 Cor. 12:27); therefore, to build up an ekklesia, the practicality is in the building up of each individual believer. If believers are built up, then the assembly is built up. Many Christians identify or associate believers based on the ministry they are following or the church they attend. Often, Christians interacting with each other or relating with each other depend on whether they are within the same group or not. If people are in the same church or follow the same ministry, they may treat each other a certain way – such as more caring and friendly. But, if one is an outsider to that group, they are treated another way, and if one departs from that group, then they are treated even worse. This happens when believers do not understand there is one Body. Believers need to treat each other the same, because each are individual members in the one Body (1 Cor. 12:25) . . . *"having the same love, being of one accord"* (Phil. 2:2). Therefore, in the Lord's ekklesia, though the people are diverse, the goal is to build up each other no matter what differences in church/ministry identification or whatever else might be contrary between them.

When any individual progresses and has genuine experiences in the following areas, "building up" occurs:

1. When the person becomes one with other diverse believers and appreciates each member (1 Cor. 12:12–14)
2. When there is no division with other believers, and the person cares for everyone the same (1 Cor. 12:25)
3. When the person functions more and more according to the gift given to each one (1 Cor. 12:4–11)
4. When they pursue love as defined by 1 Corinthians 13 (1 Cor. 14:1)
5. When they are encouraged and comforted (1 Cor. 14:3)
6. When the person receives more knowledge and revelation concerning the person and work of Jesus Christ: the mysteries of Christ and His assembly (1 Cor. 14:6)
7. When the person is motivated to go forth and bear fruit as they witness unbelievers receiving faith unto salvation (1 Cor. 14:23–25)

If the above is the experience of an individual attending and participating in a gathering, the Lord's ekklesia is being built up, God's eternal purpose is progressing, and those serving toward this end are doing their job.

Prophesying Brings Light and Understanding to the Hidden Mysteries of Christ and His Ekklesia

Prophecy is any utterance shining light and understanding into the hidden mysteries of Christ and His Body, the ekklesia. In 1 Corinthians 14:2 believers are told to desire the best gift, which is to prophesy, because prophesying builds up (1 Cor. 14:3-4). In the assembly, each believer can prophesy one by one (1 Cor. 14:24, 31). According to this chapter on building up the ekklesia, prophesying is the best and highest gift; therefore, it is critical to understand exactly what the definition is of "prophesying."

Most people automatically assume prophecy means predicting the future, but that is not the primary meaning here. According to Vine's Expository Dictionary, "prophesy," "prophecy," and "prophet" are from the same Greek word meaning, "To speak forth the counsel of God, His message." The etymology of that Greek word includes enlightening and explaining by bringing a hidden thought into light for understanding. Some Christians practice prophesying by bringing to light something hidden in another person's heart or by speaking forth what God has intended for that person in the future. This certainly can be the Spirit's special gift; moreover, there should not be a despising of any prophecy. Yet, this form of prophecy may or may not be true and may or may not come to pass; therefore, the prophecy referred to in 1 Corinthians 14 is focused on the prophesying which every believer can pursue and practice; furthermore, it is true for building up every single time.

What is hidden in God that needs to be brought to light, to be explained, for people to understand? In Ephesians 3:9 Paul reveals that he was to bring to light the economy of the mystery hidden in God (read in *One Truth*). Continuing with this thought of the hidden mystery, Paul in Colossians 1:26–27 said the hidden mystery is, "*Christ in you the hope of glory.*" He states in Colossians 2:2: Christ *is* the mystery of God. Jesus Christ manifested the hidden God; therefore, unveiling Jesus Christ is unveiling God's mystery. In Ephesians 3:4–6 Paul says the joining together in one body of believers, once previously hostile one to another, is the mystery of Christ.

Today, Jesus Christ is also hidden, but His one body of believers manifests and unveils the riches and attributes of Christ. This is His ekklesia – the mystery of Christ. When both the mystery of God and the mystery of Christ are combined as it says in Ephesians 5:32, "*Christ and the ekklesia,*" is a *great* mystery. Therefore, any speaking which unveils, teaches, brings to light, and causes people to understand and appreciate the many aspects of Christ and His ekklesia – the one body of believers – is prophesying.

Prophesying as described in this chapter can come in many forms, if it brings light and understanding concerning the mysteries of Christ and His One Body. For example, Paul said in 1 Corinthians 14:24, "*If all prophesy . . . ..*" Then in 1 Corinthians 14:26 Paul describes what he is expanding upon – what these "all" should be doing. He wrote, "*Each one has a hymn, a teaching, a revelation, each has a tongue with interpretation, let all these things be done for building up.*" Paul listed various speech-related activities as prophesying. Any of these items, when they unveil the mysteries for building up, are the goal of prophesying. Prayer, singing – even "five words" can be a prophecy if they uplift and bring to understanding and appreciation some aspect of Jesus Christ and His Body (1 Cor. 14:14–19).

No wonder all believers, men and women, can desire to be prophets; everyone can function in this way. How wonderful the building up of the Body of Christ is. It is not limited to a few gifted believers or waiting upon a miraculous manifestation; no, each believer in the ekklesia can participate directly in the building up of one another. Thus, this "gift" of prophecy really depends on a wider and deeper knowledge concerning the enjoyment of the mysteries of Christ and the one Body. Therefore, speaking, singing, and praying will be full of light and inspiration when all prophesy "*one by one.*"

What is the difference between a teacher and a prophet? Those are clearly different functions. According to the Bible, a prophet's function is more valuable and comes at a higher order of importance in the Body than that of a teacher. Teachers unlock the truth in the Scripture. People can read the Bible and may only receive stories, principles, or moral and legal requirements. A teacher can unlock the Bible so those being taught can have the knowledge of God and of Jesus Christ. For example, anyone can read 1 Corinthians 11:1-16 to understand Paul was saying women should have their heads covered. This apparent understanding has caused much debate, legalism, and division. A teacher will be able to convincingly show the truth regarding this portion to be appreciative of Jesus Christ being the Head over man (both male and female). After being taught by such a teacher the focus would shift from the actual practice of head-covering to the knowledge of Jesus being the unique male in the universe and humanity being the female. Jesus is the only Head in this union; moreover, humanity's head is covered since they are now relying on their true Head, Jesus Christ. Good teachers will be able unveil Christ from Genesis all the way through the book of Revelation, showing both God in His Trinity and His eternal purpose expressed in His ekklesia, the Body of Christ.

Prophets, on the other hand, also know the truth in the Bible as teachers; however, prophets are spiritually aware and discerning of people and environments in which they are speaking. They can specifically unveil Christ in the Scripture exactly fitting the need of the people and situation. They are speaking for and forth God which directly applies and impacts those in the circumstance in which they find themselves. They are not just systematically teaching the Bible as a teacher — they are synthesizing the people, the situation, together with the Word of God while speaking out a word by unveiling the mysteries which exactly fit what is needed. In other words, God is speaking in the context of that environment.

For example, let's say a person in the ekklesia is discouraged due to some hardship. A prophesy may be given using 2 Corinthians 4:7 to show Christ is the treasure in our fragile vessel. Yes, our vessel is weak, but the treasure of Christ in us enables us to pass victoriously through all hardship as described in subsequent verses. What if believers were generally passive and unmotivated concerning the things of Christ? Prophesies would then be needed to unveil Christ and His eternal purpose in a way which would impart a vision to motivate the saints to pursue the Lord anew.

Therefore, teachers can teach the truth from the Bible and can do so systematically. Whereas, prophets are situationally aware, people aware, and Holy Spirit aware in order to generate an instant and living speaking, using fitting Scriptures, to unveil and apply the mysteries correctly in the circumstances at hand. When there are no prophesies in an assembly, then people can go through the entire gathering without really being spoken to or speaking directly to anyone in each situation. Prophesying makes the Word current, applicable, and effective within the context of whatever circumstance taking place in the people present. Every believer should seek such a gift. This is the best gift for the building up of the ekklesia.

Preparation Needed before Assembling

Normally, when Christians go to church, they do not have to prepare to contribute anything other than some money for the tithing plate in their "Sunday best." They go to listen and watch those who have done the preparations which are in turn carried out via professional services. Therefore, there is a hard shift in the concept wherein ekklesia, according to the New Testament, is very different and will require preparation. Since an assembly's activities depend on each member's contribution; consequently, if no one prays, sings, or says anything concerning Jesus, it will be a very dead and boring gathering – or the gathering will end up focused on other inane things.

Therefore, a proper assembly requires every member to prepare something to bring and share. Again, this is why 1 Corinthians 14:26 speaks of each one having a hymn, a lesson, a revelation, etc. "Has" means it is something they already possess and bring to the assembly. During the week, believers should consider what song they can bring to share. This is not just to call a song for everyone to sing together. What if this person is so inspired and touched by the Lord whereupon he or she sings a solo to everyone? Or maybe a husband and wife enjoyed a song together – so, they sing a duet? Christians are so programmed to professional-sounding singers in church that they will not dare sing out a solo for shame it will sound out of tune. However, what feeds both God and man is a song unveiling something of

Christ sung with the person's experiential knowledge under the inspiration of the Holy Spirit. After the person initially sings the spiritual song, perhaps the entire assembly can sing together.

Or what if there is consideration on a specific testimony to give to glorify an aspect of the person or work of Christ? If every believer commits to ministering unto the Lord, each will prepare something to bring and contribute. They will not come before the Lord in His congregation "empty handed." They will not come to be spectators, but ready and willing to share. This sharing is based on each one's capacity; whether little or much, eventually everyone will be filled; moreover, there will be no lack. The point is that such preparation and sharing will fully enrich the assembly. Christ is unveiled one by one through various prayers, songs, and speaking.

The entire Hebrew Festival Calendar — the Seven Appointed Times — were ostensibly mealtimes from the early and latter harvests during the "Festival Calendar." The Israelites were to labor upon the Good Land and then bring to Jerusalem the labor of their hands (produce or livestock) where "each one has" and share it with others at these appointed feast days. Even in Ezekiel's vision of the Holy District in Ezekiel 48:18-19 it speaks of the cultivation of produce to "*be food for the workers of the city*" on either side of the Holy City . . . "*The workers of the city, from all the tribes of Israel, shall cultivate it*" and they shall be sustained by the food produced from these adjacent plots aside the Holy City — this is the eternal vision of the Holy District seen by Ezekiel — so inexhaustible is the produce of Christ!

Even though there is preparation, the prophets still need to be aware and discern a word that might be needed. A prophet may not speak what he/she prepared but will have an instant word to give by unveiling Christ based upon the situation of personalities at hand. Preparation is good, but it is necessary to be flexible and discern the moving of the Spirit.

Two or Three Prophets to Take the Lead

In every assembly, there should be two or three believers who have a fresh burden to speak for the Lord to unveil the mysteries of Christ and His Body. It should be something they have prepared from their enjoyment of fellowshipping with the Lord in the Word or a prophesy addressing a particular situation which might come to light during an ekklesia gathering. When they present their message or revelation under the Spirit's ministry, then an unveiling of mysteries will occur and an enlivening to everyone listening and discerning will spontaneously happen. When their speaking enlightens someone, and something of the riches of Christ and His Body is revealed, that person will want to speak forth what inspired them by the Spirit. Then the prophet who is speaking should stop and let the newly unveiled person speak. This becomes a kind of chain reaction, speaking to speaking; moreover, all of this can be intermingled with singing and prayer.

In fact, this kind of speaking generates more prophesying due to the increasing number of participants being inspired as mysteries are being unveiled which were previously hidden. Each one will have something to say with eagerness under the inspiration of the Spirit. This kind of excitement and enlightening will cause everyone to speak, sing, or pray at the same time, which will, in turn, become somewhat confusing. So, Paul says that they can all prophesy one by one. They should have control over their own spirit, to wait their turn to minister. There's no need to interrupt too quickly or continue speaking for too long when others are waiting to speak. Let peace prevail among the believers in the assembly.

The initial two or three prophets who started the chain reaction are not to dominate the assembly. Their burden and goal is to unveil the mysteries until the others listening and discerning are inspired to jump in and interrupt them. Interruption means the prophet(s) did their job well in sparking others to speak things that were unveiled to them, inspiring them.

Since everyone can speak and teach in the assembly, everyone should listen and discern or weigh whether the speaking is healthy — something to be taken in as from the Lord; or, contrariwise, something to be challenged and rejected as unhealthy. This type of listening to one another in conjunction with the inward teaching and witnessing of the anointing of the Spirit is needed for active participation in the assembly. Typically, once a believer joins a church, they normally become passive listeners in the sense they no longer use their discernment to consider whether what the pastor or preacher teaches is healthy or not. There is almost a mechanical acceptance to whatever is spoken. If one does not agree, the only recourse is to find another church with a different preacher. But in the ekklesia, with active listening, one can question what is being spoken or interject with a different point of view. If the "participant" shares something outside the "realm of healthy, spiritual food" — that person, if they are for the building up of the ekklesia, should not be offended if someone disagrees with their sharing. . . it's all good if the ultimate quest is the uplifting of Christ's person and work. Learn to move on — not dwelling on your mistakes or mishaps — bear with one another in love — for love covers a multitude of our "spiritual indiscretions!"

The above description is completely different from how church is practiced. Since church today is really the ministry of one person or of one school of thought, the pastor speaks the entire sermon or message, and no one interrupts the speaker. The speaker will not become silent if someone in the audience is inspired by the Spirit to say something for the Lord. There is a time and place for giving an uninterrupted message or for teaching a lesson, which is necessary. Church is more like a school with some performances to inspire the audience. Proper uninterrupted sermons and messages to expound upon the Word while teaching the truth certainly has its place, but not in the ekklesia.

The early apostles equipped believers by this kind of teaching and preaching messages in the public arena of the temple. Paul also rented a school (Tyrannus) to teach regularly for two years in Ephesus (Acts 19:9-10); notwithstanding, that school was not the ekklesia; rather, it was Paul's "ministry center" from whence "*all those who dwelt in Asia heard the word of the Lord Jesus, both Jews and Greeks*." On the other hand, the ekklesia was located at the home of Aquilla and Priscilla when they were living in Ephesus (1 Cor. 16:19). Similarly, in Jerusalem, much of the teaching and preaching were done at the temple, but the ekklesia took place in the homes, from house to house. The apostles' goal of preaching and teaching publicly or in a dedicated place (e.g., the School of Tyrannus) was so believers could be equipped with the teaching of Jesus Christ and be able to function for the building up of the ekklesia in homes.

There is a clear distinction and separation between Christian workers and their teaching and preaching in their churches or dedicated places of ministry, and believers' ekklesia from house to house where everyone is prophesying for the building up of the Body of Christ. One is where ministers exercise their gifts to equip the saints, and the other is the Lord's ekklesia where believers being equipped by differing ministers are called to assemble to practice "spiritual democracy" — diversity in unity.

No One Should Dominate the Ekklesia

Those believers who are more mature, gifted or have a dominating personality can easily control or manipulate the Lord's ekklesia. Once that happens, the ekklesia disappears and becomes the ministry of the dominating personality. There is nothing wrong with a ministry per se; in fact, they are needed and necessary. Nevertheless, once a person takes charge, then the gathering becomes his church or ministry; it is no longer the Lord's ekklesia with believers in full participation. The Lord's ekklesia belongs to the Lord and all the saints, and the controller is the Holy Spirit.

Likewise, a "cabal" of strong leaders might believe it is expedient for an ekklesia to have "direction and order." The temptation will be for that group of "leader types" to do the same as the "dominating personality" — an "ekklesia takeover" is just the same as a dominating personality who takes over the ekklesia whereupon it becomes a ministry. Call it a "church" or whatever, but it no longer resembles the participatory flavor of an ekklesia where "each one has" and all can prophesy "one by one." True ministers will equip the saints to do the "work of the ministry" — they will instruct the saints to grow up into maturity to experience ekklesia where each one is responsible and where those who are approved or genuine will be manifested to keep the unity of the Spirit in the uniting bond of peace among the brethren. Control is "handed over" to all the saints under the anointing of the Holy Spirit — not under the anointing of brother so-and-so or the "eldership" knows best.

Yes, stronger and more mature ones are needed to be a prophet to encourage believers, a peacemaker to break down walls, a pattern to see Jesus only, and a help to facilitate the functioning of the saints; however, they need to be extremely careful not to become the controller and the center of the gathering.

On the other hand, it is the responsibility of all the saints to disallow a person to rise up and dominate. The people of God have been trained over centuries of tradition to sit silently by while the professionals and the gifted perform their services. Although the Greeks knew of democracy expressed as an ekklesia — they also knew of the Orator. Tragically, prominent speakers arose early on in the initial days of the ekklesia to dominate a gathering with spectacular orations to bedazzle and entertain the gathering, the audience. The more dramatic and gifted the oratory, the more mesmerizing their appeal. No, the ekklesia is not where one pontificates, it's where everyone participates!

The gifted orators have arisen in just about all churches throughout history. Now the Lord's ekklesia is here, there must be a radical adjustment of concept and behavior when gathering as the Lord's ekklesia. Don't sit passively by and be a spectator when someone takes up disproportionate amounts of time or is constantly directing believers what to do; what not to do; when to do it; and, even how to do it.

Most of the ones with a dominate personality may not be aware the harm they are causing, but if any of the believers would speak up and say "I have something to say. . ." or, "can you shorten your sharing so others can share. . . " that should be enough to bring awareness for the one taking up inordinate amounts of time to stop. Remember, ekklesia is democracy: everyone has an equal voice in the ekklesia.

Positively, this is the reason every believer needs to attend an ekklesia prepared to share and to speak something for the Lord. Their entire week should be a kind of preparation for the Lord's ekklesia. It is easy to allow someone to excessively speak when no one else has anything to say. If no one has a hymn, a teaching, a revelation, or a testimony, then someone will try to take up the slack. It is critical every person attending an ekklesia has something ready, no matter how little or much; or, has something in reserve to "get the pot boiling." This is when, "*Let two or three prophets speak, and let the others judge . . . But if anything is revealed to another who sits by, let the first keep silent*" (1 Cor. 14:29-30). What's taking place is called "priming of the pump" — the "two or three prophets" so speaking or stirring up the saints to share should be prepared to be interrupted. Why? Because they've activated "*the spirit of the prophets is subject to the prophets*" — and, as they say, "We're off and running!"

Should Women Be Silent?

> "Women should be silent during the church meetings. It is not proper for them to speak. They should be submissive, just as the law says. If they have any questions, they should ask their husbands at home, for it is improper for women to speak in church meetings."
>
> – 1 Cor. 14:34-35 NLT

These verses have been a source of confusion and division among believers. Some have used this passage to forbid women from speaking in an assembly. However, even churches with this tradition do not forbid women from singing or praying out loud. If that is the case then women are not "silent"; therefore, their teaching on this subject is inconsistent and contrary.

In 1 Corinthians 11 where the Lord's ekklesia was described, it clearly states in verse 5 women do pray and prophesy — they are not silent. By saying women prophesy means they can do everything listed in 1 Corinthians 14: praying, singing, bringing a teaching and a revelation as described. They can do everything a man can do as far as positively contributing to the building up of the ekklesia.

The context of being "silent" is related to one specific kind of speaking, which is for a woman, who has a husband, to ask questions. The ekklesia, as a democratic assembly, tends to become unruly due to the fact everyone can speak; moreover, no one is in control. Therefore, this presents challenges to the believers, whereupon questions arise among the participants (witness many political legislative sessions are unruly). The Lord's ekklesia can also have similar tendencies when everyone has something to say while, at the same time, all are discerning: questions arise with believers speaking over each other. This is the reason Paul in verse 32 says: a prophet has control over his own spirit. They can control themselves from speaking and only speak one at a time in an orderly fashion (1 Cor. 14:31).

Since God is not the God of confusion (1 Cor. 14:33); therefore, it is not of God if in His ekklesia saints are speaking at the same time, raising questions and challenges as they are discerning what is being spoken. It is at this juncture Paul asked the married women to keep silent by not asking more questions to add to the confusion since they can ask their husbands at home.

Therefore, women can be bold to prophesy, pray, sing, speak a teaching or a revelation. However, be silent with your questions and not add fuel to any commotion among the saints in the Lord's ekklesia. Let the God of peace bring order and clarity in His ekklesia through peacemakers and approved ones turning everyone's attention back to Jesus Christ the Lord.

Dependent on the Approved Ones

"For there must also be factions among you, that those who are approved may be recognized among you. . . ..But let a man examine [approve] himself, and so let him eat of the bread and drink of the cup.

– 1 Cor. 11:19, 28

"Blessed [are] the peacemakers, for they shall be called sons of God."

– Matt. 5:9

Christians who have identified themselves with a faction typically do not fellowship with those in a contrary faction. For example, Protestant believers typically do not engage in fellowship with Catholic believers. Within a faction, there is more love, care, understanding, and communication among themselves than those outside of their faction. Members of a faction may become critical while denigrating those outside their faction. However, in the Lord's ekklesia, it is necessary for those from various factions to come together. It is in the atmosphere of potential conflict where those who are approved or who are genuine are manifested or recognized.

Let's consider again the nature of the ekklesia: An assembly of individuals called out from every quarter of a community is, by definition and practice, an assembly which should include factions of every kind, and often with conflicting interests. The Lord's ekklesia is no different. Although believers have been regenerated, having become members of the community of faith; yet, just consider all the differences which have divided believers. There are Jews and Gentiles, rich and poor, politically inclined to the left and to the right. Additionally, there are conflicting doctrines between Reform and Pentecostals, immersion and sprinkling, pre or post tribulation raptures, young earth or the gap theory of creation. Then there are preferences of teachers and ministers — conflict of personalities and styles.

Although there is a wide diversity of individuals, nevertheless, God has called them to ekklesia. That is why it is necessary an ekklesia starts with factions. In a way, if there are no factions, it would not be an ekklesia. A ministry cannot operate with factions in its midst; however, it is necessary an ekklesia starts with factions. Churches are typically homogeneous, based on teachings, practices, and emphases of respective ministers; whereas, the ekklesia is widely diverse. Therefore, she can only survive and thrive with Christ being the unique foundation and cornerstone.

How do we recognize those "approved" or "genuine" amid factions? *Faction* in Scriptures is a very negative word because it points to a hard division in the Body of Christ. It is a work of the flesh (Gal. 5:20). So, for some to stand out as approved must mean they are not factious nor divisive. The approved ones can only be manifested when they are amid believers from factions.

The word "*approved*" in Greek means "tried and accepted" or "certified genuine" (Thayer's). These individuals are approved because they are not factious. They are fellowshipping with everyone no matter which faction to which they belong.

Those approved treat every believer the same. They can easily fellowship with members of any faction; moreover, they are those who reconcile members of opposing factions. They shine among factions. They are peacemakers: bringing those who would normally be in conflict into fellowship by turning the focus to Jesus Christ. They receive and fellowship with all believers.

By the time of the participation in the bread and cup, every believer in the ekklesia must "examine" themselves to consider whether they are worthy to partake – do they discern the Body of Christ? The word "*examine*" in this verse is a derivative of the same Greek word as "*approved*" found in 1 Corinthians 11:19. No matter which faction believers identify with; they cannot stay factious and divided in the Lord's ekklesia. Each one must recognize the bread represents the entire Body of Christ which is the discerning of the Body of Christ. They need to recognize every person who has the faith of Jesus Christ is a member of His Body. If they have such discernment, they will receive and accept every believer no matter which faction from whence they affirm; they will enter fellowship with everyone. They become approved . . . tried and found to be genuine.

Being an "approved" believer does not put one into a class or category of "approved ones." There is not a category of approved or disapproved so that once a person is classified as such then there he/she remains. A person who is manifested to be approved in one ekklesia may not be so manifested when he becomes factious in the next. For example, in one ekklesia there may be believers who are from the Calvinist persuasion and others from a Pentecostal faction. A person manifested to be approved is when he is able to fellowship with both groups of believers and able to bring them together. However, the next ekklesia gathering, this same person may now avoid fellowshipping and accepting believers who consider themselves Catholics. He may even say something derogatory concerning the Catholic Church to offend them. In such a case, this one who was manifested to be approved previously now is factious – not manifested to be approved. Therefore, every ekklesia gathering is a new challenge to everyone participating. Each time, everyone will be tested concerning their genuineness in Christ. That is the reason every time the bread and cup is observed, each participant should reexamine or reapproved themselves to see whether they pass the test of accepting on behalf of the oneness with all those from various factions gathered for the Lord's ekklesia. Thus, being approved is a dynamic manifestation; always being tested by a constant stream of believers from various factions being called to ekklesia.

In every ekklesia of the Lord, there initially must be at least one approved person or a peacemaker; otherwise, those from factions will stay in their faction like the poor and rich in Corinth. It is so easy to stay in one's comfort zone and avoid fellowship with those contrary to one's faction. Therefore, it is the peacemakers who break down assorted walls between believers bringing them together into the one fellowship of the Holy Spirit. It is essential to have approved ones in the Lord's ekklesia; otherwise, the ekklesia will degenerate into conflict and segregation. The more approved ones there are, the more the Lord's ekklesia can multiply into additional homes.

The Qualification of an Approved One

> "Study to show thyself approved to God, a workman that needs not to be ashamed, rightly dividing the word of truth."
> – 2 Tim. 2:15 WEB

Typically, factions are caused by focusing on items of Scripture which are inessential to the truth. For example, there are many divisions over such things as methods of baptism, holiness, predestination or free will, etc. Defenders in each faction will confirm the correctness and superiority of their position with Scriptural verses. Those advancing the faction of once-saved-always-saved will have their Scripture; and those promoting the doctrine that a Christian can lose their salvation will have their Scriptural arsenal. A factious person studies the Bible to strengthen their position in order to win a debate. Although portions of Scripture are used, if, however, it has been used to create a faction, then it is not truth. The truth, who is Jesus Christ, can only unite His people.

"Approved" ones are the workmen who study the Scripture with a view to *rightly dividing the word of truth*. The Trinity, in the person and work of Jesus Christ, is the unique truth. He is the truth embedded throughout the Scripture from Genesis to Revelation. The approved workman is one who studies the Bible and can see and present Christ throughout Scripture. This person can divide or separate the truth from all other information in the Bible. Since there are many interesting and useful information in the Bible, it takes studying, developing skills, and enlightening of the Spirit to separate out the truth as the essence of the Bible while not dividing over the myriads of other facts. For example, there are many portions of Scripture describing the observance of baptism, which beliefs and practices have led to various factions. An approved person will be able to clearly focus on the truth: Christians are immersed into the Trinity by faith. The methods of physical baptism may vary, but the essential truth remains.

A walnut is a good illustration: the meat of the walnut is embedded on the inside crevices of a hard shell. It takes a little bit of work and skill to properly crack the walnut while separating or dividing the meat from the shell. Don't fight over the shell; it is the meat which is nourishing and tasty. The truth is embedded in the Bible. The many divisions caused by using Scripture as a basis are like Christians fighting over the walnut shell. As a person sees and presents Christ, the truth, in more and more portions of Scripture, that person will be an approved one able to handle more diverse and challenging situations among divided Christians. They will be able to present Christ as meat throughout the entire Scripture.

Truth is one of the essential gifts given for believers to become one: two books out of this trilogy have been devoted to this topic: *One Ekklesia* and *One Truth*.

". . . for the kingdom of God is not eating and drinking, but righteousness and peace and joy in the Holy Spirit. For he who serves Christ in these things [is] acceptable to God and approved by men. Therefore let us pursue the things [which make] for peace and the things by which one may edify another."
– Rom 14:17-19

Here is another portion showing how to be an approved person: One who is not judging others due to doctrinal or practice differences, but rather his/her focus is on righteousness, peace, and joy of the Holy Spirit. This person pursues peace between believers so they may be edified. All of Romans 14 concerns the manifestation of the ekklesia when two main factions (Jews and Gentiles) come together for a meal and fellowship. In such an environment it would be natural for one to judge the other and not receive those contrary for fellowship. Therefore, there is the need for persons who are acceptable to God and approved by men. These are ones who are bringing divided people into the kingdom of God; they are not distracted by non-essentials of the faith; rather, they are enjoying the Holy Spirit. They are not involved with factious behavior; instead, they are bringing peace to divided believers. They can supply and encourage everyone present no matter with which faction (Jews or Gentiles) a person is identified.

ONE Life & Glory

In 1 Corinthians 11:19, it simply made a statement that the "approved" will be made manifested in midst of factions. Deduction was made based on the context of the chapter that the meaning of an approved person is one who is not factious. Whereas here in Romans 14, an approved person is unmistakably defined by the entire chapter — one who is positively bringing previously divided believers into the Kingdom of God and peace that they may build up one another.

Here are the key characteristics of an approved person:

1. Not factious, this one can fellowship with all kinds of believers no matter with what faction they are identified.
2. A peacemaker, able to break down walls separating believers and bringing them into the righteousness, peace, and joy of the Holy Spirit; whereby they build up one another.
3. Is keenly focused on Jesus Christ as the truth throughout Scripture, so no matter which portion of the Bible is being discussed, this one can present Christ in context.
4. Accept and be at peace with differing convictions believers have from Scripture; yet, able to boldly defend the faith of Jesus Christ — the one saving faith.
5. A lowly servant in the glory of Jesus who cannot be offended or insulted so service to all can be continued with joy.

Hosting the Lord's ekklesia

"Gaius, my host and host of the whole assembly [ekklesia], greets you. Erastus, the treasurer of the city, greets you, as does Quartus, the brother."

– Rom. 16:23 HNV

"The assemblies of Asia greet you. Aquila and Priscilla greet you much in the Lord, together with the assembly [ekklesia] that is in their house."

– 1 Cor. 16:19 HNV

"Greet the brothers who are in Laodicea, and Nymphas, and the assembly [ekklesia] that is in his house."

– Col. 4:15 HNV

> "But Saul ravaged the assembly [ekklesia], entering into the houses one after another, and dragging off both men and women delivered them up to prison."
>
> ~ Acts 8:3 DBY

When Saul (before his conversion to Paul) was persecuting the ekklesia, he went from house to house to implement his persecution. The only way to devastate the assembly was to go to all the homes of believers where ekklesia was taking place (Acts 8:3). The gathering place of the ekklesia was in the homes of believers. The Lord called out people to assemble in homes to have meals, fellowship, and to build up one another in love.

Read the entire New Testament and you will find the only location mentioned for the Lord's ekklesia was in someone's home. Ministers, such as the apostles, may use different venues for their ministry: at the temple, in a public square or open market, in a school, in an upper room, in a rented house or apartment. The only spot where an actual ekklesia (assembly) was cited was in a home, someone's living space. The so-called "primitive" model of the "church" was, and should be today, the "standard model" for ekklesia — i.e., the home.

It is in the informal, unreligious, family atmosphere of a home the assembly of the Lord is associated. It is in a home where folks gather for meals, relaxation, entertainment, friends, and family — this is where the ekklesia is housed. This shows the normality and humanity which is intertwined with the heavenly, spiritual, yet pragmatic — where the ekklesia of the Lord flourishes.

Although a secular ekklesia often took place in a public arena such as the one in Acts 19, the Lord's ekklesia in the New Testament was found only in homes. This is not to say ekklesia cannot take place in other venues other than in a home, but there is no record in the New Testament other than in homes so designated where ekklesia took place[3]. Paul wrote the epistles to the Romans from Corinth. While in Corinth, he was hosted by Gaius who

---

3   The ingrained concept of holding Christian gatherings in "religious edifices" or "Temples" became standard practice as the Roman Empire terminated its persecution of Christians and demanded that pagan temples be converted into "houses of worship" between 200 to 400 A.D. Emperor Constantine in 325 A.D. at the Council of Nicene and, finally, emperor Theodosius issued the Edict of Thessalonica, making Christianity, specifically Nicene Christianity, the official religion of the Roman Empire — all pagan temples and any other Christian sects were deemed heretical, lost their legal status, and had their properties confiscated by the Roman state. The idea that one had to "find God" in a building, a basilica, a former pagan temple, was never the practice of the early ekklesia. (Ref. Wikipedia)

was also the host of the ekklesia in Corinth. Gaius not only gave hospitality to Paul; he equally opened his home for the saints to assemble as the Lord's ekklesia. Paul used the word "host" to describe the relationship between the assembly and Gaius.

The Greek word for "host" is *xenos*. This word literally means a foreigner or stranger (Thayer's). In fact, this word was used 14 times in the New Testament. In the King James Version, this word was translated 13 times as either "*stranger*" or "*strange*." Only one time, in this verse, was this word translated "*host*." When Gaius hosted the ekklesia, he welcomed strangers into his house. It is clearly consistent with the definition of *ekklesia*: God is calling out His people from all directions and diversity; therefore, a believer opening his/her home to have the Lord's ekklesia is going to expect strangers. There will be people in his house whom he will not know. They may have views and understandings which are quite different from his.

When a person hosts the ekklesia, he or she gives up the right to exclude believers due to different teachings, practices or political views while welcoming all those whom God has received — even if they are strangers and aliens. To have an ekklesia in your house, or to be a host of the assembly, means it is a gathering of "strangers."

Certainly, it does not literally mean everyone coming to Gaius' house were strangers who didn't know each other. What it does indicate is Gaius as a host was expecting strangers to show up — they were all welcome. What it also indicates is Gaius did not view the gathering at his house to be his "church" in the sense he was building up a defined group of regular attendees under his pastoral supervision. Rather, he merely opened his house to host, to be used by the Lord and His saints allowing all those whom the Lord was calling to assemble in his house.

Gaius recognized it was the Lord's ekklesia. He was simply letting the Lord and the called-out saints to use it for assembly. Finally, it also means there is only one class of people; they are all considered to be "strangers." No one has any seniority over another. Other than the person and work of Jesus Christ, there is no specifically defined doctrine or practice based on "insiders" or those considered to be "family." No, everyone is a stranger in the sense everyone has equal opportunity to speak forth what the Lord has given them without permission from an insider. Everyone is on the same level since everyone has the same status as a "stranger." Yet, over the course of an ekklesia, all strangers experience the real family of the Lord, the Commonwealth of Israel, the One Body of Christ, and all the other wonderful descriptions of the various aspects of ekklesia.

In an ekklesia, it is normal and expected to have strangers. Even when strangers are there for the first time, they are in an atmosphere where they have complete freedom to share their realization and experience of Christ. No doubt there will be some in the assembly who are more experienced in the way of assembly. They will manifest themselves as "approved" since they can fellowship freely with everyone, draw out the gifts of strangers, and bring people who are in factions together.

The matter of hosting is a critical point. It shows Gaius was not building another defined group of people in his home. He was not trying to turn his house into another church. He was not trying to create a following. He simply opened his home to be the place of the Lord's assembly where 1 Corinthians 11:17 through 1 Corinthians 14 could take place.

What a privilege it must be for the Lord's ekklesia to be in someone's home! God's eternal purpose is being fulfilled right in a home, someone's dwelling. The psalmist in Psalm 8 pondered: *"When I considered the heavens . . . what is man that You would be mindful of him and visit him. . . .."* Humans seem so insignificant amid the universe; yet, the God of the universe has chosen to join Himself — to live in such lowly human beings. All believers should have this reality, this unfathomable wonder, at the time they receive the faith of Jesus Christ. Similarly, what is a house, a home of a believer? Compared to the fancy and expensive buildings housing so many ministries; how insignificant is a home, a small house or apartment! Compared to the opulence of Solomon's temple, a home for the Lord's ekklesia seems so trivial: people sharing a meal, being who they are in Christ, loving one another, speaking, prophesying, and unveiling the wonder and mystery of Jesus Christ.

Nevertheless, it is the location of God's eternal purpose. His eternal purpose is being fulfilled. God is being manifested in their midst. This is so real and convincing whereupon unbelievers become instant worshippers of the God of the universe. Just as believers should surrender their hearts to God, for Him to dwell and have His way in their midst, even so, believers should surrender their homes to God for a place of ekklesia. This too is miraculously normal.

In a way, a person's home is really the fortress of one's life. A home is someone's protected place, a place of privacy; therefore, how can believers speak of surrendering their hearts without surrendering their homes for the Lord to use? Surrendering a heart is unseen, whereas, surrendering a home is practical and observable. God needs both the heart and the home of believers for His ekklesia.

It certainly is a blessing for a family to host an ekklesia. This is truly seeking first the kingdom, which is the Lord's ekklesia, and the Lord certainly will add everything needed to the host (Matt. 6:33). However, to host such an ekklesia of the Lord is not naturally easy. Those who are willing to open their home for hosting an ekklesia need a certain amount of maturity of the indwelling life of Christ, a solid foundation of the truth, and a heart to serve in humility — willing to become as nothing.

If a host is factious in any way, they will automatically side with their faction and have conflict with other factions who gather with them. If this is the case, the ekklesia will not be able to continue in their home, because over time, those whom they have conflict with will not feel welcome to share their perspectives. When that happens, then the gathering in such a home will no longer be an ekklesia of the Lord. At best, it will become a ministry with a point of view to help other believers or unbelievers. There is nothing wrong with that per se, it's just not an ekklesia. You can call it what you will; whereas, some ministers are under the impression what they are doing is holding an ekklesia — all the while controlling the lion's share of the gathering. No, that is not an ekklesia.

A host must have an attitude and spirit of a servant, a slave. If a host seeks self-glory, recognition, or attempts to exert control over a group of believers, they will be disappointed. Eventually, such a would-be host will not be able to host any more. Rather, such a person needs to be hospitable, ready to be a servant in food preparation or housekeeping. They need the glory of Jesus.

Although all believers meeting at the host's home should certainly contribute in all the practical areas in sustaining the ekklesia; notwithstanding, the host might be left "holding the bag" in the area of cleaning up the place, food preparation, furniture deterioration, misplaced items, and such things which are normally to be expected when "strangers" have the freedom to assemble in their house; frankly, prepare for damage control! Yet, what is a home of believers if not for God's house? What a privilege where God can build up His glorious ekklesia in the modesty of every believer's home.

The Scriptures seem to indicate homes hosting the Lord's ekklesia are a regular place of assembly. Paul could say the ekklesia at so and so person's house — that is why Peter knew where to go after getting out of prison (Acts 12:12). So, a stable and permanent home where the Lord's ekklesia is hosted is preferred over moving the location or the assembly from house to house. However, with today's ease of communication and travel from one house to the next, it may work just as well to move a location for gathering from house to house. The objective is people know where to go when they want to go to the Lord's assembly.

Truly, the Lord's ekklesia is His. It does not belong to any person or group. No one can claim ownership or be the head of the Lord's assembly. The best a follower of Christ can do is become manifested as "approved", be a peacemaker, participate, receive the wealth of Christian experience from other members, and be an example by allowing the Lord to use him/her for the building up of God's ekklesia.

The Lord needs to raise up more believers with this vision motivating them to open their homes to host an ekklesia. It seems when there is persecution, such as what happened in China during the Cultural Revolution or in Muslim countries, believers were forced to meet in homes. They spontaneously opened their homes to host the Lord's ekklesia without considering denominational affiliation. Christians in the West have the freedom and luxury of going to "the church of your choice"; therefore, it's easy to stay segregated into various sects or ministries. Let's pray our Lord will recover ekklesia from house to house among more and more followers of Jesus without the need of persecution. Let's be those with a vision of the ekklesia and do it willingly.

Furthermore, it is critical for believers gathering in a home to care for the host. A home where the Lord's ekklesia is hosted needs to be cared for so the host would not be overburdened. Those going to such a home should be aware when there is a meal, they should contribute food or money to help if possible. Before or after the meeting, there may be the need to prepare, clean up or put things back where they belong; thus, different ones should volunteer to help with the dishes, vacuuming, restroom cleaning, etc. The best practice is to leave the home as clean if not cleaner than when you first entered.

This is a real and practical cherishing, love and care for the host family. If this matter is not practiced, it can become too difficult for anyone hosting to continue to be open for ekklesia. Therefore, since the goal is to have homes for would-be hosts of an ekklesia (a regular gathering place), then it is critical the matter of food and cleanup be lovingly attended. While performing these chores, fellowship can and should start or continue. As ones are preparing meals or washing dishes, they can sing, pray or share the Word together. How practical and enjoyable! This is the way to insure more and more homes will be receptive to host and eventually become a regular place of assembly.

Every Ekklesia in a Home Represents the Whole

Though this gathering in Corinth happened in a home (it was in Gaius' house according to Romans 16:23), it was the "whole assembly" coming together. If the whole assembly today were in Jerusalem (or let's say in Los Angeles), it would include tens or hundreds of thousands of people, since every believer is part of the assembly. If that were the case, it would be impossible for each person to practice taking turns to speak; and it would not be practical to gather so many believers all at once in each locality. Therefore, the only way to understand this verse in 1 Corinthians 14:23 is every ekklesia in the homes represents the whole ekklesia coming together. Even though there may only be twelve believers gathered in a home in a city of 100,000 believers, those twelve believers represent the whole ekklesia if they have the characteristics and activities of the ekklesia.

When Jesus said He was in the midst of any two or three people who were gathered into His name, it was the *whole* Jesus — not a part of Him. In 1 Corinthians 12:27, referring to the assembly in Corinth, Paul said, "*Now you are the body of Christ.*" The Body of Christ should include every believer throughout time and space, but Paul referred to the believers in Corinth at that time as the Body of Christ. Shouldn't he have said, "*Now you are a part of the Body of Christ*"?

Just as any two or three who gather have the entire Jesus with them, and as the assembly in Corinth was the entire Body of Christ, so too, any ekklesia in a home today is also the whole ekklesia, the Body of Christ. This is significant: even though an ekklesia may be a small group of believers, it does not lack the gifts of the whole Body. If all the members in the home assembly participate and exercise the gifts and functions given to them by the Spirit, then there is no lack. Everyone will be supplied, filled with joy and love. There will be spiritual growth and increase. This is the practical building up of the ekklesia in homes — house by house. The "whole assembly" is present and represented by any home gathering in the Lord's name as the one Body of Christ. As a result of this, there will be a realization of the utmost importance of home gatherings as the Lord's ekklesia.

Concerning Elders in Ekklesia

Christians are programmed by over 1500 years of tradition in which the dominance of ministries has prevailed; consequently, one of the first questions concerning the ekklesia is: Who are the elders or leaders? This question was answered in detailed in the book, *One Ekklesia*, but since it is a common and potentially confusing topic, it will be answered briefly here. In short, clear leadership and direction are needed for churches or ministries, but ekklesia is distinctly different to the extent the historical and traditional thoughts concerning this topic simply do not apply.

In ministries, people are gathered to support or follow a specific minister. Where in ekklesia, the assembly is not gathered around any particular person or doctrine; rather, it is around the Lord with no one particular person or doctrine. Ekklesia is likened to a free-for-all democracy where every person is equal with equal rights to speak regarding the Christ they see and experience. Whereas, a church or ministry cannot allow any factions which leads to confusion, the Lord's ekklesia with every person able to speak and question will have a tendency toward chaos. Notwithstanding the propensity toward chaotic behavior the ekklesia shouldn't actually cross into confusion since believers can control their spirit and speak one by one (viz., "*For God is not the author of confusion* [i.e., "disorder"] *but of peace, as in all the ekklesia of the saints*" (1 Cor. 14:33).

Yes, Paul did tell Timothy and Titus to appoint elders in every ekklesia, but that was not for the purpose of control; rather, they were *pointed out* as patterns who have already shown themselves to be approved by bringing factions together, peace makers, and facilitating the Lord's ekklesia. They were not pointed out until 15 to 20 years after the ekklesias were founded in various cities. None of the early epistles relating to the vision or practice of ekklesia such as 1 Corinthians and Romans mentioned elders. So, getting bogged down by a discussion concerning elders before practicing true ekklesia for at least 10 years is like the tail wagging the dog. Therefore, every believer should forget about the tail and be empowered with the freedom to practice ekklesia via holding on to the one true Head, Jesus Christ.

Yes, the especially gifted ministers, also known as the five-fold ministries in Ephesians 4, are still very much needed. However, their function is to equip the saints then let them loose to practice and build up the ekklesia. They may continually equip, teach, instruct and guide saints for years, but they have no control or dictation over any of the Lord's ekklesia. Their goal of equipping believers is so they may mature and be able to fellowship with all kinds of believers influenced by diverse ministers in the ekklesia. They cannot influence those under their equipping to form a division or a clique. Believers causing a division due to their preferences of ministers are spiritual babes. The goal for any gifted minister is to bring those under their care to maturity where they can go on to live the Christian life and serve God and humanity on their own. When regular believers can live and serve in miraculous normality, then those especially gifted have done their job.

Practice: Prepare to Prophesy

Remember your goal in prophesying is to inspire others to see and appreciate something concerning Christ so they will be motivated to speak and participate in fellowship. In fact, if those listening are so inspired to the extent, they interrupt you, then you are a good prophet. Therefore, don't be prepared to give an oration — a fancy message or "three-point sermon." Typically, material for about three minutes is enough to inspire; anything more than five minutes can be too much, since it may appear you are dominating the time. There are three things you should consider as a preparation:

1. A scriptural portion — Consider verses which recently inspired you in your reading — write some notes on how these verses unveil something of Jesus Christ concerning His person or work. Ponder on the verses with the points while prayerfully considering those who might be at the gathering. As you do this, the Spirit may give you a special word which you can speak to the assembly.

2. A song or hymn — During the week you could be singing and praying over some hymns and songs. You may even compose your own lyrics with some familiar tunes. These songs you are enjoying before the Lord — which have inspired you — should be brought to the assembly. Then in the assembly you can sing the hymn or a portion of it. Before or after your singing, you can speak a word concerning the song. This is very different from just singing a hymn in a program or calling a hymn for everyone to sing; rather, this is bringing a song as your portion to share. You may bring a song or

hymn via electronic communication – great; but remember, you're not the only "tune in town" – let others do likewise.

3. A testimony – Do you have a testimony of your experience this week that would give glory to God and highlight the Lord Jesus in your experience? If you do, then testimonies are always inspiring, real, and applicable for the assembly to enjoy.

Typically, you will not be able to do all three of the above within 3–5 minutes so just one or two of the above items will be adequate. But if you have all three readied, then the Spirit during the gathering will move you according to His will as to what and when to share without dominating the meeting and taking up all the time. It is better to share multiple times than one long period of time. How rich will the assembly be even if just some of the believers have such preparation handy – then all those assembling will be inspired and speak their inspiration concerning Jesus Christ!

Open Your Home for Fellowship

It is critical that there are open homes for fellowship and ekklesia. Therefore, it is a good practice to invite fellow Christians to your house for fellowship, or some unbelieving friends or relatives, for the sake of speaking the gospel to them. Inviting people into your house means that you are open to them, that you have nothing to hide from them, and that they are welcomed to be comfortable around you.

Immediately begin to pray and consider whom you can invite to your house; then take action and invite them. It can be for a meal, it can be for a Bible reading and discussion, it can be for a snack – it can just be to hang out so that an opportunity for the Word can be spoken.

You can start this casually and conveniently, or better yet, do it regularly. It is not hard to decide to do this once a month; eventually it may be once a week. Ideally, you can host the assembly in your house once a week according to the pattern set up by Paul. In any case, it is good to just start.

I will have someone over to my house on before this date: _____

_____

Potential people that I can invite: _____

_____

14

CONCLUSION

The Heavenly Vision

"Where there is no vision, the people cast off restraint. . . .."
                                        – Proverbs 29:18 ASV

"But rise and stand on your feet; for I have appeared to you for this purpose, to make you a minister and a witness . . . to open their eyes, [in order] to turn [them] from darkness to light, and [from] the power of Satan to God, that they may receive forgiveness of sins and an inheritance among those who are sanctified by faith in Me."

"Therefore, King Agrippa, I was not disobedient to the heavenly vision."
                                        – Acts 26:16, 18–19

There are so many topics for Christians to focus on today: signs and wonders, holiness, deliverance, systematic theology, styles of worship, the end times, evangelism, Jewish laws and festivals, ecclesiology, Calvinism or Arminianism, on and on. Those with these emphases may envision these are the goals of their ministries. For example, if the focus is evangelism, one may envision bringing an entire stadium full of people to salvation. If one is concentrated on the miraculous, the goal may be to heal people from stage 4 cancer and to raise the dead. Therefore, among Christians and Christian ministries, there are myriads of visions and goals to pursue. With such diversity in these "spiritual aspirations" it is easy to understand how Christians with their ministries are so divided.

However, shouldn't all believers and ministers have one overarching vision? Isn't there only one ultimate purpose for Christians which is God's eternal purpose? Do ministers in the New Testament have different goals or the same? Paul, Apollos, and Peter were three independent ministers in the

New Testament. They had different temporal goals, but they were all for one eternal purpose. Paul's immediate goal was for the gospel to Gentiles. Peter's vision was to see more Jews become followers of Jesus Christ by ministering to them. Nevertheless, they had the same ultimate goal, one vision: the building up of the Lord's ekklesia.

If they didn't have the ekklesia as their vision and goal, then Paul would have raised up a Gentile church, and Peter a Jewish church. They didn't. All their ministries built up God's ekklesia, because that was their vision. They may have had temporal and intermediate goals, but their vision and purpose was God's ekklesia. Here in America today there are Chinese churches, Nigerian churches, Churches catered to one form of doctrine or another; yet, the manifestation of the Lord's ekklesia is hard to find.

Proverbs states: where there is no vision, people cast off restraint — they are in confusion. This is the case among God's people today. Since there is a lack of vision concerning God's eternal purpose of the oneness of His people, there is no restraint as to multiplying divisions and factions. Everyone can run wild in their own ministry since there is no central focus as to what their ministry is ultimately producing. There must be one central vision for all Christian living and service; otherwise, the fulfillment of the Lord's prayer for the oneness of His people will be delayed.

That is the reason all God's people — especially those desiring to serve God and humanity — must have a clear vision of God's eternal purpose. Understanding God's eternal purpose is critical and essential for all Christians. Shouldn't every follower of Jesus Christ have full understanding and confidence in the purpose of their vision to be completely aligned with God's eternal purpose?

Therefore, again, the intention of these three books has been to provide believers Scriptural basics for understanding God's eternal purpose; additionally, this trilogy is designed to provide clear guidance concerning how one should live and serve (minister) — how one can participate and contribute to the ultimate purpose of God. These three volumes are not just theoretical and theological, but pragmatic for the here and now — whatever your condition or environment.

Paul's Vision

Have you seen *ONE*? Have you seen this heavenly vision from the Lord after considering all the verses highlighted in this book together with *One*

Ekklesia and **One Truth**? God's people need an overarching vision. Without a dominant vision, there is no guidance — confusion will reign. This will cause a person to flounder; there will be nothing to restrain them from living a destructive or at least an unproductive spiritual life.

Paul, on the other hand, could declare that he was not disobedient to the heavenly vision the Lord showed him. God appeared to Paul to make him a minister and a witness, so he would turn people from darkness to light, from the power of Satan to God, bringing about the forgiveness of sins. Up to this point, almost all ministers of the gospel would agree with the above declaring this is their goal of ministry. However, just about all have neglected the last part of Paul's "heavenly vision" statement: "*an inheritance among those who are sanctified by faith in Me.*"

Where is the inheritance of each believer? It is among all other believers — those who are sanctified by faith. For any one believer to receive his inheritance, he needs all the saints. Believers in division will not be able to locate their inheritance. God's inheritance for each believer is among all His people. Without accepting and having fellowship with all of God's people, then the inheritance will be missed. In other words, oneness is needed to obtain this inheritance.

Inheritance also points to maturity. Only in maturity can a son or daughter have the right to claim inheritance. By most legal standards, a child, although an heir, is not qualified for inheritance until reaching the age of maturity. We have also seen from 1 Corinthians that divisions among believers is due to immaturity — babes in Christ. Therefore, Paul's heavenly vision was not just to bring people to individual salvation but to maturity so they would be in unity with all kinds of other believers in the Body of Christ where they might enjoy their inheritance.

This is both the gospel of grace and the gospel of peace which Paul preached. This was the entirety of His heavenly vision. This matched the very first revelation at his conversion when Jesus from the heavens said: *Why are you persecuting ME.* Paul was persecuting the followers of Jesus on earth, but Jesus in heaven declared those followers are just Jesus Himself. This is the inheritance among the saints. Those in division and factions will miss out on this inheritance until they have the maturity to receive and fellowship with all the saints in His Body.

What a calling — what a vision! God is giving this same vision to all His people — calling them to awake and stand on their feet. Have you seen this heavenly vision? Will you rise up? Will you be a minister and witness with the life and power of God to bring people around you into righteousness, peace, and joy in the Holy Spirit? Will you be a person bringing people into ONE?

The Vision of the One Body

I have no doubt if you see God's eternal purpose, you will be motivated to commit yourself to living and service directed toward God's purpose. Are you seeing this vision of God's eternal purpose of the oneness among believers is the building up of the Lord's ekklesia, His Body? Seeing this vision will fundamentally change your view toward other believers, toward the world around you, and toward your own earthly purposes. Seeing and living according to God's purpose and keeping this as a priority, will make clear your own personal pursuits and goals, whether earthly or spiritual. You will have peace, joy, and direction in life as you align yourself to God's eternal purpose as clearly unveiled in the Scriptures.

Oneness as unveiled in John 17 is the building up of the Lord's ekklesia. Receiving God's eternal *life* is for this. Knowing and understanding the *truth* is for this. And receiving the Lord's *glory* is for this. If you see this, then you will also recognize many things among Christians which are being used by Satan to distract believers from this oneness. Keeping and obeying this vision will cause you to stay true and abandon all distracting things, no matter how scriptural they may appear to be. You will live and act according to the heavenly vision for the building up of His ekklesia.

This heavenly vision will cause you to enjoy and steadily grow in His divine-eternal life through eating, drinking, breathing, exercising, and sleeping in Christ. You will love the truth, which is the knowledge of Jesus Christ. This love will cause you to study the Bible with a hunger to expand your knowledge of the truth, and to have your mind renewed by it; in order for you to become a solid foundation for the building of the ekklesia. Finally, you will find joy and purpose in serving and ministering Jesus Christ to people for salvation and building up. There is glory in being nothing but a servant for God's purpose. In this glory, self-pride is absent; you will be a peacemaker in the Body of Christ — a humble, yet peaceful and joyful servant. Your function is truly as a member of Christ to fulfill the mission of accomplishing God's eternal purpose.

Take Action

"... but the people who know their God shall stand firm and take action."

~ Daniel 11:32 ESV

What has been highlighted in this trilogy: *One Ekklesia, One Truth*, and *One Life & Glory* has not been just a vision, since there are many practical actions which need to be taken in order to fulfill the heavenly vision of ONE. For growth in life — eating, drinking, breathing, exercising, and resting must occur — consequently, actions are needed. For practicing ekklesia, actions are needed whereby expansion of this one fellowship with other believers will increase. Certainly, for a life in the Lord's glory, actions are needed to be a minister — in sharing the gospel, cherishing, nourishing, discipling, and in the building up of ekklesia house by house.

If you know God and His purpose, then you are ready to take action. One of the best ways for consistent action is to connect with or find companions who have the same heavenly vision and take action together. To do this, it is recommended you gather a few people together as a study/action group. Go over with them the verses with associated points in these books — chapter by chapter. Set up a regular time (preferably once a week) to consider and fellowship over the verses. It is not a matter of whether you agree with all the points; rather, the exercise to fellowship and pray over what is presented through the Scriptures in these chapters will cause a fresh move of the Lord in your group.

I can assure you with testimonies if you do this with just one or two other people, you will be instrumental in the building up of the Lord's ekklesia according to the Scriptures. This is living, pragmatic, fruitful, and full of the joy of the Lord.

Remember, such a study/action group can include those attending institutional churches, those already meeting in homes, or even those unassociated with any group. What you will build up is an independent assembly existing in oneness with all believers, with no human hierarchy, and where everyone can participate just as they are — members of Christ's One Body.

The study/action group itself should be considered as a class to learn and to help keep each other accountable. It is what you will do outside of this class which will become the real building up of the assembly. If you will practice according to what is highlighted here chapter by chapter, within 4–8 months you will be able to testify to a transformation in your living — a witness to the Lord using you for the building up of his ekklesia, His Body. Something fresh and dynamic of the Holy Spirit will transpire as you take action in accordance with the heavenly vision.

Let's Have the Same Dream: Reset to ONE; Revival Next!

May the Lord's Prayer in John 17 continue to be fulfilled through you. May the Lord Jesus bless you and be with you. Grace and peace to you. Amen.

SHARE THE VISION AND DREAM OF ONE

It is our hope that the matter of ONEness among people and specifically among the followers of Jesus Christ becomes a major topic of conversation. This discussion would not just be on a theoretical level or relegated only to a future reality. Neither can it be a political mediation among Christian organizations. Becoming, functioning, and manifesting ONE among believers requires it start with each individual on a "grass roots" level. The ONEness of the Trinity among believers cannot happen organizationally; it can only flourish organically.

Therefore, if you have come to the same dream of "Reset to ONE; Revival Next!" — then it is up to you to spread the word and bring others into this conversation and vision. In other words, ONEness cannot be dictated from the top down. ONEness must be viral, spreading from one to another at a personal level.

The book, *ONE*, now disbursed into this trilogy, is not intended to be a concluding word, nor a terminal definition of the practice of oneness among Christians. Rather, our hope is it will be a catalyst for expanding fellowship which will allow the Spirit to move freely among God's people for new and fresh discoveries, insights, and experiences.

Here are a few suggested ways to make use of this trilogy in order to spread the conversation of *ONE*, God's eternal purpose:

1. Quote from these pages and reference them throughout your social media postings. Use the content found in the trilogy to start and expand on the topics of *ONE*: life, truth, and glory.
2. Refer people to our website where the content is freely available to be read online: www.ONEbody.life.
3. Buy the book(s) at bulk pricing to give away in order to spread the message of *ONE*.
4. Sell the book through your channel by either purchasing the book at wholesale or be an Amazon Associate direct purchasing *ONE* at www.amazon.com.

For more information contact us at:
www.ONEbody.life

Bibliography

Austin-Sparks, T. *The Centrality and Supremacy of the Lord Jesus Christ*. Online Library of T. Austin-Sparks.

Brother Lawrence. *Practice the Presence of God*. London: Epworth Press.

Cannon, Michael. *The Prayer of Jesus*. Eugene, OR: Resource Publications.

Coneybeare and Howson. *The Life and Epistles of St Paul*. Grand Rapid, MI: WM. B. Eerdmans Publishing Co.

Dale, Felicity. *Army of Ordinary People*. Barna and Tyndale House Publishers.

Freeman, Bill. *Our Common Oneness*. Scottsdale, AZ: Ministry Publication.

Giles, Keith. *Jesus Unveiled*. Orange, CA: Quoir.

Jacobson, Richard. *Unchurching*. Murfreesboro, TN: Unchurching Books.

Jacobson, Wayne. *Finding Church*. Newbury Park, CA: Trailview Media.

Krieger, Doug. *So, You Want to do Ekklesia?* Sacramento, CA: Tribnet Publications.

Lee, Witness. *The All-Inclusive Christ*. Anaheim, CA: Living Stream Ministry.

Lee, Witness. *The Economy of God*. Anaheim, CA; Anaheim, CA: Living Stream Ministry.

Lee, Witness. *Exercise and Practice of the God Ordained Way*: Anaheim, CA: Living Stream Ministry.

Lloyd-Jones, Martyn. *The Assurance of Our Salvation*. Wheaton, IL: Crossway.

Mackintosh, C.H. *Genesis to Deuteronomy*. Neptune, NJ: Loizeaux Brothers.

Mackintosh, C.H. *The Mackintosh Treasury*. Neptune, NJ: Loizeaux Brothers.

Murray, Andrew. *The Two Covenants*. New Jersey: Spire Books.

Murray, Andrew. *Abide in Christ*. New Kensington, PA: Whitaker House.

Murray, Andrew. *The Spirit of Christ*. Minneapolis, MN: Bethany House Publisher.

Nee, Watchman. *The Normal Christian Life*. PA: CLC.

Nee, Watchman. *The Normal Christian Church Life*. Colorado Springs, CO: ISP.

New Testament Recovery Version (with footnotes). Anaheim, CA: Living Stream Ministry.

Newton, George. *John 17*. Carlisle, PA: The Banner of Trust Trust.

Rainsford, Marcus. *Our Lord Prays for His Own*. Grand Rapids, MI: Kregel Classics.

Rodriguez, Milt. *The Priesthood of All Believers*. Box Elder, SD: The Rebuilders.

Scroggie, W. Graham. *The Unfolding Drama of Redemption*. Grand Rapid, MI: Zondervan Publishing House.

Silvoso, Ed. *Ekklesia*. Minneapolis, MI: Chosen

Simms, Steve. *The Joy of Early Christianity*. Nashville, TN. Harper Simms Press.

Vine, W. E. *Vine's Expository Dictionary of New Testament Words*. Public domain: www.blueletter.org.

Viola, Frank. *Reimagining Church*. Colorado Springs, CO: David C. Cook.

Zens, Jon. *58 to 0*. Lincoln, NE: Ekklesia Press.

BIBLE VERSIONS USED

Unless otherwise noted, all scriptural verses are taken from New King James Version (NKJV). Copyright © 1982 by Thomas Nelson. Used by permission. All rights reserved.

[DBY] Some of the scriptural verses taken from Darby Version have been revised to conform to modern English. Public domain version.

[ESV] English Standard Version copyright © 2001, 2007 by Crossway Bibles, a publishing ministry of Good News Publishers. Used by permission. All rights reserved.

[RSV] from the Revised Standard Version of the Bible, copyright © 1946, 1952, and 1971 the Division of Christian Education of the National Council of the Churches of Christ in the United States of America. Used by permission. All rights reserved.

[NET] THE NET BIBLE®, NEW ENGLISH TRANSLATION COPYRIGHT © 1996 BY BIBLICAL STUDIES PRESS, L.L.C. NET Bible® IS A REGISTERED TRADEMARK THE NET BIBLE® LOGO, SERVICE MARK COPYRIGHT © 1997 BY BIBLICAL STUDIES PRESS, L.L.C. ALL RIGHTS RESERVED

[NIV] THE HOLY BIBLE, NEW INTERNATIONAL VERSION®, NIV® Copyright © 1973, 1978, 1984, 2011 by Biblica, Inc.® Used by permission. All rights reserved worldwide.

[ASV] Thomas Nelson & Sons first published the American Standard Version in 1901. This translation of the Bible is in the public domain.

[WBT] The Webster Bible was translated by Noah Webster in 1833 in order to bring the language of the Bible up to date. This version of the Bible is in the public domain.

[HNV] The Hebrew Names Version is based off the World English Bible, an update of the American Standard Version of 1901. This version of the Bible is in the public domain.

[KJV] The King James Version. Outside of the United Kingdom, the KJV is in the public domain. Within the United Kingdom, the rights to the KJV are vested in the Crown. This Bible is printed and published by Cambridge University Press, the Queen's royal printer, under royal letters patent. The text commonly available now is actually that of the 1769 revision, not that of 1611.

[HCSB] Scripture quotations marked HCSB are taken from the Holman Christian Standard Bible®, Copyright © 1999, 2000, 2002, 2003, 2009 by Holman Bible Publishers. Used by permission. Holman Christian Standard Bible®, Holman CSB®, and HCSB® are federally registered trademarks of Holman Bible Publishers.

[WEB] The World English Bible is a 1997 revision of the American Standard Version of the Holy Bible, first published in 1901. It is in the Public Domain.

Made in the USA
Monee, IL
12 June 2020